"*A Therapist's Guide to Adolescent Development* is a necessary book for therapists who work with adolescents. Expert knowledge in both development and clinical practice come together to create a one-stop guidebook for all things adolescent, including in-depth details of each age and quick handouts for reference. This is an excellent resource for all levels of practitioners."

Hayley Stulmaker, *PhD, LPC-S, RPT-S, owner of HLS Counseling PLLC*

"It's finally here! By bringing together experts in adolescence, Jayne and Purswell have created an invaluable resource for mental health professionals. This volume provides a detailed and practical look at each year of adolescence, grounded in research and evidence. Counselors will use this book to expand their knowledge and as an invaluable resource tool for practice with adolescents and their families."

Dee C. Ray, *PhD, regents professor and director of the Center for Play Therapy at University of North Texas*

"In this much-needed book, the authors share astute perspectives that look closely into an exciting stage of life that is often stereotyped as a 'difficult period.' This book not only motivates us to effectively work with adolescents; it also helps us examine our own adolescent lives and cultivate deeper self-understanding. It is a unique and exceptional book."

Yumiko Ogawa, *PhD, associate professor of clinical mental health counseling at Marist College*

A Therapist's Guide to Adolescent Development

A Therapist's Guide to Adolescent Development is a practical guide to understanding adolescent development and applying that knowledge in therapeutic practice.

Chapters explore development and therapeutic considerations for specific age ranges in pre-adolescence and early, middle, and late adolescence. The final chapter includes reproducible, age-specific handouts about adolescent development for use by counselors and therapists to educate and collaborate with adolescents and their significant adults, including parents, caregivers, teachers, and mentors. Clinical examples representing diverse clients are provided throughout the book to support culturally sustaining practice and practical application.

This unique and meaningful book will benefit any mental health professional or student who wants to integrate developmental knowledge into practice in a way that educates, empowers, and promotes collaboration with adolescents rather than pathologizing them.

Kimberly M. Jayne, PhD, LPC, NCC, RPT-S, is an associate professor at Saybrook University and a licensed professional counselor working with children, adolescents, and families in Oregon.

Katherine E. Purswell, PhD, LPC-S, RPT, is the owner of a private practice in San Marcos, Texas and a licensed professional counselor in the state of Texas.

A Therapist's Guide to Adolescent Development

Supporting Teens and Young Adults in Their Families and Communities

Edited by Kimberly M. Jayne and Katherine E. Purswell

NEW YORK AND LONDON

Designed cover image: Prostock-Studio / Getty Images

First published 2025
by Routledge
605 Third Avenue, New York, NY 10158

and by Routledge
4 Park Square, Milton Park, Abingdon, Oxon, OX14 4RN

Routledge is an imprint of the Taylor & Francis Group, an informa business

ISBN: 978-1-032-05043-0 (hbk)
ISBN: 978-1-032-05042-3 (pbk)
ISBN: 978-1-003-19629-7 (ebk)

DOI: 10.4324/9781003196297

Typeset in Sabon
by Apex CoVantage, LLC

To all the teens and young adults who have opened their lives and worlds to me. And for Ollie, Ruby, and Ezra.

Kimberly M. Jayne

To the clients who taught me that adolescents are not so scary after all. Most of all, for Sofi.

Katherine E. Purswell

Contents

Contributors

Dominique A. Avery, PhD, NCC, LMHC, is a clinical mental health counselor and counselor educator with a passion for developmental, contextual, trauma-informed, and culturally responsive clinical work and counselor education. She has experience in EMDR counseling survivors of childhood sexual abuse, has worked with refugee children and families by bringing play-based therapy into their homes, and has supported emerging adults' LGBTQIA+ identity development. Before becoming a counselor, Dominique spent a decade working with children and adolescents in shelter home settings, wilderness therapy in the deserts of Idaho, and forest schools in the woodlands of England.

Taylor Falardeau, PhD, LPCC (OH), NCC, has clinical experience ranging from inpatient psychiatric hospitalization to outpatient practice. Currently, Taylor provides counseling services in a private practice setting. Working with individuals across the lifespan, Taylor strives to align therapeutic approaches and techniques to each individual client she works with. Along with her clinical practice, she enjoys adjunct opportunities at counseling institutions and engaging in research pursuits.

Ryan D. Foster, PhD, LPC-S, CHST, is an associate professor of counseling at Tarleton State University and founder of the Humanistic Sandtray Therapy Institute in Fort Worth, TX. He is a licensed professional counselor (LPC) and board-approved supervisor with over 15 years of professional counseling experience in outpatient clinics, college counseling centers, and private practice. His research and scholarly interests include humanistic sandtray therapy, ethics of psychotherapy, and transpersonal counseling.

Ali Hamilton-Fay, MS, LPC, NCC, is a licensed professional counselor maintaining a private practice specializing in working with children, adolescents, and their families. In addition to providing counseling services, she facilitates community education programs and has served as a guest lecturer and adjunct professor at the University of Scranton. Ali is also involved in curriculum and program development related to adolescent and child mental health, burn out prevention, and counselor education.

Rachel Jacoby, PhD, LPCC-S, NCC, ACS, CFLE, is an assistant professor at Palo Alto University and served as a past president (2022–2023) of the Association for Child and Adolescent Counseling. A dedicated professional with a wealth of experience, her research focuses on trauma-informed counseling practices for children and adolescents as well as effective supervision methods. Rachel continues to work clinically, having experience working in community mental health, private practice, and school settings.

Kimberly M. Jayne, PhD, LPC, LPCC, NCC, RPT-S, PMH-C, is an associate professor at Saybrook University and sustains a private practice providing play therapy, family therapy, supervision, and training for child and adolescent counselors. Kimberly has worked as a counselor and play therapist with children, adolescents, and their adults in schools, community settings, and private practice for 15 years. Kimberly is endlessly curious and passionate about learning and integrating developmental knowledge into therapeutic practice.

Karen Jubert, MEd, LPC-S, NCC, is a licensed professional counselor supervisor and board-certified counselor who works as a university mental health counselor and community mental health support group facilitator. Karen is currently pursuing a PhD in counselor education and supervision at Saybrook University. Karen has more than 20 years of combined professional experience in higher education, corporate, community, and private mental health agency settings. Karen's primary counseling experience has been working with college students and emerging adults supporting their stressors associated with career decisions, performance anxiety, life transitions, cultural identity, and navigating change. Karen also specializes in supporting and empowering the LGBTQIA2S+ community, persons living with chronic health conditions, individuals struggling with addiction, and students experiencing grief/loss or depression.

Amanda Lara, MS, LPCC, is a licensed professional counselor in Colorado and is currently a compliance director for a community mental health center that serves the northwestern region of Colorado. Amanda has a master of arts degree in clinical mental health counseling from the University of Scranton. She has been a counselor for six years, primarily working with adolescents and young adults in Pennsylvania and Colorado. She has worked in various mental health settings including clinics, not-for-profit organizations, private and public schools, and private practice. Amanda specializes in trauma-related disorders related to immigration, discrimination, violence, and abuse. She enjoys conducting program evaluations and creating counselor training content.

Emily Michero, PhD, LPC-S, has been passionate about counseling adolescents, especially 15-year-olds, for over 18 years. She has worked with adolescents in a variety of settings and continues to be inspired by their insight, resilience, and growth potential. Emily is currently an assistant professor of professional practice at Texas Christian University where she serves as an instructor and the clinic director, along with maintaining a small private practice in Fort Worth, TX.

Kimberly Molnar, PhD, LPSC (OH), is a professional lecturer at DePaul University in Chicago, IL. A practiced school counselor, her research focuses on the intersection of school counseling and school-based mental health counseling, as well as mothers' issues in counseling. Kimberly has expertise working with adolescents and young adults in multiple school levels and settings as well as experience supervising both school counselors and clinical mental health counselors work with these populations.

Molly Moran, PhD, LPC, Licensed School Counselor, is a clinical assistant professor in counselor education and supervision at Oregon State University–Cascades. She is a licensed professional counselor in the state of Idaho and a licensed school counselor in the state of Oregon. She has over two decades of experience working with children and adolescents primarily in school settings. Her passion lies in supporting historically marginalized K–12 students, advocating for their unique needs, and striving to bridge educational gaps through her research endeavors.

Katherine E. Purswell, PhD, LPC-S, RPT, is the owner of a private practice serving children, adolescents, and adults. She is also a regular visiting professor at Concordia University in Montreal, Quebec. Katherine has experience working with children, adolescents, and families in school, agency, and private practice settings and has taught graduate level counseling classes for the past 10 years. She is passionate about helping new and experienced counselors apply child and adolescent development concepts to their clinical practice.

Alyssa M. Swan, PhD, LCPC, NCC, RPT, is a core faculty member in the School of Social and Behavioral Sciences at Capella University. Alyssa is a licensed clinical professional counselor in Illinois and a registered play therapist through the Association for Play Therapy. She is a certified child-centered play therapist-supervisor/trainer and a certified child-parent relationship therapist-supervisor/trainer with the University of North Texas Center for Play Therapy.

Chris Wilder, PhD, LPC-S, is an assistant professor, school counseling coordinator, and clinic director at Tarleton State University. He is a licensed professional counselor and board-approved supervisor with over 30 years of professional counseling experience in outpatient clinics, college counseling centers, public high schools, and faith-based settings.

Acknowledgments

Many people contributed to the success of this book. We would like to thank all our chapter authors for their perseverance and dedication to the project. A huge thanks to Titan Page for their help reviewing the initial drafts and supporting the literature review for the introductory chapters and to Tahira Lopez Benevelli for her assistance with the final details of the book.

We want to thank Dee Ray, who, in addition to helping us become the counselors we are today, supported us in building off her idea for an age-by-age guide to development that began with her edited book, *The Therapist's Guide to Child Development: The Extraordinarily Normal Years*.

Katie would like to thank Mom, Dad, and Rachel not just for the significant amount of childcare they provided during the editing and writing process for this book but also for their ongoing support and encouragement. Thank you to Joshua and Caleb for being my resident experts in adolescent development.

Kimberly would like to thank Cory for being my greatest support and for all the many ways you care for me every day. Thank you to Ollie, Ruby, and Ezra for inspiring me always to be curious and ask big important questions and doing your best to understand why I spent so much time on my computer working on this book. I am beyond grateful I get to grow and learn with each of you. And, thank you to Katie for being a steadfast friend and writing partner and for sharing a love for development.

Part I

Fundamentals of Adolescent Development

Chapter 1

Introduction to Adolescent Development

Katherine E. Purswell

Adolescence is a time of rapid growth and change. Many psychotherapists find adolescent clients to be engaging, interesting, and refreshing. Others feel intimidated by this age group. This book is for both of those groups and everyone in between. We hope that reading this book will provide therapists with insight into the developmental context of adolescence and, by doing so, help them serve their clients and their clients' communities in ways that honor and support the developmental tasks of adolescence. To that end, many examples are included throughout the book. Some of these are fictional examples that are based on chapter authors' general experiences. If a real client is used, their name and identifying information has been changed to protect client confidentiality.

For many helping professionals, human development knowledge may be something relegated to their graduate school days with seemingly limited relevance to the real world of therapy. However, understanding theories and models of typical development can help therapists better understand their teen clients, improve case conceptualization, and select developmentally relevant interventions. Further, providing developmental information to the adults in adolescents' lives can help those adults have age-appropriate expectations and develop greater empathy for their teens, thus improving adolescent-adult relationships. Although it is beyond the scope of this book, a comprehensive understanding of child development and preteen development is an important foundation for counselors and therapist to work effectively with early, middle, and late adolescents/emerging adults.

Adolescence can be defined broadly as the start of puberty around age 9 to the mid-20s (NASEM, 2019). In this book, our focus is on the period of adolescence from 13 to 25, teens to emerging adulthood, and we will consider the term *adolescent* to include younger teens as well as emerging adults in their early- to mid-20s and "adolescent therapist or counselor" to include those who work with this population. However, because young people over the age of 18 typically do not appreciate being labeled an adolescent, they will be referred to as "young or emerging adults" in the chapters that specifically address the later end of adolescence.

Clearly, much variability exists within this expanded age range for adolescence. In this book, authors with experience with the various stages of development share their experience and the available research that pertains to each age. We hope that breaking down the broad swath of adolescence into smaller ranges will assist therapists in applying the

DOI: 10.4324/9781003196297-2

unique developmental landmarks of each age to their clients. As with any discussion of development, the concepts and milestones discussed in each age-specific chapter are only intended to represent what most individuals of that age in the United States experience. We recognize that many adolescents in the US will have different developmental experiences than the ones described at each age in this book and that certain normative experiences in the US are not normative in other cultures and countries. Therapists should always use their clinical judgment and individual assessment of the client when applying developmental concepts. We have found that, when used in an empathic and intentional way, sensitive application of theories of development can make a difference for clients and for the adults in their lives.

Key Developmental Theories and Models

Brain Development in Adolescence

Understanding brain development can help therapists better understand the experiences of adolescents (NASEM, 2019). This section includes a brief refresher on brain development, including the unique changes that take place during adolescence. What follows is a simplified explanation of brain development. The interested reader can access the cited resources for a greater depth of specificity and research.

Brain cells (neurons) are composed of three parts: the cell body, a long projection (axon), and information-gathering extensions that branch off the cell body (dendrites; Lally & Valentine-French, 2019). The brain contains both gray and white matter. Gray matter refers to parts of the brain where cell bodies are stored and includes the dendrites and connections between neurons (synapses; NASEM, 2019). Synapses develop based on experience so that they represent memory and learning. Unused synapses disappear; thus, memory and learning are use-dependent. The development of synapses (synaptogenesis) and pruning of synapses result in nets of connections such that one memory or piece of learning may be tied to another based on the way that information was encoded in the brain (Badenoch, 2008; NASEM, 2019). For example, if a person experienced a traumatic event on a boat, just seeing a boat may activate some of the same neural responses as the traumatic event. Whereas the synaptic nets of gray matter can be considered to represent the breadth of memory and learning, white matter impacts the speed and efficiency of communication between neurons. White matter gets its name from a fatty sheath called myelin that coats axons and acts as a superhighway for information. Greater myelination indicates stronger and more efficient neural pathways.

Understanding the function of gray and white matter can help therapists understand how an adolescent brain is processing information (NASEM, 2019). For example, if a teen has experienced consistent rejection throughout their lives, they may have an expansive neural net and highly myelinated pathways that quickly and efficiently allow them to identify risk of rejection and act in a protective way. While this system may have developed as an adaptive mechanism in their family of origin, it may not serve them as well in other relationships they develop as teenagers and young adults outside the home. If one instance of perceived rejection leads to significant relational withdrawal due to those heavily myelinated neural pathways, the resulting isolating behavior may impact the adolescent's ability to form healthy interpersonal relationships.

Structure of the Brain

In addition to a basic understanding of the cellular structure of the brain, it is also important to be familiar with the main regions of the brain and their functions. The brainstem is responsible for autonomous actions such as breathing and temperature control, and this part of the brain completes its development early in life (Siegel, 2011). The next part of the brain to mature is the limbic region. This region includes the amygdala, which is responsible for basic survival emotions, especially anger and fear (NASEM, 2019; Siegel, 2011). When a person of any age has lost control of their behavior and is reacting almost exclusively from an emotional place, they are primarily operating from the amygdala. By the end of early childhood, the limbic region has completed most of its development. However, in adolescence, the limbic system appears to go through changes that result in the inhibition of the fear response meaning that adolescents are more likely to respond impulsively to threats or perceived threats. These changes also result in an increase in sensitivity to rewards, novelty, and peers (NASEM, 2019).

Although these changes may feel frightening to worried adults in adolescents' lives, the suppressed fear response and increase in sensation-seeking actually serve to aid teens and young adults in having the courage to face the many new experiences they encounter in the transition to adulthood, such as increased self-responsibility, starting a career, or participating in higher education (NASEM, 2019; Romer et al., 2017). In other words, exploration and risk-taking, when undertaken in the context of a supportive environment and otherwise adaptive development, are necessary to develop skills needed for adulthood (NASEM, 2019).

The cerebral cortex of the brain is the last to mature, something that does not happen until the late 20s. The prefrontal cortex is of particular relevance to therapists because it is responsible for integrative functions such as attuned communication, emotional regulation, and insight (Badenoch, 2008). When a teen takes deep breaths to avoid losing their temper, they are using the integrative functions of the prefrontal cortex. Development of the prefrontal cortex during adolescence means teens are increasingly more adept at behavior inhibition and self-regulation. However, they are still less efficient at these skills than are people in their 30s and later, and they are less likely to be able to access such executive functioning when emotions are high. The adults in teens lives may be confused when an adolescent who can plan ahead and be very disciplined about schoolwork, for example, engages in behavior with friends that shows almost no awareness of the consequences. In the latter situation, the teen brain's orientation toward reward, novelty, and peers likely overrode the fledgling abilities of their prefrontal cortex. Rather than seeing the increased executive functioning of the prefrontal cortex and the increased sensation-seeking and inhibition of risk as an imbalance of the brain, adolescent therapists can utilize their understanding of brain development to celebrate the readiness of the adolescent brain for exploration and growth (NASEM, 2019).

One misconception that results from the "imbalance" approach to adolescent development is the idea that maladaptive behaviors often considered to be "normal" adolescent behavior, such as substance misuse, repeated risky sexual behaviors, and reckless risk-taking, are inevitable (Romer et al., 2017). Rather, they are more likely to be indicative of individual risk factors such as heightened impulsivity or behavioral trauma responses that first appeared in childhood and can be better understood through knowledge of brain development across the lifespan.

All the neural and structural changes in adolescent brains mean that these brains are ready to adapt and change and are exceptionally resilient. As such, positive neurobiological changes during this time can have an outsized influence on future development, and adolescent therapists have a unique opportunity to be part of that transformation. By providing a supportive, caring relational environment and allowing adolescents space to work through changes and challenges at their own pace, adolescent therapists take advantage of the unique adaptability of the adolescent brain to help teens create new neural connections that can set them up for current and future success (NASEM, 2019).

Cognitive Development

Piaget's Stages of Cognitive Development

Piaget proposed that children's cognitive development progresses in stages in which children can think and use logic in qualitatively different ways. Research has broadly supported Piaget's theory, with some results indicating that children are able to reason in more complex ways even earlier that Piaget suggested when the tasks are presented in ways that are meaningful to the child (Lally & Valentine-French, 2019). Following is a brief summary of Piaget's stages with an emphasis on adolescence.

In the sensorimotor stage, infants and toddlers use their senses to make sense of the world around them and to solve problems. Once they move into the preoperational stage, preschoolers use intuitive thought to understand their environment and problem-solve. For example, a 4-year-old may "intuit" that if a glass of water is taller, it must hold more water than the shorter glass, even when an adult has just poured water from one glass to the other. In the concrete operational stage, school-age children can engage in logical thinking when they have physical objects to represent the components of the problem (e.g., using sticks they can reason that if A > B and B > C, then A > C). Piaget said that around age 11 most children begin to move into the formal operations stage. In this stage, they develop abstract thought and can solve the A > C problem without the use of visual aids. They are also able to engage in hypothetico-deductive reasoning (e.g., using the scientific method by testing one hypothesis at a time while controlling the other variables).

As children are moving from the concrete operational stage to formal operations in preadolescence, they often begin to practice using their enhanced reasoning abilities. Teachers and caregivers may experience this change as the preteen being more argumentative or needing to question the logic of every decision. Preteens are beginning to understand more complex concepts such as love, racism, social justice, or sacrifice. Although younger children may know the meanings of these words, they tend to tie them to more concrete behaviors (e.g., love is when a caregiver makes you a special dinner or reads you a book before bed), whereas a preteen may start to understand the general concept of love (e.g., you could love a person and still hurt them). When faced with a problem, preteens are better able to isolate specific variables and work to only change one thing at a time to find out how that changes the outcome. However, preteens will still need significant support around these cognitive tasks and may fluctuate frequently between concrete and abstract thought.

As children move into adolescence, they become even more adept at using abstract thought, logic, and hypothetico-deductive reasoning. They are often becoming more aware of social injustices (or perceived injustices) and may become frustrated when solutions that make sense logically are not being implemented. Often, they do not have the life experience to understand that solutions to complex problems are often not that simple. For example, if a teen from a privileged group is noticing discrimination against other groups at school for the first time, they may think the solution is to require all the employees at the school to do a diversity training with the idea, "If everyone could see what I see, things would be different." This teen does not have the life experience to realize the myriad of systemic and individual factors that impact microaggressions and discrimination against minoritized groups. One way the move into formal operations may show up in therapy sessions is that teens may begin to analyze and critique their caregivers' parenting style. Adolescents may not consider that they do not likely have access to the whole picture and that the "obvious" parenting technique may not be within the emotional capabilities of their caregiver.

Perry's Stages of Epistemic Cognition

One of the limitations of Piaget's theory is that he ended his exploration of cognitive development with the development of abstract thought. Perry (1968, 1981) proposed a scheme of cognitive and ethical development that focuses on individuals who have reached Piaget's formal operations stage. Perry's complex theory can be described in four phases of development, and like Piaget, he suggested not all adults reach the final stages.

The first stage in Perry's model is dualism. Individuals in this stage generally see knowledge as singular and knowable. They highly value the word of people they consider to be an authority on the matter and believe everyone should view an issue in the same way they do because that is the "right" answer. For example, a 14-year-old may believe their parents' political party is the best one because their parents and their parents' like-minded friends are the authority on the matter. Some adults stay in dualism for most of their lives.

The second stage is multiplicity. In this stage individuals become aware that there are multiple solutions to problems or multiple answers to a complicated issue. They also realize that authority is not always correct and that it can be challenging to find the best answer. People in this stage typically hold the belief that truth is relative and most solutions to a given problem are equal. A 20-year-old in this stage may say, "I shouldn't be criticized for my opinion. After all, there is no way of proving what the best answer is."

In Perry's third stage of development, relativism, individuals consider that context impacts "truth," and they use perspective-taking to see people's good reasons for holding their beliefs. An 18-year-old may say, "Given that mom's life experience, I see why she is against abortion. But I also get why my other friend is advocating to make abortion legal. It's really hard to make a decision about my own stance when they both have such well-thought-out arguments." Again, according to Perry, every adult may not reach this stage.

Perry's final stage is commitment within relativism. In this stage, individuals are still able to see others' good reasons for their views, but they are also able to use the available evidence to explain why they selected their own perspective or course of action. A 24-year-old might say, "I understand why my friend doesn't believe in a higher power, and I can respect that. For me, I just can't deny the evidence of a supernatural being in my life and in my cultural heritage." Perry's theory can be useful to therapists in understanding how clients are using their formal operational skills to understand their world and form values.

Social/Emotional Development

Attachment Theory

Bowlby's theory of attachment resulted from observations of children who were separated from their caregivers (O'Shaughnessy, 2023a). Based on his experiences, Bowlby developed the belief that the need for connection was inborn and that it served a survival function. Bowlby (1969), and later Ainsworth and Bell (1970), characterized attachment as a persistent, emotional bond between two individuals that is maintained over time and space. Understanding attachment theory can help adolescent counselors better understand the manifestations of early childhood attachment in the teen and young adult years.

In her work, Ainsworth developed three categorizations of attachment (Ainsworth et al., 1978). A child with a secure pattern of attachment is able to leave the attachment figure's side and explore the environment with confidence that the attachment figure will meet the child's emotional and physical needs when necessary. The child also feels confident in being welcomed back to the attachment figure when the child returns from exploring. In this sense, the attachment figure is a secure base. Children who have insecure patterns of attachment are unable to use their attachment figure as a secure base because they are either unsure of being welcomed back and are, therefore, afraid to explore (ambivalent attachment), or they are sure of not being welcomed back, so they appear disengaged and do not attempt to return to the attachment figure (avoidant attachment). A fourth classification of attachment (disorganized) was developed to include children whose interactions with their caregiver did not seem to fall fully into any of Ainsworth's classifications. It is characterized by the outward display of internal dilemmas, such as taking two steps toward the caregiver and then falling to the floor in uncertainty (Main & Solomon, 1990).

Crittenden (2000, 2016) conceptualized Ainsworth's patterns of attachment as self-protective strategies that fall along a continuum. Although Crittenden agreed that secure attachment in a safe environment is the ideal situation for every child, in her view, insecure patterns of attachment are the most adaptive behavior for some children given their environment. For a child growing up with an abusive parent, distancing themselves from that parent is likely the most protective strategy for that child. Problems arise when the child's insecure attachment pattern becomes so rigid that the child continues to adhere to that pattern of attachment in safe relationships. Crittenden emphasized providing a safe environment in therapy in which the individual can try out new behaviors and responses without fear of negative repercussions.

In adolescence, attachment experiences from childhood continue to have an important influence on teens as they work through the developmental tasks of adolescence (Dallos, 2023). Results of a meta-analysis indicated youth with a secure attachment style were more likely to have higher self-esteem than those with insecure attachment styles (Pinquart, 2023). Secure attachment may also impact identity development. A teen with a secure attachment to an aunt, for instance, may use the aunt as a secure base from which to explore new identities as well as their growing independence. In this example, the teen could trust that the aunt would be a consistently caring presence as the teen tried out different ways of being in the world. Another teen with an overall pattern of avoidant attachment may cease to reach out for support from adults in their life and become overly independent. Without a secure base from which to explore, the teen may feel untethered and may have difficulty engaging in healthy identity exploration.

In addition to the continued importance of adult relationships, peers increasingly serve as attachment relationships in adolescence (Dallos, 2023). Increases in cognitive and emotional development allow teens to develop deeper relationships with peers, and these romantically or emotionally intimate relationships can serve as important attachments. Adolescents with insecure attachment patterns may seek to meet their attachment needs through substance use or risky sexual relationships (Crittenden, 2016; Dallos, 2023). Conversely, for adolescents with difficult attachment histories, positive peer attachments can serve an important role in healing attachment wounds.

Attachment theory has been criticized for applying primarily in Western individualistic contexts and for lacking studies that take into account children's larger cultural context (Vicedo, 2017). Proponents of attachment as a universal phenomenon have emphasized that context is important and that attachment patterns and attachment behavior must be interpreted within the unique cultural context of each society, family, and individual (O'Shaughnessy, 2023b). In addition, current attachment theorists recognize the potential for many attachments and de-emphasize the mother as the "default" attachment figure (e.g., Crittenden, 2016; O'Shaughnessy, 2023b). When cultural considerations are centered, attachment theory can still be a helpful framework for viewing relational patterns.

Erikson's Stages of Psychosocial Development

Erik Erikson was one of the first theorists to propose a lifespan model of development, and his thinking continues to impact the mental health field today (Lally & Valentine-French, 2019). He developed his theory of psychosocial development as a reaction to Freud's psychosexual stages, emphasizing ego development over sexual development (Newman & Newman, 2020). Erikson conceived his stages as progressive, meaning that an individual would proceed in an orderly way from the earlier stages to the subsequent ones. How well an individual progresses through what Erikson termed the central crisis of each stage – normal stress based on societal expectations –would help determine how successfully they would be able to resolve the crises of the upcoming stages (Newman & Newman, 2020).

However, he believed that a person could more positively resolve a crisis from an earlier stage later in life. For example, a teen who exited their infancy with a sense of mistrust and thus is now struggling to positively resolve the crisis of identity vs. identity confusion may develop trust through their work with a therapist and be able to continue their psychosocial development in more healthy ways.

Although Erikson emphasized positive resolution of each stage, he also defined healthy development as grappling with the more challenging side of the stage (Erikson, 1963; Newman & Newman, 2020). For example, within Erikson's theory, it is a healthy part of development for young adults to struggle with isolation in the early years of adulthood as part of the process of finding emotional intimacy in relationships. Further, progress through each crisis can be viewed as a continuum rather than achievement of a particular status. An individual making positive progress through industry vs. inferiority may enter the teen years with some self-doubt in certain areas and still be considered to have healthy development.

Familiarity with Erikson's early stages is necessary for adolescent counselors to understand how challenges from early development inform current development. Table 1.1 provides an overview of Erikson's first six stages. The final stages of generativity vs. stagnation (middle adulthood) and ego integrity vs. despair (late adulthood) are not listed. Erikson did not provide age ranges for his stages (Cross & Cross, 2017), but others have ascribed general ages to each stage, and those are listed in Table 1.1.

Identity Development

Although identity development is a complex process (Willis & Cashwell, 2017) that occurs throughout the lifespan, the cognitive changes taking place in adolescence allow teens to engage in new levels of self-examination and reflection (Crocetti, 2017). Erikson believed that healthy development in adolescence meant entering adulthood with a cohesive (not unchanging) identity (Newman & Newman, 2020). James Marcia expanded on the identity formation stage of Erikson's theory and developed four identity statuses. Scholars continue to explore more specific areas of identity development such as ethnic/racial identity development, gender identity development, and other important aspects of identity. Today, many scholars consider this focused period of identity development to continue through at least the mid-20s (Willis & Cashwell, 2017). In the 21st century, we must also consider the impact of digital (e.g., social media, video games) engagement on the identity development of adolescents (Granic et al., 2020). In this section, we explore just some of the many models of identity development and hope that these can be a starting place for understanding the development of adolescents' diverse identities.

Marcia's Identity Statuses

In his work on identity, Marcia posited that there were two processes in identity development: exploration and commitment. He also proposed four statuses based on a person's level of exploration and commitment. Table 1.2 provides a summary of Marcia's identity statuses.

Table 1.1 Erikson's First Six Stages of Development

Approximate Age	*Positive Resolution*	*Negative Resolution*
Infancy (birth – 18 mo)	**Trust** – Facilitated by consistent, responsive caregiving; Child leaves infancy trusting their physical/emotional needs will generally be met by their environment	**Mistrust** – May result from inconsistent or abusive caregiving; Child leaves infancy believing they cannot count on their environment to meet their physical/emotional needs
Toddlerhood (18 mo – 2 yrs)	**Autonomy** – Facilitated by caregivers who allow child space to explore independent action and provide support when needed; Child leaves toddlerhood believing they can be their own person	**Shame/Doubt** – May result from controlling or disengaged caregiving; Child leaves toddlerhood believing they are bad or unable to function independently
Preschool Age (3yrs – 5 yrs)	**Initiative** – Facilitated by caregivers who allow child to imagine and explore possibilities; Child leaves preschool age with confidence they can work with others to imagine and carry out plans	**Guilt** – May result from frequent criticism or rejection of ideas or from inability to follow through with any plans; Child leaves preschool age believing they cannot accomplish something without negatively impacting others
School Age (6 yrs – 12 yrs)	**Industry** – Facilitated by an environment in which child can find their strengths and experience small failures; Child leaves this age with a sense of competence and a belief in their ability to learn the tools of adulthood	**Inferiority** – May result from lack of challenges or frequent perception of being "less than" peers; Child leaves this age with a lack of motivation and low confidence in their ability to be successful
Adolescence (13 yrs – 18+ yrs)	**Identity formation** – Facilitated by an environment that supports role exploration, self-reflection, and relational feedback; Individual leaves adolescence with a sense of agency and a cohesive self-concept that integrates childhood experiences with newly developed values	**Identity confusion** – May result from lack of confidence and difficulty integrating various aspects of their lives; Individual may leave adolescence with a lack of agency, lower self-esteem, and/or vulnerability to peer pressure
Early Adulthood (18 yrs to 40 yrs)	**Intimacy** – Facilitated by a strong sense of self and opportunities to sacrifice for others; Individual leaves early adulthood with the ability to form emotionally intimate relationships	**Isolation** – May result from a lack of cohesive identity or lower self-esteem; Individual may leave early adulthood without being able to sustain emotionally intimate relationships

Note: For more detailed information see: (Cross & Cross, 2017; Lally & Valentine-French, 2019; Newman & Newman, 2020).

Table 1.2 Marcia's Identity Statuses

	Low Commitment	*High Commitment*
Low Exploration	Diffusion	Foreclosure
High Exploration	Moratorium	Achievement

Religious identity provides a useful context for understanding these statuses. A 16-year-old in identity diffusion might go through the motions of attending religious services with their family but would show neither exploration (e.g., questioning or trying to learn more about the religious teachings) nor commitment (e.g., making choices that aligned with the family's religious views or refusing to attend services). A 14-year-old in identity foreclosure might be actively engaged in the family's religious community and espouse those ideas to their friends (high commitment). However, when questioned, this teen would not have considered that they have the option to have a different belief system and may not be able to explain their own personal reasons for following the religion (low exploration). A 17-year-old in identity moratorium might be actively exploring their family's religion (e.g., questioning or seeking to learn more) but has not yet come to a personal conclusion about their beliefs. A 23-year-old in identity achievement will have gone through a process of questioning and/or learning more about their religion or components of the religion and will make choices aligned with their chosen identity. They may decide they no longer want to be involved in the religion or they may continue to identify with the religious group. Either way, they will "own" their identity in a way that was not possible when they had not engaged in the process of exploration.

Research has consistently demonstrated that statuses with high commitment (foreclosure and achievement) are associated with higher levels of wellness (Willis & Cashwell, 2017). However, experiencing periods of questioning (moratorium) is an important developmental process for adolescents (Crocetti, 2017) and only becomes problematic if it extends indefinitely. Identity formation is an ongoing process throughout the lifespan, and people may re-examine committed identities at any time, something that often leads to at least minor distress (Crocetti, 2017). Although they should not be viewed as static, Marcia's framework can help therapists identify an adolescent's status and articulate shifts in identity over time.

Ethnic/Racial Identity Development

Researchers have used Marcia's identity statuses as a starting point to develop models of ethnic/racial identity (ERI) development. Next, we discuss two of the many models of identity development that exist.

RACIAL/CULTURAL IDENTITY MODEL

Atkinson et al. (1998) and later Sue et al. (2019) proposed another general model of ethnic/racial/cultural identity development that drew heavily from Cross' (1971, 1995) pioneering work on Black identity development. In the first stage, conformity, the individual expresses a preference for the values of the dominant group. For minoritized individuals, this preference may or may not be accompanied by negative feelings about their own group. The second stage is dissonance. In this stage, the individual has an experience or a series of experiences that cause them to begin to question their previously held views. A person with a minoritized identity for whom race/ethnicity has not been particularly salient may experience blatant discrimination for the first time. A minoritized person with internalized racism may encounter a person of their own group who challenges their stereotypes. A person in the dominant group may develop a relationship with a minoritized person and begin to see the instances of discrimination through their eyes.

In the third stage, resistance and immersion, individuals tend to reject the ideals of the dominant society and embrace the values of minoritized groups. This stage tends to be characterized by anger toward the dominant culture. The fourth stage, introspection, involves the realization that spending so much energy on anger toward White society is, by itself, exhausting and not helping the individual move forward. The individual then begins a period of introspection where they may begin to experience incongruence and discomfort with the near-absolute thinking of White = bad; other groups = good. In this stage, the individual may begin to reassess the usefulness of dominant group and minoritized group values. However, in this stage, the reassessment is not coming from a place of disparagement for the minoritized group as it was in the first stage. The final stage is the integrative awareness phase. People in this stage are able to feel secure in their own culture and can recognize that there are positive and negative elements of all cultures. In this phase, individuals recognize and desire to eliminate forms of oppression, but, different from other stages, they are able to separate their own identity and esteem from the dominant narrative. They are also able to target the root of problems more accurately. Rather than seeing all Whiteness as bad, they are able to direct their anger toward specific behaviors and systems of oppression.

HELMS' MODEL OF WHITE RACIAL CONSCIOUSNESS

Janet Helms (1984) proposed a model of White racial consciousness that continues to contribute to the identity development literature today. Helms described five stages and emphasized that, due to their status as the dominant group, most White people have the option to ignore their Whiteness or avoid encountering situations that challenge their views on race. Thus, in each of Helms' five stages, the person has the option to resolve challenges positively and move forward or remain stuck.

In the first stage, contact, White people become aware that people of other races exist. However, they may still have a tendency toward minimizing differences between races. In the next stage, disintegration, the person begins to accept the reality of racism and White privilege and may feel guilty and depressed. The person may attempt unsuccessful strategies to deal with their feelings, such as overidentification with the minoritized group or trying to become a "protector." These efforts will inevitably be rejected, and a White person working to resolve their feelings of helplessness moves into the third stage, reintegration. In this stage, the person may become more hostile toward the minoritized group and increase dominant-group identification. If the person is able to continue to explore their feelings of anger and guilt and explore their Whiteness, then they begin to develop an understanding of what it means to be White in a society that is racist and they are able to move into the next stage, pseudo-independent. In this stage, the White person's exploration of racial differences tends to be more intellectual, and there is less naivete and fewer intense emotions than in the previous stages. Successfully moving through this stage leads to the final stage, autonomy, when the person is able to both understand and accept differences between races, seeks out cross-cultural experiences, demonstrates security in their own racial identity, and is respectful and appreciative of the differences between groups.

Gender Identity Development

The field of gender identity is perhaps one of the most rapidly changing areas of the mental health world. Gender can be defined as one's internal sense of one's gender (sense of being male, female, trans, nonbinary, etc.; Ginicola & Filmore, 2017), who a person knows themselves to be. Traditional approaches to gender development have emphasized the gender binary, the idea that there are only two genders (male and female) and that people are one of those two genders, usually the one associated with a person's sex assigned at birth based on their observed genitalia. Anderson (2018) used the term *gender expansive* to describe individuals who do not identify with either gender binary. Anderson noted three areas that can help therapists understand gender development for all youth. These are biological, social, and cognitive influences. Each of these influences interacts with one another, and they are influenced by the person's family, cultural, and social environments.

Research strongly supports a biological explanation for gendered differences in the brain (Ginicola et al., 2017). In addition, it is well-documented that certain specific conditions (e.g., exposure to hormones in utero) are linked to particular expressions of gendered behavior in childhood that are not traditionally associated with an individual's sex assigned at birth (Anderson, 2018). According to evolutionary theory, differences that persist over time must have developed to help the species survive. Thus, from a biological perspective, various gender identities, including no gender identity, can be seen as a normal part of human development as they have been documented across human history (Ginicola et al., 2017). It is also important to note that, while there are some biological influences on gendered behaviors, the idea of gender is a social construct.

Social influences on gender have also been well-documented (Lally & Valentine-French, 2019). Children are adept at picking up on the social expectations of others and use this information to understand their gender identity. For example, if a child assigned male at birth tries on a princess dress, the response the child gets will impact the child's view of their own and others' genders. Bandura's (1977) social learning theory has frequently been used to describe gender development. This theory suggests that children develop their own sense of gender by modeling their behavior after same-gendered adults. Bandura also emphasized the role of direct teaching in social learning. If gender identity is developed through this type of learning, then an understanding of a person's gender identity and gendered experiences must take into account structural inequities that exist in society (Robbins & McGowan, 2016).

The cognitive perspective on gender development suggests that children develop a cognitive schema of gender that includes stereotypes and norms of their society as well as their immediate environment (Anderson, 2018). Children are socialized through interactions with their families, caregiving and educational environments, and experiences in their larger cultural context. Children learn gender behavior and expectations through modeling and by how they are treated by others based on their perceived gender. For example, an adolescent who grew up in a community that only viewed gender in the binary may have developed some traditional schemas about what it means to be a man or a woman. If that adolescent now attends a more diverse high school, the adolescent will likely be exposed to more varied conceptions of gender, including gender expansive identities. This experience would likely result in a more complex gender schema, which would allow the adolescent to self-identify in new ways.

Current conceptions of gender development are rapidly shifting, and some of the ways gender is described in this book may be out of date by the time it reaches readers. However, it is clear conceptualizations of gender are moving in a more inclusive and expansive direction in the mental health community. For example, gender identities outside the gender binary were once seen as pathologies, but all major health and psychological organizations accept and understand these identities as normal, healthy variations of the human experience (Anderson, 2018). Adolescent therapists can support their clients' gender identity development by engaging in current continuing education and by listening to and affirming their client's identities and ways of describing and expressing themselves.

Sexual/Affectional Orientation Development

Sexual or affectional orientation is defined as the "biological and physiological impulse of attraction or arousal and the psychological impulse for romantic and emotional attraction, both of which provide a foundation for sexual behavior and bonding" (Ginicola et al., 2017, p. 22). Using the term *affectional orientation* in place of the more common *sexual orientation* de-emphasizes the importance of sexual attraction and allows for more overt inclusion of asexual individuals who are not sexually attracted or minimally sexually attracted to others. It is important to emphasize that the components of physical attraction, romantic attraction, and sexual behavior included in this definition may or may not be aligned. For example, a person could identify as pansexual (experiencing physical and/or romantic attraction for all genders), but they may currently only engage in sexual behavior with one gender. The many ways people identify themselves in terms of their sexual and romantic identities is beyond the scope of this brief introduction. We recommend exploring the online glossaries provided by LGBTQIA+ advocacy groups such as PFLAG and the Human Rights Campaign for more information.

CASS' MODEL OF GAY IDENTITY DEVELOPMENT

Cass (1979) developed a six-stage model of LGBTQIA+ identity development that emphasizes the person's active role in forming their identity. Although the model was originally intended to explain gay and lesbian identity development, it is now considered to be applicable to any minoritized sexual identity (Brandon-Friedman, 2019). In the first stage, identity confusion, an individual becomes aware of LGBTQIA+ relationships and begins to apply the information learned about these relationships to the self. The individual develops the belief that they might be queer. In the second stage, identity comparison, the individual begins to feel some social isolation due to the sense of feeling different than others in a heteronormative society. In identity tolerance, the third stage, the individual begins to interact with other queer people and can articulate the belief that they are probably queer. The increased contact with the LGBTQIA+ community leads to the fourth stage, identity acceptance, when the individual's involvement in the LGBTQIA+ subculture normalizes their developing identity. In this stage, they may only be out to the queer community and trusted allies.

The fifth and sixth stages are reminiscent of the last two stages of the ethnic/racial identity models discussed before (Cross, 1971; Sue et al., 2019). In the fifth stage, identity pride, the individual places a high value on the opinions of the LGBTQIA+ community and a low value on the opinion of the heteronormative society. Anger and pride tend to co-exist together in this stage, and people tend to hold their queerness as the most salient aspect of their identity. In the final stage, identity synthesis, the individual is able to recognize both positive and negative aspects of the heterosexual world and the LGBTQIA+ world. They are also better able to see themselves more holistically, with their LGBTQIA+ identity being one of many important aspects of their identity.

Although LGBTQIA+ persons still experience significant discrimination in the US, much has changed since the time Cass developed the model. In certain communities and families, adolescents and young adults may be met with affirmation and support as they explore their sexuality and affective orientation. For this reason, some have suggested that adolescents and young adults in more affirming environments may skip the early stages of Cass' model (Taylor & Neppl, 2023). For example, an adolescent with gay parents will not remember a time they did not know about same-sex relationships (Stage 1) and will be less likely to feel isolation if they experience same-sex attraction (Stage 2). They probably also already have many connections to the LGBTQIA+ community (Stages 3–4). Thus, progression through Cass' stages could look very different for a teen who has been exposed to LGBTQIA+ individuals and communities for most of their life versus a young person with little or no exposure.

Minority stress theory (Meyer, 2003; Frost & Meyer, 2023) was developed to better articulate the mental health difficulties present in sexual minoritized populations. Meyer (2003; Frost & Meyer, 2023) posited that the negative health outcomes experienced by these groups are a result of discrimination, not some problem inherent with that group's sexuality. The term *minority stress* refers to the stress that results specifically from experiences of discrimination. This stress can be distal (coming from the outside and acting on the person) or proximal (directly related to the person; Frost & Meyer, 2023). Distal stress comes from discriminatory policies, events, and chronic daily stressors. For example, a polyamorous young adult is asked to fill out forms that do not have an option or space to accurately reflect their relationship status. Each time this happens, the person is then faced with the decision of whether to say something or only represent part of their experience on the form. Although one such experience in isolation may not be particularly stressful, repeated experiences such as this can result in an accumulation of stress. Another example could be a transgender adolescent who is forced to use the restroom associated with their sex assigned at birth. This teen would experience daily stress due to the discriminatory policy. Proximal stress in minority stress theory involves stressors that involve the LGBT person's internalization of stigma through socialization. These proximal stressors could manifest as expectation of rejection or in concealment of their LGBT identity, for example. Application of this theory can help adolescent therapists conceptualize and advocate with and for their teen and young adult clients.

Identity Development and Ability

Disability status is another identity that some adolescents may need to integrate into their self-concept. Because a disability can begin at any point across the lifespan, researchers do not agree on any one model of disability identity development. Frank (1993) and Charmaz (1995) were some of the first to research disability identity, and their models emphasize the perception of self in relation to others and the acquisition of a disability respectively (Forber-Pratt et al., 2017). A more recent systematic review of disability identity research summarized some key components of the existing disability identity models. First, disability identity itself is a meaning-making experience that impacts how people view themselves and their interactions with the world. This means that individuals with disabilities must work with both the manifestations of their disability as well as the social messaging around it (Forber-Pratt et al., 2017). For example, a first-year high school student who uses a wheelchair must find the accessible routes on campus and must deal with stares, questions, and well-meaning sympathy or infantilization from others. For youth in more disability-affirming and accessible environments, their experience of disability and disability identity development would be vastly different.

A second finding of the review was that most data on disability identity research has been qualitative (Forber-Pratt et al., 2017). This result is consistent with a philosophy that honors the unique experiences of each person and each disability. However, the lack of research with larger sample sizes makes it more difficult to understand commonalities of disability identity development across a wide range of diverse experiences. A third area of emphasis in many of the models examined by the researchers was the impact health care professionals have on individuals' perceptions of themselves and their disability. One example of a way a health care professional might have a negative impact on a person's development of a disability identity is to underestimate what the person can do. Similarly, they might extend well-meaning pity or unneeded sympathy that ranges from unhelpful to harmful to the person with the disability. Finally, more recent models of disability identity development emphasize community and disability pride (Forber-Pratt et al., 2017). Connecting with the disability community can help individuals with disabilities see themselves more positively and can normalize some of their experiences with stigma and prejudice. Adolescent therapists working with young people with new or existing disabilities can follow the client's lead to better understand their unique experience of disability.

Intersectionality

In any discussion of identity development, it is important to remember that people are much more complex than any one identity and that the "intersection" (Crenshaw, 1989) of a person's various minoritized identities provides them with a unique experience of discrimination that cannot be explained by simply looking at each individual identity (Cho et al., 2013; Crenshaw, 1989; Grzanka, 2020). Crenshaw's (1989) definition of intersectionality originated within the context of the legal system to understand discrimination and injustice that was uniquely experienced by people with multiple marginalized identities. She identified that the intersectional identity of Black women had to be understood to understand their distinct experiences of oppression.

In recent years, intersectionality has been applied to other professions, including mental health, and serves as a useful tool for conceptualizing individual's experiences of oppression (Cho et al., 2013; Grzanka, 2020). Application of intersectionality includes three key components (Robbins & McGowan, 2016): recognizing a person's experience of discrimination is more than just the sum of their various identities (as described previously); understanding identities must be understood within a larger social system and highlighting existing inequities; and taking action toward changing those systems (Crenshaw, 1989; Grzanka, 2020; Robbins & McGowan, 2016). Adolescent and young adult therapists can apply these principles to understand marginalized clients' unique experiences with oppression as well as client activism that might stem from those experiences.

Bronfenbrenner's Bioecological Theory

To wrap up our discussion of theories of development, we turn to one theorist who sought to explain development from a systemic perspective. Urie Bronfenbrenner developed his theory of human development from his post-World War II experiences researching child development in both the US and in what was then Soviet Russia (Hayes et al., 2023). Although the iteration of his model that describes the context of development is most well-known (i.e., ecological systems theory), Bronfenbrenner also emphasized other concepts such as interpersonal interactions, time/history, and the impact of the individual on their own development (Navarro et al., 2022).

To describe the context of development, Bronfenbrenner envisioned nested systems with the individual at the center (Bronfenbrenner & Morris, 2006; Hayes et al., 2023). The innermost system, the microsystem, includes the people and environments that have a direct influence on the person, such as household members, teachers, and friends. Recent scholars have suggested that for adolescents today, the microsystem can be divided into a physical (i.e., face-to-face relationships) and a virtual (i.e., relationships on any given digital platform) microsystems (Navarro & Tudge, 2023). The next system is the mesosystem, which can be described as the interaction between microsystems. For example, if an adolescents' parents strongly disapprove of the adolescent's best friend, that would have an impact on the development of the adolescent. The exosystem encompasses both the mesosystem and the microsystem and include actions that impact microsystems in an individual's life but do not directly involve the individual (Bronfenbrenner & Morris,

2006). For example, a parent's workplace environment or school district policies would affect a teen, even if the teen never goes to their parent's place of work or talks with the superintendent. Next, the macrosystem includes even more distant influences on development, such as cultural values and national laws. For example, if a young adult's culture values self-discovery and exploration, they may be able to experience a period of self-focused emerging adulthood, whereas if a young adult's culture values providing for family members, they may not have a similar experience of focusing on their own goals and identity development. Digital culture can also impact an adolescent's macrosystem as they have constant access and exposure to cultural values online and through social media (Navarro & Tudge, 2023). Finally, the chronosystem includes a person's place in history (e.g., experiencing the COVID-19 pandemic and the Black Lives Matter movement) as well as transitions throughout their life (e.g., moving from middle school to high school, experiencing parental divorce).

Understanding the context of development based on Bronfenbrenner's theory can help adolescent and young adult therapists better understand the whole picture of a client's development, including social factors that may impact the individual or family. Therapists can also consider the way an individual's characteristics (both innate and learned) have an impact on their environment (Hayes et al., 2023). For example, a Black gay cisgender man may elicit a different reaction and treatment from others in the environment than an Asian trans woman due to others' preconceived ideas about these individuals' various identities. This example illustrates an important component of Bronfenbrenner's theory. Namely, that the environment acts on individuals while individuals act on the environment. Bronfenbrenner said that reciprocal actions repeated over time were the impetus for development (Bronfenbrenner & Morris, 2006), and therapists can consider what kinds of interactions have contributed to and are currently impacting adolescents' development.

A Word on Developmental Models

Developmental models can be useful in understanding adolescent development. They can help adolescent therapists better conceptualize their clients leading to improved intentionality and better communication with the adults in clients' lives. However, therapists must also remember developmental models are just that – models. Most models are based on a normative perspective. That is, the theorists attempted to describe what was typical development in a given domain versus the many unique paths of development an individual might take. Further, the development of these models was influenced by the identities of theorists who conceived of them who were, in turn, influenced by their historical and social contexts. This observation does not negate the usefulness of these models to modern therapists. Rather, it reminds adolescent therapists that application of developmental models must be done with sensitivity to the lived experiences of the adolescent. When a model is being forced onto a person's experience or becomes pathologizing rather than assisting in development of empathy, the model is no longer being used in an ethical and therapeutic manner. As is evident by the amount of space given to developmental theories in this chapter, we believe they are extremely useful when applied in a considered way and with the understanding that they may not fit for everyone. In our practice, a deeper understanding of human development has helped us respond with greater empathy, assisted in explaining adolescent behavior to adults in ways that enhance understanding and respect of the adolescent, and provided a way to advocate for developmentally sensitive solutions to difficult adolescent behavior.

Other Key Issues in Adolescent Development

In addition to the many development theories discussed in this chapter, there are other significant impacts on adolescent development that bear mentioning, such as the role of pre-adolescent development and the impact of trauma.

Pre-Adolescent Development

Pre-adolescence, here defined as approximately ages 9 to 12, is a time of significant variance. In my clinical practice, I have worked with preteens who could articulate their parents unique parenting styles and said things like, "I know I shouldn't care so much about what my friends think, but that's something I've always struggled with," as well as preteens who spent the entire session building imaginary worlds out of sandtray figures or engaging in sword fights.

Although there is much variation, most pre-adolescents have begun puberty (NIH, 2021). Researchers have found the average age of menarche (first period) is 12.4 years for individuals assigned female at birth (Marques et al., 2022) and spermarche (first ejaculation) is about 13 for those assigned male at birth (Tomova et al., 2011). Some individuals in this age range will begin to experience the appearance of secondary sex characteristics, such as breasts, pubic hair, facial hair, and a deeper voice (Lally & Valentine-French, 2019). Preteens exhibit a greater desire for privacy and independence and are becoming more interested in romantic relationships (NSVRC, 2013). They also tend to be more curious about adult bodies and may seek out media with sexual content (NSVRC, 2013). Many preteens begin to articulate a sexual orientation (Second Step, 2014). When provided an accurate sex education, preteens can understand reproduction, puberty, pregnancy, and childbirth. Otherwise, they may seek out (inaccurate) information elsewhere, such as friends or the internet.

Older preteens are also experiencing the first signs of the explosion in synapses that takes place in adolescence. These physical and cognitive changes can leave preteens feeling alienated from their bodies and brains. I have a distinct memory of angrily yelling at my parents when I was in sixth grade, something that was out of character for me. I remember part of me recognizing that they were being perfectly reasonable, but I felt like I had no control over what my brain and body were doing.

Along with the changes in brain development, cognitive development makes a big shift in the 9- to 12-year-old age range. Piaget said that children developed the capacity for abstract thought and hypothetico-deductive reasoning around age 11 (Lally & Valentine-French, 2019). However, as illustrated by the examples at the beginning of this section, the cognitive development of individual children vary considerably. Regardless, pre-adolescents still need considerable support in accessing their growing cognitive skills.

Social/emotional skills and needs of preteens vary as well. However, throughout this age, an increasing depth of and reliance on peer relationships is seen. Preteens are firmly in Erikson's industry vs. inferiority stage and benefit from a supportive environment at home and school where they can practice taking risks and experiencing both success and low-stakes failures (Cross & Cross, 2017). Children in this stage want to feel they can make meaningful contributions to their environments. Preteens who resolve this phase in a more positive way enter their teen years with a sense that they can use adult tools to move forward in their lives and have a real impact in their relationships and world. In adolescence, they can use these tools to explore their identity. Those who more negatively resolve this stage may feel a sense of inferiority that stays with them into adolescence.

The physical, cognitive, and social changes experienced by pre-adolescents impact the ways they understand their various identities. Younger preteens tend to focus on group membership and may take increased ownership of cultural practices (Wilson, 2016). There tends to be high group-esteem for their own group, which can be a particularly important part of positive identity development for those with marginalized identities (Ojiambo & Taylor, 2016). Older pre-adolescents are able to describe their identities in more complex ways but still lack the ability to think about -isms (e.g., racism, sexism, ablism) in systematic ways (Purswell, 2016).

Overall, pre-adolescence is a time of feeling in-between childhood and adolescence, but the age at which a young person feels this in-betweenness can vary considerably and is based on both socialization and biological development. Experiences in pre-adolescence can set the tone for development in the teen years, and it is often useful for adolescent therapists to ask about late elementary and middle school experiences of their clients.

Adverse Childhood Experiences, Trauma, and Adolescents

Understanding the development of adolescent clients also entails understanding the impact of trauma and adverse childhood experiences (ACEs) on their lives. Trauma can be both the big, life-threatening traumas that might result in a PTSD diagnosis and the smaller, but significant, stressors such as emotional abuse, racist microaggressions, or persistent financial stress (McBride, 2021). During the COVID-19 pandemic, most children, who are today's adolescents, experienced persistent stressors as they saw their caregivers worrying about health, finances, loved ones, and racial injustice. Others experienced more acute traumas such as the death of a family member, loss of financial stability, and severe disruption of childcare/school environments. The impacts of the COVID-19 pandemic will continue to show up in counseling rooms for years to come.

Many adolescents, particularly older adolescents and young adults, may be identifying previous experiences as trauma for the first time. Others may be experiencing the impact of past ACEs in new ways as they reach certain milestones. For example, a 16-year-old who lost a parent in a car accident will likely have to face that loss again when learning to drive. They may miss the parent being there during an important milestone and also fear the responsibility of being a driver knowing how painful it is to lose a loved one in a car wreck. Whether the event(s) occurred in childhood or adolescence, trauma and adverse experiences are very relevant to the great task of adolescence: identity development.

In adults, having multiple ACEs is associated with greater incidence of substance use as well as many health problems such as cancer, diabetes, and HIV (Felitti et al., 1998). The results of one study found that adolescents with four or more ACEs were three times more likely to have a diagnosis of depression (McGowan et al., 2023), and another study showed that each individual ACE is associated with an increased risk of substance use (Afifi et al., 2020). However, even for adolescents with higher numbers of ACEs, family resilience was associated with a lower risk of depression (McGowan et al., 2023). Furthermore, being future-oriented, getting sufficient sleep, having positive family and school relationships, and feeling knowledgeable about one's culture and language were protective factors for decreased use of substances among adolescents with higher ACEs scores (Afifi et al., 2023). The results of these studies show that adolescents are already being impacted by their ACEs but that many factors can decrease the negative impact of these experiences. Adolescent therapists are uniquely positioned to support adolescents and their families in building these protective factors.

Some Final Thoughts and How to Use This Book

Adolescence is a time full of change, challenges, and opportunity. Due to the adaptability of the adolescent brain, adolescent therapists are in a unique position to facilitate and support lifelong growth and transformation in their 13- to 25-year-old clients. The next chapter in this book provides a framework for understanding the culture and context of adolescence when working with teen and young adult clients as well as important therapeutic considerations for counseling adolescents. Then, Chapters 3 through 10 apply developmental concepts and best practices to each age/age range of adolescence and emerging adulthood. Finally, the last chapter includes handouts summarizing key points of development for each age, including when to seek help and tips for supporting adolescents. These handouts can be shared with parents/caregivers and other important adults or used to support psychoeducation with the adolescents themselves. We hope that the information contained in this book will assist adolescent therapists in increasing empathy, intentionality, and communication with adults who impact the lives of their clients.

References

Afifi, T. O., Taillieu, T., Salmon, S., Garcés Davila, I., Stewart-Tufescu, A., Fortier, J., Stuck, S., Asmundson, G. J. G., Sareen, J., & MacMillan, H. L. (2020). Adverse childhood experiences (ACEs), peer victimization, and substance use among adolescents. *Child Abuse and Neglect*, *106*, 1–12. https://doi.org/10.1016/j.chiabu.2020.104504

Afifi, T. O., Taillieu, T., Salmon, S., Stewart-Tufescu, A., Stuck, S., Fortier, J., MacMillan, H. L., Sareen, J., Tonmyr, L., & Katz, L. Y. (2023). Protective factors for decreasing nicotine, alcohol, and cannabis use among adolescents with a history of adverse childhood experiences (ACEs). *Journal of Mental Health and Addiction*, *21*, 2255–2273. https://doi.org/10.1007/s11469-021-00720-x

Ainsworth, M. D. S., & Bell, S. M. (1970). Attachment, exploration, and separation: Illustrated by the behavior of one-year-olds in a strange situation. *Child Development*, *41*, 49–67.

Ainsworth, M. D. S., Blehar, M. C., Waters, E., & Wall, S. (1978). *Patterns of attachment: A psychological study of the strange situation*. Lawrence Erlbaum Associates.
Anderson, E. E. (2018). The unfolding and exploration of gender from a gender affirmative perspective. In C. Keo-Meier & D. Ehrensaft (Eds.), *The gender affirmative model: An interdisciplinary approach to supporting transgender and gender expansive children* (pp. 21–36). American Psychological Association. https://doi.org/10.1037/0000095-002
Atkinson, D. R., Morten, G., & Sue, D. W. (1998). *Counseling American minorities: A cross-cultural perspective* (5th ed). McGraw-Hill.
Badenoch, B. (2008). *Being a brain-wise therapist: A practical guide to interpersonal neurobiology*. Norton & Norton.
Bandura, A. (1977). Self-efficacy: Toward a unifying theory of behavioral change. *Psychological Review*, *84*(2), 191–215. https://doi.org/10.1037/0033-295X.84.2.191
Bowlby, J. (1969). *Attachment and loss: Vol 1. Attachment*. Basic Books.
Brandon-Friedman, R. A. (2019). Youth sexual development: A primer for social workers. *Social Work*, *64*(4), 356–364. https://doi.org/10.1093/sw/swz027
Bronfenbrenner, U., & Morris, P. A. (2006). The bioecological model of human development. In W. Damon & R. M. Lerner (Eds.), *Handbook of child psychology* (pp. 793–828). Wiley.
Cass, V. C. (1979). Homosexual identity formation: A theoretical model. *Journal of Homosexuality*, *4*, 219–235.
Charmaz, K. (1995). The body, identity, and self: Adapting to impairment. *The Sociological Quarterly*, *35*, 269–288. http://doi.org/10.111/j.1533-8525
Cho, S., Williams Crenshaw, K., & McCall, L. (2013). Toward a field of intersectionality studies: Theory, applications, and praxis. *Signs: Journal of Women in Culture and Society*, *38*(4), 785–810. https://doi.org/10.1086/669608
Crenshaw, K. (1989). Demarginalizing the intersection of race and sex: A black feminist critique of antidiscrimination doctrine, feminist theory, and antiracist politics. *University of Chicago Legal Forum*, *1989*(1), 139–167.
Crittenden, P. M. (2000). Introduction. In P. M. Crittenden & A. H. Claussen (Eds.), *The organization of attachment relationships: Maturation, culture, and context* (pp. 1–12). Cambridge University Press.
Crittenden, P. M. (2016). *Raising parents: Attachment, representation, and treatment* (2nd ed.). Routledge. https://doi.org/10.4324/9781315726
Crocetti, E. (2017). Identity formation in adolescence: The dynamic of forming and consolidating identity commitments. *Child Development Perspectives*, *11*(2), 145–150. https://doi.org/10.1111/cdep.12226
Cross, T. L., & Cross, J. R. (2017). Maximizing potential: A school-based conception of psychosocial development. *High Ability Studies*, *28*(1), 43–58. https://doi.org/10.1080/13598139.2017.1292896
Cross, W. E. (1971). The Negro-to-black conversion experience: Towards a psychology of Black liberation. *Black World*, *20*, 13–27.
Cross, W. E. (1995). The psychology of nigrescence: Revising the cross model. In J. G. Ponterotto, J. M. Casas, L. A. Suzuki, & C. M. Alexander (Eds.), *Handbook of multicultural counseling* (pp. 93–122). SAGE.
Dallos, R. (2023). Attachment in adolescence. In K. B. O'Shaughnessy, R. Dallos, & K. Bateson (Eds.), *Attachment theory: The basics* (pp. 75–88). Routledge. https://doi.org/10.4324/9780203703878
Erikson, E. (1963). *Childhood & society* (2nd ed.). W.W. Norton.

Felitti, V. J., Anda, R. F., Nordenberg, D., Williamson, D. F., Spitz, A. M., Edwards, V., Koss, M. P., & Marks, J. S. (1998). Relationship of childhood abuse and household disfunction to many of the leading causes of death in adults: The adverse childhood experiences study. *American Journal of Preventative Medicine*, *14*(4), 245–258. https://doi.org/10.1016/S0749-3797(98)00017-8

Forber-Pratt, A. J., Lyew, D. A., Mueller, C., & Samples, L. B. (2017). Disability identity development: A systematic review of the literature. *Rehabilitation Psychology*, *62*(2), 198–207. https://doi.org/10.1037/rep0000134

Frank, A. W. (1993). The rhetoric of self-change: Illness experience as narrative. *The Sociological Quarterly*, *34*, 39–52. http:// doi.org/10.111/j.1533-8525.1993.tb00129.x

Frost, D. M., & Meyer, I. H. (2023). Minority stress theory: Application, critique, and continued relevance. *Current Opinion in Psychology*, *51*, 1–6. https://doi.org/10.1016.j.copsyc.2023.101579

Ginicola, M. M., Smith, C., & Filmore, J. (2017). *Affirmative counseling with LGBTQI+ people*. American Counseling Association. https://doi.org/10.1002/9781119375517

Granic, I., Hiromitsu, M., & Hanneke, S. (2020). Beyond screen time: Identity development in the digital age. *Psychological Inquiry*, *31*(3), 195–223. https://doi.org/10.1080/1047840X.2020.1820214

Grzanka, P. (2020). From buzzword to critical psychology: An invitation to take intersectionality seriously. *Women and Therapy*, *43*(3–4), 244–261. https://doi.org/10.1080/02703149.2020.1729473

Hayes, N., O'Toole, L., & Halpenny, A. M. (2023). *Introducing Bronfenbrenner: A guide for practitioners and students in early years education* (2nd ed.). Routledge. https://doi.org/10.4324/9781003247760

Helms, J. (1984). Toward a theoretical explanation of the effects of race on counseling: A Black and White model. *The Counseling Psychologist*, *12*(4), 115–185. https://doi.org/10.1177/0011000084124013

Lally, M., & Valentine-French, S. (2019). *Lifespan development: A psychological perspective* (2nd ed.). Creative Commons. http://dept.clcillinois.edu/psy/LifespanDevelopment.pdf

Main, M., & Solomon, J. (1990). Procedures for identifying infants as disorganized/disoriented during the Ainsworth Strange Situation. In M. T. Greenberg, D. Cicchetti, & E. M. Cummings (Eds.), *Attachment in the preschool years: Theory, research, and intervention* (pp. 121–160). University of Chicago Press.

Marques, P., Madiera, T., & Gama, A. (2022). Menstrual cycle among adolescents: Girls' awareness and age at menarche and overweight. *Revista Paulista de Pediatria*, *40*. https://doi.org/10.1590/1984-0462/2022/40/2020494

McBride, H. (2021). *The wisdom of your body*. Brazos.

McGowan, E., Oyeku, S. O., & Lim, S. W. (2023). Family, neighborhood, and parent resilience are inversely associated with reported depression in adolescents exposed to ACEs. *Academic Pediatrics*, *23*, 773–781. https://doi.org/10.1016/j.acap.2022.10.009

Meyer, I. H. (2003). Prejudice, social stress, and mental health in lesbian, gay, and bisexual populations. *Psychological Bulletin*, *129*, 674–697.

National Academies of Sciences, Engineering, and Medicine (NASEM). (2019). *The promise of adolescence: Realizing opportunity for all youth*. The National Academies Press. https://doi.org/10.17226/25388

National Institutes of Health. (2021). *Precocious puberty*. www.nichd.nih.gov/health/topics/pubertyhttps://medlineplus.gov/ency/article/001168.htm

National Sexual Violence Resource Center (NSVRC). (2013, January). *An overview of healthy childhood sexual development*. National Sexual Violence Resource Center. www.nsvrc.org/sites/default/files/2013-01/saam_2013_an-overview-of-healthy-childhood-sexual-development.pdf

Navarro, J. L., Stephens, C., Rodrigues, B. C., Walker, I. A., Cook, O., O'Toole, L., Hayes, N., & Tudge, J. R. H. (2022). Bored of the rings: Methodological and analytic approaches to operationalizing Bronfenbrenner's PPCT model in research practice. *Journal of Family Theory and Review*, *14*, 233–253. https://doi.org/10.1111/jftr.12459

Navarro, J. L., & Tudge, J. R. H. (2023). Technologizing Bronfenbrenner: Neo-ecological theory. *Current Psychology*, *42*, 19338–19354. https://doi.org/10.1007/s12144-022-02738-3

Newman, B., & Newman, P. (2020). *Theories of adolescent development*. Academic Press. https://doi.org/10.1016/B978-0-12-815450-2.00006-1

Ojiambo, D., & Taylor, L. (2016). The extraordinary 10-year-old. In D. C. Ray (Ed.), *A therapist's guide to child development: The extraordinarily ordinary years* (pp. 136–151). Routledge.

O'Shaughnessy, K. B. (2023a). Attachment and caregiving. In K. B. O'Shaughnessy, R. Dallos, & K. Bateson (Eds.), *Attachment theory: The basics* (pp. 1–14). Routledge. https://doi.org/10.4324/9780203703878

O'Shaughnessy, K. B. (2023b). Individual and cultural differences in attachment. In K. B. O'Shaughnessy, R. Dallos, & K. Bateson (Eds.), *Attachment theory: The basics* (pp. 15–34). Routledge. https://doi.org/10.4324/9780203703878

Perry, W. G., Jr. (1968). *Patterns of development in thought and values of students in a liberal arts college: A validation of a scheme*. US Department of Health, Education, and Welfare.

Perry, W. G., Jr. (1981). Cognitive and ethical growth: The making of meaning. In A. W. Chickering (Ed.), *The modern American college*. Jossey-Bass.

Pinquart, M. (2023). Associations of self-esteem with attachment to parents: A meta-analysis. *Psychological Reports*, *126*(5), 2101–2118. https://doi.org/101177/00332941221079732

Purswell, K. E. (2016). The extraordinary 9-year-old. In D. C. Ray (Ed.), *A therapist's guide to child development: The extraordinarily ordinary years* (pp. 153–164). Routledge.

Robbins, C. K., & McGowan, B. L. (2016). Intersectional perspectives on gender and gender identity development. *New Directions for Student Services*, *2016*(154), 71–83. https://doi.org/10.1002/ss.20176

Romer, D., Reyna, V. F., & Satterthwaite, T. D. (2017). Beyond sterotypes of adolescent risk taking: Placing the adolescent brain in a developmental context. *Developmental Cognitive Neuroscience*, *27*, 19–34. https://doi.org/10.1016/j.dcn.2017.07.007

Second Step. (2014). *Childhood sexual development chart*. Author. www.earlyopenoften.org/wp-content/uploads/child-sex-development.pdf

Siegel, D. (2011). *Mindsight: The new science of personal transformation*. Bantam Books.

Sue, D. W., Sue, D., Neville, H. A., & Smith, L. (2019). *Counseling the culturally diverse: Theory and practice*. Wiley.

Taylor, A. B., & Neppl, T. (2023). Sexual identity development in lesbian, gay, bisexual, transgender, and queer or questioning emerging adults: The role of parental rejection, sexuality, and specific family support. *Journal of Family Issues*, *44*(2), 409–428. https://doi.org/10.1177/0192513X211050663

Tomova, A., Robeva, R., & Kumanov, P. (2011). Timing of pubertal maturation according to the age at first conscious ejaculation. *Andrologia*, *43*, 63–166. https://doi.org/10.1111/j.1439-0272.2009.01037.x

Vicedo, M. (2017). Putting attachment in its place: Disciplinary and cultural contexts. *European Journal of Developmental Psychology*, *14*(6), 684–699. https://doi.org/10.1080/17405629.2017.1289838

Willis, B. T., & Cashwell, C. (2017). Predicting identity status: The role of attachment, differentiation, and meaning-making. *Adultspan Journal*, *16*(2), 80–92. https://doi.org/10.1002/adsp.12037

Wilson, B. J. (2016). The extraordinary 9-year-old. In D. C. Ray (Ed.), *A therapist's guide to child development: The extraordinarily ordinary years* (pp. 123–135). Routledge.

Chapter 2

The Culture and Context of Adolescence

Considerations for Therapeutic Practice

Kimberly M. Jayne

Adolescence as a developmental period and adolescents as individuals are often misunderstood. Because of this misunderstanding, adolescence is often viewed negatively as a tumultuous, awkward, rebellious, and risky time. As we saw in Chapter 1, when viewed within a developmental framework, adolescence can be seen as both a unique time of opportunity and growth as well as a time of potential challenge. In this chapter, we take a deeper look at the context of adolescent counseling in the 21st century, including implications for the culture of adolescence, key factors impacting adolescent health and well-being today like sleep and technology, and developmentally and culturally sustaining conditions for and approaches to adolescent therapy.

Culture of Adolescence

With puberty – the biological onset of adolescence – beginning at younger and younger ages, (Eckert-Lind et al., 2020) and adolescence lasting longer physiologically and socially than ever before (Sawyer et al., 2018), modern adolescence now spans 15–20 years of an individual's life. Researchers have found that the onset of puberty for children assigned female at birth (AFAB) has decreased an average of almost 3 months per decade from 1977 to 2013 (Eckert-Lind et al., 2020). As the average age of college graduation, home ownership, marriage, and parenthood continue to increase in the US (NAR, 2023; National Center for Health Statistics, 2017; United States Census Bureau, 2024), we see that many of the social markers of adulthood are shifting and occurring later and later in life or not at all. With this extended adolescence and shifts in the how adulthood is socially defined, adolescent counselors and therapists must work to understand a new and changing context and culture of adolescence.

Adolescence is neither childhood nor adulthood while also serving as a bridge between the world of childhood and the world of adulthood. Adolescents and adults often may feel that adolescents exist in a different world, and in many ways, this is true. In their exploration of the culture of adolescence, Nelson and Nelson (2010) identified three core features of adolescent culture – the centrality of peers, importance of technology and social media in daily life, and the challenge of identity development and individuation. These three core features persist across early, middle, and late adolescence even as they show up uniquely

DOI: 10.4324/9781003196297-3

in each period. When we are grounded in developmental perspective, it is evident that adolescence is not only a unique stage in life but also its own culture embedded with distinct values, experiences, language, economics, and artifacts.

In the US, adolescents are known for an intense focus on their social worlds and friendships, active pursuit of belonging and acceptance with peers, and ubiquitous use of technology and social media. Teens engage in active exploration of their identity through experimentation, seek novelty and adventure, and are driven toward greater independence and autonomy. Adolescents are often on the cutting edge of social change and movements, defining and setting trends and shaping the language and communication of the times through their use of slang, memes, and emojis. Older adolescents – emerging adults – embody the in-betweenness of adulthood and adolescence with lives that are marked by continual transition and change. In late adolescence, these almost-but-not-yet adults experience more frequent changes in their geographical location and living environments, educational programs and jobs, and friendships and romantic and sexual relationships. While seemingly a time of less internal change than early and middle adolescence, emerging adults continue to experience many changes in their external worlds and their sense of identity as they focus intensely on who they are, what they want in life, and establishing themselves within the adult world.

When we understand adolescence as its own culture, we are able to relate and respond with greater cultural humility and empathy in our interactions with adolescents. Rather than seeing aspects of adolescent culture as a challenge or problem, both adolescents and adults can approach their experiences and behavior with an understanding that adolescents are often navigating an adult world that was not made for them and with an appreciation for the cross-cultural nature of adolescent-adult relationships. When adults neglect to see adolescents and emerging adults in the context of their culture, we often draw the wrong conclusions about their behavior and experiences (Plank, 2016). When we hold adult expectations for adolescents, adolescents will always fall short. For example, when a teen breaks curfew to spend time with their friends or stays up late scrolling through social media rather than studying or sleeping before a big exam, we can easily become frustrated at their poor decision-making or angry at their defiance or disregard for rules. However, in the context of their culture, being deeply focused on peers and intensely engaged with social media and technology even at the cost of consequences for breaking rules, not getting enough sleep, or poor academic outcomes makes sense. Using Plank's (2016) work on the culture of childhood as a model, we have identified the central values, beliefs, behavior, language, artifacts, and economics of the culture of adolescence in Table 2.1.

When adolescents are understood within their own culture and context, parents, teachers, and other adults can appreciate and support youth more holistically and effectively (Nelson & Nelson, 2010). Within the culture of adolescence framework, adolescents can also be empowered to navigate their own development with greater self-understanding and regard. Within counseling and therapy, understanding the culture of adolescence and seeing adolescents in context become the foundation for the therapeutic relationship and therapeutic practice from intake through termination.

Table 2.1 Characteristics of Adolescent Culture

Cultural Element	*Definition*	*Characteristics*
Values	What is most important and central to adolescents:	• Peer relationships • Social dynamics and status • Sense of identity • Independence • Autonomy
Beliefs	What adolescents understand, share, and hold as true, is shaped by their:	• Emotions • Peers • Novelty-seeking • Reward-seeking • Social Context • Life Experience
Behavior	How adolescents act in their relationships and the world:	• Verbal • Nonverbal • Peer-focused • Present-focused • Mediated through and by technology and social media
Language	How adolescents communicate and make meaning:	• Activity and play • Talk • Slang • Texting • Emojis • Memes • Videos
Artifacts	The objects and items adolescents collect and use reflects their:	• Focus on peers • Focus on the present • Focus on social status • Use of technology and social media • Drive for individuality and autonomy • Identity Exploration
Economics	What adolescents perceive as worthwhile and valuable:	• Acceptance • Belonging • Attention • Influence • Social Status

Context of Modern Adolescence

Adolescents live and grow within environments and systems that profoundly impact their long-term development and well-being. In this section, we consider three highly interrelated aspects of contemporary adolescent development – adolescent mental health and well-being, technology and social media use, and sleep. While many other factors influence adolescent experiences and development, these three interconnected issues illustrate some central developmental and contextual factors for adolescents today.

Social Determinants of Mental Health

When we first encounter our adolescent clients, we are usually just starting to see a glimpse of all the individual and systemic factors that have shaped the constellation of experiences that influence their development. Within the social determinants of mental health model, it is understood that adolescent development, well-being, and mental health are profoundly impacted by social and environmental factors including: 1) economic stability, 2) educational access and quality, 3) healthcare access and quality, 4) neighborhood and built environment, 5) and social and community relationships (Johnson et al., 2023).

Youth experience better mental health outcomes and decreased risk of mental health concerns over their lifetimes when they have sufficient financial resources; food and housing security; access to high-quality, equitable education; access to high-quality healthcare services that are geographically and financially accessible; live in neighborhoods and communities that are safe and include strong social support systems; have access to high water and air quality, nature, and physical spaces that support their needs; and have strong, caring, and supportive relationships with family, friends, teachers, neighbors, and their broader community (Johnson et al., 2023). In the absence of some or all these supportive environmental factors and systems, adolescents are at increased risk for poor mental, emotional, and physical health outcomes. These social determinants of mental health can also serve as bridges or barriers to important developmental experiences and milestones. For example, an adolescent may not have the opportunity or time to explore their identity through diverse activities and engagement with peer groups if they are excluded from extracurricular activities because they cannot afford the cost of participation or must change schools frequently because their family is experiencing eviction and insecure housing. If an adolescent has access to a strong recreational program and community centers in their neighborhood, they are likely to have more opportunities for adult mentorship, activities that support physical health, and a stronger and more extensive social support system.

Understanding adolescent development within the broader social and environmental context broadly and specifically for individual clients is critical for identifying the nature and scope of a client's challenges and for providing holistic, socially just, and effective mental health care. In many cases, the work of adolescent counselors and therapists is to advocate with and for adolescents within their environments and social systems to eliminate barriers that impede their development and well-being.

Adolescent Mental Health and Well-Being

Adolescent counseling and therapy continue to be shaped and influenced by a myriad of dynamic and complex factors. The COVID-19 pandemic has had deep and lasting impacts on children and youth. Today's adolescents continue to experience the reverberations of navigating a global pandemic at critical times in their child or adolescent development. For those that were actively in adolescence during the early years of the pandemic, isolation from peers, disruptions to education and family routines, and the many associated stressors and losses continue to impact their social, emotional, and identity development. Teens and emerging adults are navigating an increasingly complex and interconnected world. In the US, adolescents exist in a society navigating the challenges of racial and social injustice, climate change and crises, economic instability, national and state legislation limiting access to healthcare and bodily autonomy, school and community violence, and a growing adolescent mental health crisis (CDC, 2023).

The state of adolescent mental health continues to shift reflecting both increased resilience and health and increased stressors and risk. In the US, youth ages 10 to 24 are decreasing their use of substances and risky sexual behavior and reporting a decrease in experiences of being bullied (CDC, 2023). However, youth also report decreased use of protective sexual behaviors and increases in experiences of violence. Adolescents are experiencing more depressive symptoms and higher rates of suicidal thoughts and attempts. Adolescence and young adulthood are especially critical periods for the identification and intervention for mental health issues. In fact, 50% of mental health disorders begin before the age of 18 and 75% begin by the time youth are 24 years of age (Solmi et al., 2022). Prevention, early intervention, and access to quality care are crucial during adolescence, yet only half of adolescents who seek mental health care can access mental health services (SAMHSA, 2020). When youth do not have access to needed mental health support, they are at greater risk for substance use and misuse and unsafe sexual behavior and sexually transmitted illnesses, are more likely to experience violence, and have poor educational outcomes (CDC, 2023) with consequences that last far into adulthood.

Due to oppression and systemic injustice, AFAB adolescents; Black, Indigenous, and people of color (BIPOC) adolescents; and lesbian, gay, bisexual, and queer/questioning (LGBQ) adolescents report higher rates of depressive symptoms, experiences of violence, substance use, suicidality, and poorer mental health than assigned male at birth (AMAB) adolescents, White adolescents, and adolescents who do not identify as LGBQ (CDC, 2023). Furthermore, researchers continue to find that adolescents with marginalized identities who experience discrimination and oppression have increased mental health challenges and often decreased access to mental health services (OPA, 2023). Due to this stark gap in mental health support, there is a growing need to improve access to mental health care for adolescents and to eliminate barriers to quality counseling and therapy services for marginalized youth and their adults and families.

Currently, within the US, schools and outpatient settings are the environments where adolescents access mental health care most frequently (Duong et al., 2021). As we work to address the gap in adolescent counseling and therapy services, it is critical for the mental health community to consider how to improve access to quality mental health services within educational settings, clinics, and community centers that already serve adolescents and to think creatively and intentionally about how to integrate mental health supports in the environments and spaces where adolescents spend their time including online and on social media. As adolescents discuss and share more about mental health topics through social media, we can consider how to best join the conversation and help them access accurate knowledge and resources that can support their health and well-being.

Adolescent Technology and Social Media Use

Today's adolescents were born into a world defined by widespread use of technology and the internet and grew up during the rapid development and expansion of social media into daily life. Social media is *a* and, sometimes, *the* primary context of adolescent development. Applications and websites that promote the creation and sharing of content and social networking are a key means and focus of adolescent social interaction, communication, access to information, and exposure to many facets of the world.

Ninety-five percent of adolescents ages 13 to 17 have access to a smartphone and use social media, with YouTube, TikTok, Instagram, Snapchat, and Facebook topping the charts of the most frequently used social media platforms by teens (Vogels et al., 2022). In addition, 36% of teens identify that they spend too much time on social media, and 35% of adolescents report using social media "almost constantly." Furthermore, 54% of teens report that it would be hard to discontinue social media use, and 50% of teens report using the internet almost constantly. The statistics on adolescent social media and internet use are revealing and highlight the need for careful consideration of social media and technology use within the context of adolescent mental health and therapy.

Based on developing research, the U.S. Surgeon General (2023) identified social media and youth mental health as an urgent public health issue. While the Surgeon General's advisory recognized there may be some benefits to social media use for some children and adolescents, they highlighted the many risks and potential harms of social media use especially for younger adolescents. Because of the sensitive period of brain development, adolescents, in general, and younger adolescents, specifically, may be especially vulnerable to its impacts. The individual risks and benefits of social media are related to the frequency and duration of social media use, the type of content youth are consuming, and if and how social media causes disruptions or barriers to physical activity, sleep, and social development. For an adolescent who uses social media a few hours a day to connect with peers through Snapchat and watch YouTube videos related to their interests, social media may be a positive or more benign influence. For a teen that feels anxious when separated from their phone for even a few minutes, who stays up all night till the early morning watching TikTok videos or accessing pornography, or who experiences bullying through Instagram, social media has a much more negative and harmful impact.

Social media may provide opportunities for peer connection and social support, especially for teens with marginalized identities, and may also be an entry point to improving mental health access and support (U.S. Surgeon General, 2023). However, researchers have identified that adolescents' increased social media use is also related to increased risk for anxiety, depression, eating disorders, low self-esteem, bullying, and harassment (U.S. Surgeon General, 2023). Additionally, social media can negatively impact social skill and relationship development; attention, decision-making, and impulsivity; and learning and educational outcomes. The constant distraction and connection to the online world may be a barrier to teens and emerging adults' presence and focus in their face-to-face and direct interactions with the real world. It is common for a family to be eating a meal together and rather than holding a conversation about the day for both teens and adults to be texting or scrolling on their phones. High school teachers and undergraduate professors may struggle to keep students engaged in learning activities when students are constantly being pulled and rewarded for engaging in online content or being distracted by notifications on their phones.

Social media has fundamentally changed the context for and increased the risk of bullying, predatory behavior and exploitation from adults, and youth accessing content that is not developmentally beneficial or appropriate including violence and pornography. With the prevalence of social media and internet use for adolescents, it is imperative that counselors and therapist build knowledge and skills to support adolescents and their families in navigating the benefits and risks of social media and internet use as well as consider the role and impact of technology and social media on adolescents' mental health and well-being and therapeutic practice and interventions.

Adolescent Sleep

In adolescence, sleep plays a critical role in global development, mental health, and well-being for adolescents. Adolescents ages 13 to 18 need 8 to 10 hours of sleep per night. However, most teens only get 6 to 7.5 hours of sleep a night with over 78% of teens not getting adequate sleep on school nights (CDC, 2019). The vast majority of teenagers in high school are sleep deprived. Inadequate sleep impacts teens' moods, energy levels, concentration, physical health and development, and it puts them at higher risk for depression, anxiety, and poor academic performance. Sleep effects every domain of development and has far-reaching impacts on the daily lives of adolescents.

Nearly 1 in 3 adolescents report using screen media until midnight or later during the week with social media applications being the most common media used by teens late at night (CDC, 2023). As adolescents navigate new social dynamics and strive to stay connected with peers in-person and online and as they juggle increased expectations related to school, work, or extracurricular activities, they experience competition between their social needs and their physical needs. Presented with this consistent dilemma, most often it is their sleep duration and quality that suffers. Teens are more likely to prioritize short-term rewards – staying up late and texting with friends or staying up late to finish an assignment due the next day – over the less immediate and longer-term consequences of poor sleep and sleep deprivation.

Adolescents' circadian rhythms shift dramatically from childhood as their brains begin to make and release melatonin hours later than their child or adult counterparts. This delay often makes it difficult for them to fall asleep until much later at night. What used to be an 7 or 8 o'clock bedtime is now often 10, 11, or later at night. With this natural change in their circadian rhythms leading to later sleep onset and later wake times, adolescents' biological sleep patterns and needs may no longer align with school and family schedules or routines. It is common for teens to go to sleep later and sleep in later. While this may be a common point of challenge or conflict for adolescents, parents/caregivers, and teachers, it is also an opportunity for counselors to support, educate, and advocate with teenagers and their families to help support teens in getting adequate, quality sleep and adjust social expectations to meet their changing biological cycles.

As adolescents move toward adulthood, their sleep needs decrease to 7 to 9 hours of sleep per night. With age, adolescents often experience more transitions in their living environments and continue to focus on developing their social and professional lives all of which can impact sleep quality and sufficiency. Emerging adults may sacrifice sleep to prioritize educational or career responsibilities, financial goals, and/or romantic relationships and friendships. As counselors work with individuals and families across early, middle, and late adolescence, it is important to consider the impact of sleep on mental health and overall well-being as part of the therapeutic process.

Developmentally and Culturally Sustaining Therapeutic Conditions

The Therapeutic Relationship

At the core of effective counseling practice with adolescents is the person of the therapist and the therapeutic relationship. Beyond any specific treatment modalities or approaches, the quality and strength of the therapeutic relationship are the most influential on adolescents' overall experience in therapy and therapeutic outcomes (Karver et al., 2018; Shirk & Karver, 2003). Of the factors the therapist most directly influences in the counseling process, therapist warmth, genuineness, empathy, and unconditional positive regard are strongly correlated with positive therapeutic outcomes.

Fostering these attitudes and developing these interpersonal skills in relationships with youth is uniquely informed by the culture and context of adolescence. Genuineness may look different in a therapeutic relationship with an adolescent than it does with a child or adult client (Holliman & Foster, 2016). Authenticity with adolescents may include using more self-disclosure, conversational tone and vocabulary, and transparent and developmentally centered communication about confidentiality and creating spaces specifically with the culture, needs, and comfort of teens and emerging adults in mind.

How a teen or young adult perceives empathy from the therapist is informed by their cognitive and emotional development, identity development, and relationships with peers and other adults. For adolescent therapists, empathy develops through a strong desire and commitment to know and understand the adolescent and understand the way they see and experience the world. Learning more about adolescent development can be particularly helpful for experiencing and conveying greater empathy to adolescents. Additionally, it takes time to create a shared understanding, flow, and language within the therapeutic relationship as the therapist pays attention to how the client is experiencing their empathy and what aspects of the interaction are most connecting or facilitative. While consistent in many ways across clients, the adolescent counselor's way of being with each adolescent will also be unique and idiosyncratic to each relationship.

As adolescents feel more deeply known and understood in the therapeutic relationship, they are more likely to experience the therapist's acceptance and unconditional positive regard. If the teen does not feel safe to share themselves openly or does not believe that the therapist truly understands them, they may dismiss the therapist's acceptance of them, or it may feel empty because it is not based on a true or felt understanding of who they really are as a person. Especially as adolescents are so engaged and focused on exploring, defining, and expressing their sense of self, it is essential that they experience the therapist as deeply valuing and accepting their changing and growing identity and all the bumpy happenings and learning that support this key developmental task.

The Context of Adolescent Therapy

While some adolescents seek or initiate counseling on their own, many come to therapy because a parent, teacher, or other adult initiates the process or refers them for mental health services. Adolescents may be reluctant to start or engage in therapy when it is not of their choosing and may resent being required to navigate a relationship with a new, unknown adult. Additionally, they may not see the need for counseling and may have very different goals for treatment than their parents/caregivers. Even when it is intended to support the adolescent and provide needed care, adult-initiated counseling for an adolescent may be experienced as punitive, intrusive, or irrelevant as adolescents seek greater independence and autonomy from adults and are more focused on and influenced by relationships with peers.

Because of these factors, adolescents are more likely than adults to leave or end counseling prematurely. Developing a strong therapeutic alliance with teens and young adults may also be more challenging. In a study that utilized adolescent reports on therapeutic factors, the only variable that accurately predicted premature therapeutic dropout was how the adolescent perceived the therapeutic alliance (Bullock, 2017). In their meta-analysis on premature termination in child and adolescent outpatient mental health care, de Haan et al. (2013) found that treatment and therapist variables were the most important and reliable predictors of premature therapeutic dropout for adolescents (de Haan et al., 2013).

Adolescents were more likely to prematurely end therapy if the quality of the therapeutic alliance was poor or the therapist was perceived as less caring, communicative, or supportive. When therapists were more directive, controlling, and/or confrontational in therapy or treatment was perceived as less relevant to the adolescent's needs or concerns, adolescents were more likely to dropout or terminate from therapy prematurely either by their own choosing or because their parent decided to discontinue services. More than any pre-treatment adolescent or family variables, the factors the therapist has the most power to influence – the therapeutic relationship and the structure and process of counseling – predict whether are not youth stay in counseling or terminate prematurely.

In their research on adult-referred adolescents ages 15–19, Stige et al. (2021) identified that the therapist played a central role in whether mental health treatment was experienced positively or negatively by the teens. In these cases, mental health services were initiated by a parent/caregiver or child welfare professional. Youth found therapy to be a positive and beneficial experience when they experienced their therapists as warm, accepting, open, authentic, transparent, and trustworthy. Confidentiality and a comfortable setting further supported the youth's sense of safety and openness in the therapeutic process. When treatment was flexible, predictable, and supportive, youth were able to engage and benefit even when they did not initiate therapy.

Additionally, youth identified they were more engaged and benefited from treatment when their therapists were genuinely interested in their perspective and experiences and could see beyond their problem behaviors (Stige et al., 2021). The therapist focused on the person of the adolescent rather than on their presenting problems or concerning behaviors. Being able to respond to the whole person and understand the world from their perspective is especially relevant for teens or emerging adults who are mandated or required to attend counseling or are reluctant to seek counseling for themselves.

Furthermore, the therapist's genuine acceptance of and ability to competently respond to silence, conflict, and/or challenges in the therapeutic relationship were often a turning point for the youth in their relationship with the therapist and in the counseling process overall (Stige et al., 2021). When the therapist demonstrated the ability to be flexible and sensitive to the adolescent's often unpredictable needs, energy and capacity, and preferences across therapeutic interactions, youth experienced treatment more positively. Consistency over time with the same therapist was experienced as fundamental to building trust and supporting therapeutic outcomes. Even brief disruptions in a strong therapeutic relationship were experienced negatively by youth. Although counselors may not always see direct evidence of it, their presence and absence can make a big difference to their adolescent clients.

Although it is clear the therapeutic relationship is central to the success of adolescent counseling, it is also important to consider that an adolescent's reluctance or refusal to participate in counseling may be reflective of their focus on autonomy and independence. Therapy may be fertile ground for an adolescent to assert themselves and practice individuating from their parents or caregivers. Especially for adolescents with limited opportunities to express their independence in other environments, "resistance" may be an essential process for them in the context of a counseling relationship. Through acceptance and understanding, the counselor may be setting a foundation for the teen's future engagement in therapy either with them or with a future therapist.

For adolescent counselors, being able to hold, empathize, and honor the developmental experiences of adolescents within the therapeutic process is key. It is also important for adolescent counselors to view adolescents holistically and within their contexts and environments and understand the distinct experience of adolescents who are required to come to therapy by important adults in their lives. Perhaps most importantly, counselors who foster strong relationships through genuine warmth, unconditional positive regard, and care and who can weather challenges and repair ruptures in the relationship are able to provide the context for adolescents to benefit from and experience counseling positively.

Developmentally and Culturally Sustaining Therapeutic Approaches

While the culture, context, and developmental needs of adolescents are distinct from children and adults, the development of and research on adolescent-specific counseling and therapy approaches are much more limited in comparison to counseling approaches for adults (Chen et al., 2023) and even children. While some evidenced-based approaches for working with adolescents with specific concerns or diagnoses exist, clinicians must navigate the large gap in adolescent counseling outcome research and the limitations of using approaches that were not developed specifically for adolescents. Adolescent counselors and therapists rely on the best available research, their clinical expertise, and intentional consideration of a client's culture, identities, and context – including the culture and context of adolescence – to inform best practices and interventions (Nelson & Nelson, 2010). Across theoretical orientations and approaches, it is essential for adolescent counselors to appreciate an adolescent's individual development within the context of their environments, social groups, and culture. This includes considerations related to the structure of therapy including individual, group, and family therapy; how and when to involve parents/caregivers in the therapeutic process; the type of therapy including talk, play, activity, and expressive arts therapy; and the format of therapy in-person or telehealth.

Individual Therapy

Adolescents are commonly seen in individual counseling as this is the primary delivery method for therapy within the healthcare system. Individual counseling allows for therapists to provide undivided attention and focus on the client. Many adolescents value the opportunity to share their experiences openly and deeply in an accepting and supportive relationship without having to compete for attention. The privacy and safety of individual counseling may also be beneficial in fostering a strong therapeutic relationship between client and counselor. Individual therapy may also provide greater flexibility and ease of scheduling for adolescents.

Typically, individual counseling is more expensive overall but is also more likely to be covered than other forms of therapy by private insurance and through state and nationally funded insurance programs. For some teens, individual counseling can feel intrusive and exacerbate their sense of being under a microscope by the counselor and the important adults in their life. Awareness of the client's desire to be in therapy, prior experiences in counseling, and relational history with adults can be helpful for determining if individual counseling is the best approach for an adolescent client.

Group Therapy

Group therapy is less prevalent than individual counseling, especially in outpatient settings, but it is a powerful approach that reflects and honors adolescents' developmental experiences and needs. In group therapy, adolescents have the benefit of directly relating to and experiencing peer support at a time when peers play a central and defining role in their development. Group therapy may promote a more egalitarian and less hierarchical dynamic than individual therapy and help adolescents feel more comfortable and open in sharing their experiences. Additionally, in group therapy, adolescents' development and culture can serve to foster the therapeutic factors of cohesion, identification, imitative behavior, universality, interpersonal learning, and development of socializing techniques.

Because of the power of peer influence, it is important that group therapists facilitate groups in ways that support positive peer influence and reduce the risk of negative peer pressure or social contagion. Group focus, structure, and composition are essential to providing an environment that supports positive social support, influence, and interaction. Group therapy may not be the best fit for adolescents that need more individualized support or who are in a state of crisis, adolescents who feel inhibited within a group setting, or adolescents who may be more susceptible to social contagion or negative peer pressure. Screening and assessment are critical processes for identifying if individual adolescents will benefit from group therapy and can participate in a way that supports the needs of the whole group. Therapists need to consider age; development; culture, identity, and social context; history or current experiences of trauma; and how socially motivated a client is to determine if group therapy is the best approach for a teen or young adult.

Family Therapy

Even as adolescents seek independence and autonomy and do the important work of individuating from their parents and families, they still need and benefit from strong relationships with parents, teachers, and other adults. In addition to positively impacting the mental health of the adolescent, family therapy can promote change within the home environment and family system and improve family functioning, attachment, and communication (Carr, 2014).

In many cases, family therapy is a beneficial approach for supporting adolescents especially if their needs and concerns are centered within the family system or the parent-child relationship(s) or high involvement of the parent/caregiver is necessary within the therapeutic process. Like group therapy, family therapy is typically used less frequently than individual therapy for adolescents. Yet it is an important modality for therapists to consider to promote systemic change and advocate for adolescents in the context of one of their primary environments.

For family therapy to be beneficial, the counselor needs to assess the readiness, capacity, and willingness of all involved family members to engage in the therapeutic process – this may include the adolescent(s), parents/caregivers, and siblings. Karver et al. (2006) identified that in addition to the therapeutic relationship with the adolescent client and the therapist's interpersonal skills (empathy, warmth, genuineness), the parent's willingness to participate and participation in treatment and youth willingness to participate and participation in treatment were correlated with positive therapeutic outcomes in family therapy. When adolescents and their family members are open and engaged in the therapeutic process, family therapy may be an essential tool for supporting the mental health and development of teens and emerging adults.

Parent/Family Involvement

Beyond family therapy, therapists often feel challenged in identifying if, how, and when to involve parents/caregivers and other family members in the therapeutic process. Based on research, parental involvement and support is shown to improve therapeutic outcomes for children and youth (Dowell & Ogles, 2010). In some states and settings, parental involvement is required for minors to access mental health care, and in other states, teens can consent to counseling services on their own without parental involvement. Emerging adults are more likely to access counseling and therapy independently from parents and caregivers but still may benefit from or desire parental involvement.

When parental involvement is necessary and/or beneficial, it is helpful for therapists to work collaboratively and transparently with the adolescent on why it is helpful and how best to involve family members in the process. Typically, parent/caregiver sessions are conducted jointly with the adolescent, and the counselor works to invite direct communication between family members while centering the adolescent's needs, experiences, and goals. These collaborative sessions may be held on a consistent basis depending on the adolescent's needs and parental capacity, or on a more periodic basis. When a counselor meets with a parent without the adolescent present, it is valuable to discuss the purpose and agenda, what the counselor is planning to discuss, and the adolescent's feelings, questions, and concerns prior to the parent-only session. It is also helpful to debrief with the adolescent following the parent-only session to support trust and safety in the therapeutic relationship, honor the identity development and autonomy of the adolescent, and empower them in their counseling experience.

A therapist may also choose to work solely with parents/adult family members when a parent wants to initiate services for an adolescent who does not want therapy or when the focus of the concerns is related to parenting or the parent-child relationship. Working with an engaged parent or parents/caregivers is likely more beneficial than working with an adolescent that does not want to be in counseling. This approach may also shift the focus from the adolescent as the problem to be fixed and support the parent/caregiver in navigating the changes to their role, parenting practices, and relationship with their adolescent during this new developmental period.

Play, Activity, and Expressive Arts

Adolescents may engage in therapy in a variety of ways as they develop cognitively, emotionally, and socially. At times, they may engage in therapy primarily through play and creative expression, or they may be very talkative and express themselves primarily through verbal communication. Often adolescents relate and communicate through a blend of talk, play, and creativity. For younger adolescents specifically, access to play, art, and sandtray as means of expression and exploration is critical to developing a strong therapeutic relationship and being able to engage meaningfully in the therapeutic process.

Like play and activity, expressive arts are often utilized in adolescent counseling to support teens and young adults in exploring and integrating their experiences through nonverbal, process-oriented, and multimodal approaches. Expressive arts therapy includes integration of visual arts, writing, music, dance, and/or drama as means of expression, communication, and exploration in counseling. For many teens who may not want to sit directly across from an adult and discuss their lives or challenges, expressive arts provide a doorway for them to engage in counseling in a way that honors their mutual needs for connection and autonomy and privacy and intimacy and their fluctuations between the worlds of childhood and adulthood.

While older adolescents may be more adept or comfortable expressing themselves verbally, many young adult clients find it helpful to express themselves through multiple mediums and in ways that do not require or go beyond talking. Sandtray therapy has been found effective in use with adolescents and adults and in both individual and group formats (Holliman & Foster, 2023). Likewise, art therapy and creative mediums are widely used with adolescents and adults. As adolescents are deep in the process of identity formation and individuation, creative expression can be especially helpful in supporting their needs for identity exploration and individuality within the therapeutic relationship.

Telehealth and Technology

With the COVID-19 pandemic, use of telecommunications or videoconferencing to provide adolescent counseling and therapy increased exponentially and with lasting impact on the profession. Following the height of the pandemic, counselors continue to navigate the benefits and limitations of using telehealth with youth. Outcome research on the benefits of telehealth counseling and therapy with adolescents is very limited. Care, intentionality, and proper assessment and consent processes are necessary to determine if telehealth is beneficial for individuals across early, middle, and late adolescence.

For some youth, the use of telehealth increases access to counseling and reduces barriers related to finding a therapist, scheduling weekly sessions, and transportation. For adolescents with disabilities and chronic illness, telehealth can make consistent participation in therapy more accessible. For some adolescents, experiencing therapy sessions in the context of their own living or educational environments can support their sense of safety, comfort, openness, and integration of their family and school life into therapy sessions. Adolescents are often comfortable with using and relating to others through technology, which may increase their engagement in a telehealth session. Telehealth may also make it more accessible and reduce some of the logistical barriers to offering group therapy to adolescents and emerging adults.

As adolescents typically require more time to develop trust in the therapeutic relationship and require a high need for authenticity and presence in the therapeutic relationship, telehealth can further delay or impede this process due to the challenge of experiencing someone in an embodied way online, and the use of technology and screens can create distance and distraction. Many adolescent therapists have experienced adolescents multitasking or being distracted by notifications or open applications on their phones or computers during therapy sessions. This can negatively impact the therapeutic relationship and limit the development of social and emotional skills that are supported in the context of meaningful relational contact and interaction.

Privacy is an additional concern as it may be challenging to protect a client's confidentiality when they are having sessions in their homes, cars, or other settings. With their focus on peers, adolescents may not value the need for privacy from friends in their telehealth counseling sessions. Alternatively, they can be very inhibited if they are concerned that parents, other family members, or teachers may overhear or be privy to what they are sharing in a telehealth session. Economic and social barriers may also be exacerbated through telehealth delivery as not all youth or families have access to technology, internet, or environments to support access to telehealth services.

For younger adolescents who engage more fully in therapy through play and activity, telehealth is often not responsive to their needs as telehealth requires more static and talk-based engagement in front of a screen or device. Even for adolescents who can engage within the technological boundaries in a telehealth session, it can be challenging and sometimes impossible to translate play, activity, and expressive activities to telehealth. Like any therapeutic intervention, the use of telehealth is considered with intentionality and understanding of the client's development, context, culture, and needs.

In addition to considerations for using telehealth in adolescent counseling, counselors need to consider what role technology plays in their face-to-face counseling relationships. Adolescents will often bring smartphones and internet-connected devices into the therapeutic space and want to share parts of their lives lived online and through social media. Counselors must explore the benefit and limitations of integrating technology into the therapeutic process as well as identify how to create boundaries to support the therapeutic relationship and provide safety and confidentiality.

Conclusion

Adolescence in the 21st century is dynamic, complex, and reflective of the current social and cultural context and systems that teens and emerging adults are experiencing. Adolescent counselors and therapists are in a unique position to support and impact the trajectory of teens' and emerging adults' lives. Understanding the culture and context of adolescence and using developmental knowledge to foster strong therapeutic relationships and inform therapeutic practice is essential for supporting teens and emerging adults effectively within and beyond therapy.

References

Bullock, M. M. (2017). *Rates and predictors of adolescent premature termination: Applying clinically significant change* (All Theses and Dissertations. 6687). https://scholarsarchive.byu.edu/etd/6687

Carr, A. (2014). The evidence base for family therapy and systemic interventions for child-focused problems. *Journal of Family Therapy*, *36*(2), 107–157. https://doi.org/10.1111/1467-6427.12032

Centers for Disease Control and Prevention. (2019). *Youth risk behavior survey*. www.cdc.gov/sleep/data-and-statistics/high-school-students.html

Centers for Disease Control and Prevention. (2023). *Youth risk behavior survey: Data summary and trends report*. www.cdc.gov/healthyyouth/data/yrbs/yrbs_data_summary_and_trends.htm

Chen, S., Chen, C., Su, Y., Hyun, J. H., & Pietrantoni, Z. (2023). Content analysis of child and adolescent counseling outcome studies in counseling journals. *Journal of Child and Adolescent Counseling*, *9*(2), 84–100. https://doi.org/10.1080/23727810.2023.2232140

de Haan, A. M., Boon, A. E., de Jong, J. M., Hoeve, M., & Vermeiren, R. M. (2013). A meta-analytic review on treatment dropout in child and adolescent outpatient mental health care. *Clinical Psychology Review*, *33*(5), 698–711. https://doi.org/10.1016/j.cpr.2013.04.005

Dowell, K. A., & Ogles, B. M. (2010). The effects of parent participation on child psychotherapy outcome: A meta-analytic review. *Journal of Clinical Child and Adolescent Psychology*, *39*(2), 151–162. https://doi.org/10.1080/15374410903532585

Duong, M. T., Bruns, E. J., Lee, K., Cox, S., Coifman, J., Mayworm, A., & Lyon, A. R. (2021). Rates of mental health service utilization by children and adolescents in schools and other common service settings: A systematic review and meta-analysis. *Administration and Policy in Mental Health*, *48*(3), 420–439. https://doi.org/10.1007/s10488-020-01080-9

Eckert-Lind, C., Busch, A. S., Petersen, J. H., Biro, F. M., Butler, G., Bräuner, E. V., & Juul, A. (2020). Worldwide secular trends in age at pubertal onset assessed by breast development among girls: A systematic review and meta-analysis. *JAMA Pediatrics*, *174*(4), e195881. https://doi.org/10.1001/jamapediatrics.2019.5881

Holliman, R. P., & Foster, R. D. (2016). Embodying and communicating authenticity in adolescent counseling. *Journal of Child and Adolescent Counseling*, 2(1), 61–76. https://doi.org/10.1080/23727810.2016.1160353

Holliman, R. P., & Foster, R. D. (2023). The way we play in the sand: A meta-analytic investigation of sand therapy, its formats, and presenting problems. *Journal of Child and Adolescent Counseling*, 9(2), 205–221. https://doi.org/10.1080/23727810.2023.2232142

Johnson, K. F., Cunningham, P. D., Tirado, C., Moreno, O., Gillespie, N. N., Duyile, B., Hughes, D. C., Scott, E. G., & Brookover, D. (2023). Social determinants of mental health: Considerations for counseling children and adolescents. *Journal of Child and Adolescent Counseling*, 9(1), 21–33. https://doi.org/10.1080/23727810.2023.2169223

Karver, M. S., De Nadai, A. S., Monahan, M., & Shirk, S. R. (2018). Meta-analysis of the prospective relation between alliance and outcome in child and adolescent psychotherapy. *Psychotherapy*, 55(4), 341–355.

Karver, M. S., Handelsman, J. B., Fields, S., & Bickman, L. (2006). Meta-analysis of therapeutic relationship variables in youth and family therapy: The evidence for different relationship variables in the child and adolescent treatment outcome literature. *Clinical Psychology Review*, 26(1), 50–65. https://doi.org/10.1016/j.cpr.2005.09.001

National Association of Realtors. (2023). *Profile of home buyers and sellers*. National Association of Realtors. https://www.nar.realtor/sites/default/files/documents/2023-profile-of-home-buyers-and-sellers-highlights-11-13-2023.pdf

National Center for Health Statistics. (2017). *Key statistics from the national survey of family growth – b listing*. www.cdc.gov/nchs/nsfg/key_statistics/b.htm

Nelson, T. D., & Nelson, J. M. (2010). Evidence-based practice and the culture of adolescence. *Professional Psychology: Research and Practice*, 41(4), 305–311.

Office of Population Affairs. (2023, December). *Access to adolescent mental health care*. https://opa.hhs.gov/adolescent-health/mental-health-adolescents/access-adolescent-mental-health-care

Office of the Surgeon General. (2023). *Social media and youth mental health: The U.S. Surgeon General's Advisory*. www.hhs.gov/sites/default/files/sg-youth-mental-health-social-media-advisory.pdf

Plank, E. (2016). *Discovering the culture of childhood*. Redleaf Press.

Sawyer, S. M., Azzopardi, P. S., Wickremarathne, D., & Patton, G. C. (2018). The age of adolescence. *The Lancet. Child & Adolescent Health*, 2(3), 223–228. https://doi.org/10.1016/S2352-4642(18)30022-1

Shirk, S. R., & Karver, M. (2003). Prediction of treatment outcome from relationship variables in child and adolescent therapy: A meta-analytic review. *Journal of Counseling and Clinical Psychology*, 71(3), 452–464.

Solmi, M., Radua, J., Olivola, M., et al. (2022). Age at onset of mental disorders worldwide: Large-scale meta-analysis of 192 epidemiological studies. *Molecular Psychiatry*, 27, 281–295. https://doi.org/10.1038/s41380-021-01161-7

Stige, S. H., Barca, T., Lavik, K. O., & Moltu, C. (2021). Barriers and facilitators in adolescent psychotherapy initiated by adults: Experiences that differentiate adolescents' trajectories through mental health care. *Frontiers in Psychology*, 12, 633663. https://doi.org/10.3389/fpsyg.2021.633663

Substance Abuse and Mental Health Services Administration. (2020). *Key substance use and mental health indicators in the United States: Results from the 2019 National Survey on Drug Use and Health* (HHS Publication No. PEP20-07-01-001, NSDUH Series H-55). Rockville, MD:

Center for Behavioral Health Statistics and Quality, Substance Abuse and Mental Health Services Administration. www.samhsa.gov/data/

United States Census Bureau. (2024). *Households and families: 2020* (2020 Census Briefs C2020BR-10). https://www2.census.gov/library/publications/decennial/2020/census-briefs/c2020br-10.pdf

Vogels, E., Gelles-Watnick, R., & Massarat, N. (2022). Teens, social media and technology 2022. *Pew Research Center: Internet, Science & Tech*. www.pewresearch.org/internet/2022/08/10/teens-social-media-and-technology-2022/

Part II

Early Adolescence

Chapter 3

The 13-Year-Old

Alyssa M. Swan

Evie is a 13-year-old cisgender Latino girl who lives in a rural town with her mother, maternal grandmother, and two younger sisters. She attended an assembly last week about registering for high school courses; she and the entire eighth-grade class are touring the high school today. Evie wears a new outfit that she carefully chose to match her friend Sierra, finishes breakfast with her younger siblings, and walks to meet Sierra at the sidewalk before school. Last week they planned to sit together on the bus that will drive them to the high school so they could walk together during the tour. Evie is both excited and nervous about attending high school next year. As they approach the high school, she glances down at her jeans and sees the price tag still attached; she hopes no one else saw that she forgot to remove it. She glances hesitantly at her reflection in the glass of the trophy case as they walk through the high school halls. As Evie talks with her friends on the bus ride back to their school building, she reminds herself there will be a social studies quiz in fifth period today.

Gus, who lives down the street from Evie, is a 13-year-old Latino cisgender boy. He grabs a breakfast bar from the cupboard on his way out the door with his older brother Jac; their parents have both left for work already. Jac's best friend Tony, a junior in high school and a new driver, pulls his car in front of their house. As Tony stops at the middle school to let Gus climb out of the backseat, they are all laughing at Tony's joke about pranking their coach at football practice after school. Gus can't wait to be on the high school football team with Jac and Tony next year although he hopes he will have his "growth spurt," as his mother termed it, between now and then. Enviously, he watched Jac grow almost six inches this past year; his brother now towers above Gus in size and boasts about the density of his facial hair. On the bus ride to the high school tour today, Gus talks with a group of peers about what's for lunch.

Thirteen-year-olds are transitioning from childhood to adolescence. This transition is marked by distinct physical, cognitive, and social development, an age of enormous exploration and learning. Thirteen-year-olds are driven to learn new things and embrace new experiences. Characteristic of 13-year-olds is a motivation to spend an increased amount of time and focus forming and navigating social relationships (i.e., friendships, dating, online engagement, and peer groups). Around age 13, adolescents initiate greater independence from their caregivers. Typically, puberty begins prior to or around the age of 13, a process that begins internally prior to the onset of characteristics commonly associated

DOI: 10.4324/9781003196297-5

with beginning puberty (e.g., menstruation and voice change). At 13, adolescents are experiencing primary and secondary bodily changes associated with puberty at varying rates.

Although many 13-year-olds will have common experiences, the progression and expression of adolescent development are highly dependent on individual experiences and genetics. In this chapter, I will intentionally refrain from portraying 13-year-olds as individuals necessitating a "survival guide" with which to be understood or managed. Rather, the purpose of this chapter is to describe and explain development at this age as a natural and purposeful period of human development. At age 13, as the number itself suggests in English, an individual enters "teen" years. Developmentalists regard 13 as early adolescence (e.g., Galván, 2017; Steinberg, 2017), as opposed to childhood or late adolescence, and this transition is ritualized in many cultures to mark a child becoming more adultlike in stature and socialization. For example, 13-year-old boys who practice Judaism may celebrate with bar mitzvahs, an acknowledgement and celebration of a Jewish child's transition into adulthood (girls can make the transition at 12).

Physical Development

Early adolescence is characterized by changes that occur both inside and outside the body because of puberty (Blakemore et al., 2010). Chronological age, such as age 13, can but does not always align with pubertal aging. Some 13-year-olds may be advanced or delayed in the timing of their observable bodily changes compared to their peers. Pubertal differences that may be observed or experienced can include timing of voice changes, breast development, growth spurts, and menarche. Typically, puberty begins between 8 and 14 years in people assigned female at birth (AFAB) and between 9 and 15 years in people assigned male at birth (AMAB; Blakemore et al., 2010).

During puberty, the human body activates maturation of the gonads (ovaries/testes) that coincide with the secretion of hormones (estrogen/testosterone), signaling additional changes in the reproductive organs, referred to as primary sex characteristics. Secondary sex characteristics, such as pubic hair and body odor continue to mature throughout puberty until early adulthood. Other examples of secondary sex characteristics include breast development and body fat in AFAB people and vocal changes and body hair in AMAB teens. Body composition and stress are two factors that impact the onset of puberty. Thirteen-year-olds are developing an internal sense of their gender; for youth who are transgender or gender nonconforming, their internal sense of their gender may not align with the externally observed sex. This period of bodily changes can be challenging and distressing to trans and gender nonconforming youth who identify less with the physical and sexual changes they are experiencing in their bodies (Pullen Sansfaçon et al., 2020).

Blanton et al. (2012) studied puberty among 54 cisgender females between the ages of 9 and 15 years old. Less than half of the individuals in this study had started menarche; of those who had had their first menstrual cycle, the average age of their first cycle was 13 years of age. Tomova and colleagues (2011) studied puberty in cisgender males, one marker being the timing of first conscious ejaculation. Among the 1,582 participants, the mean age of first ejaculation was reported as 13.27 years of age with a standard deviation of 1.08 years. Pubertal milestones and age estimates can vary across geographic locations, populations of people, generational data, and research studies (Biro et al., 2010; Herman-Giddens et al., 2012; Lee & Styne, 2013). Later pubertal timing may delay the timing of first intercourse (Meschke et al., 2000). For pre-adolescents who are not cisgender, pubertal change can be particularly distressing as physical changes may not match their gender identity.

Another related physical development, initiated by patterns of hormonal secretion, that occurs around the age of 13 is sometimes referred to as a "growth spurt." Adolescents will likely experience notable growth in body size and shape between the average ages of 12 (AFAB) and 14 (AMAB); this growth requires energy expenditure from their developing bodies (Dorn et al., 2019). It is typical that AMAB adolescents increase in height one to two years later than their AFAB counterparts.

Adolescents at age 13 are developing an understanding of sex and romantic relationships. Some adolescents at age 13 will have experimented and/or engaged in different types of sexual contact with their own bodies and/or with peers to whom they are attracted. Discussions about consent, types of sexual activity, sexual health, sexually transmitted infections, and contraception are timely at 13 years of age. For example, the human papillomavirus (HPV) vaccination is recommended by health providers by the age of 13 in the United States (Centers for Disease Control and Protection, 2021).

Relatedly, while experiencing significant bodily changes during puberty, it is common to desire privacy in personal spaces, such as bathrooms and bedrooms. Thirteen-year-old adolescents may have questions or concerns about their bodies. Inherent to physical maturation, 13-year-olds develop body consciousness; they are aware that they are developing and may overtly or discretely compare their body development to the bodies of same-age peers, older siblings, and/or adults. Advanced or delayed physical development across sexes can impact social recognition and self-esteem. For transgender and gender nonconforming youth, physical development can initiate or advance internal and social explorations of gender identity and gender expression. For example, transgender or non-binary 13-year-olds may be questioning their gender and experimenting with presenting differently gendered versions of themselves, such as through clothing, names/pronouns, and social media.

Brain and Cognitive Development

Have you ever heard of adolescents being characterized by mood swings and acting irrationally? Fluctuations in mood and different reasoning abilities, compared to adult counterparts, are a natural part of a 13-year-old's maturation process. Brain development research illuminates a richer story of what is occurring in the brain during this period. Researchers have gained considerable knowledge about adolescent brain functioning from nonhuman animal brain research; nowadays, brain scans and magnetic resonance imaging (MRI) allow researchers to look directly at processes of human brain functioning and make comparisons throughout human lifespans. Neuroscience evidence is ever developing and remains limited by the constraints of studying living beings. Notable from neuroscience research: the 13-year-old brain is uniquely different from its child or adult version (Rice & Sher, 2017).

Regarding reward circuitry, brain development during adolescence assists adolescents in relying less on their parents and becoming gradually more independent. The engagement of reward circuitry in the brain and the release of dopamine during pleasurable or evocative experiences are underlying rationales for a young person's newfound motivation toward independence-seeking behaviors (Galván, 2017). Riskier choices are more enjoyable, and 13-year-olds experience curiosity and a proclivity toward experimentation.

Animal research suggests that during early puberty, the human brain overproduces axons and synapses, followed by a distinct initiation of a process called pruning beginning in early adolescence (Casey et al., 2008). The brain is readying itself for distinct neural connections that will prolong adult life. Neural networks in the 13-year-old brain are reworking and advancing. Brain imaging portrays that subcortical regions of the brain (e.g., amygdala) are increasingly activated throughout adolescence (Casey et al., 2008). Coupled with hormonal and social development, emotional information processing and novelty-seeking behavior are extenuated beginning around early adolescence.

Brain development coupled with an increased propensity to seek out independence from caregivers can culminate in naturally riskier situations for a 13-year-old, particularly in situations that are novel. As one example, at age 13, Evie attended the high school track meet without adult supervision for the first time (usually her mother drives their group of friends and sits in the bleachers; this time they walked without an adult). The novelty of this experience is exciting, and a gradual increase in independence-seeking can become a point of necessary negotiation between teenagers and parents. By balancing safety and learning opportunities, it is possible for young teenagers to experience independence and understand natural consequences. How freedom and limits are contextualized for each 13-year-old is dependent on family, social, cultural, and individual circumstances and principles. Decisions and discussions about autonomy should be taken seriously and develop with age. For example, the American Psychological Association recommended that "13-year-olds should be given earlier curfews and be more closely supervised than older teens, even if they physically appear to be much older" (2002, p. 8).

In an effort to deepen the understanding of how the adolescent brain responds to emotional regulation in the context of the parent–child relationship and provide neurological support for the impact of parental attunement on adolescents' ability to self-regulate, Whittle et al. (2008) investigated the impact of parent–child interactions on a sample of 137 early adolescents' brain structure and affective behavior. Higher frequency and intensity of emotional parent-child interactions, which can result in increased amygdala volume (part of the brain linked to emotions), can lead to increases in aggressive behavior exhibited by adolescents during parent–child interactions. As adolescence marks a critical period of both biological and relational maturation, increased volume in the amygdala increases the risk and illuminates the predisposition toward sustained negative affect that can interfere with regulation and manifest externally as aggression even later in life (Whittle et al., 2008).

Emotional Development

Wendelken et al. (2016) researched adolescent brain development (particularly impulsivity) and found that adolescents can learn to control their impulses and disregard irrelevant information in an effort to focus. However, the task of focusing and learning to control impulses is more difficult for adolescents compared to children and adults when the stimuli are emotionally evocative rather than neutral. Thirteen-year-olds are increasingly attuned to the feelings and experiences of others. Their developing skills in empathic understanding and perspective-taking help them to understand and to connect in family and social contexts. Despite these new skills, 13-year-olds can misperceive others' emotions as related to their own perception of self. For example, when parents of younger children express sadness, a younger child is likely to also feel sad; when parents of adolescent children express sadness, adolescents may express and internalize a complementary emotion to their parents' sadness, like fear or disappointment (Harter, 1983). The presence of alexithymia, defined by an inability to identify emotions in oneself, declines after age 14 (Gatta et al., 2017).

Feelings of worry and anxiety are not uncommon for 13-year-olds due to transitions in their social and physical experiences. Pressures at school, home, and online can impact a 13-year-old's ability to cope with everyday stresses of physical development and energy expenditure. Teens will naturally strive to cope with these new stressors by employing strategies that may be effective in the short term (e.g., isolating, distraction, pleasing peers) but present long-term consequences (e.g., self-esteem, depression, anxiety). In a recent study, Hemberg et al. (2021) described that involuntary loneliness among adolescents precipitated shame and self-contempt; self-chosen solitude among adolescents in this study was associated with experiences of creativity and meaning-making.

Social and Relationship Development

Aligned with nuanced physical, cognitive, and emotional growth and changes at age 13, adolescents embrace new social experiences and experiment with peer and romantic relationships. Adolescence is a period of learning and practicing, honing resources, skills, and relationships that will sustain longevity throughout adulthood. Hewlett (2013) distinguished between biological adolescence, signaled by biological expression, and social adolescence, defined by cultural meanings and expectations. Kunnen (2012) described a particularly interesting component of adolescent autonomy beyond brain-based motivation for dopamine secretion. From an evolutionary perspective, autonomy-seeking during early adolescence is maintained through a series of conflicts and fights over autonomy-related issues with caregivers, which, in turn, further sustains adolescents' desire for increased autonomy. Theoretically, with decreased feelings of connectedness to their primary family unit, adolescents are freer to connect with and find a sense of belonging outside of the family system, with friends and peer groups, and eventually in pursuit of a potential mate (Schlegel, 2015). Thirteen-year-old Gus asked his parents for permission to meet his buddies at the football field on a Sunday evening. His parents gave him permission to ride his bike to the football field if he agreed to come home by 6:00 p.m. that evening to eat dinner with the family. Caught up in the excitement of playing football and chatting with his friends, Gus lost track of time and returned home at 6:30 p.m. His parents were worried about him, and Gus knew he had disappointed them. After dinner, Gus texted with his friends about his frustration with his parent's rules. Gus is navigating how to balance his parents' expectations of him with his own desires for social connection and autonomy.

Caregiver–child relationships remain essential, even at age 13, when parents might naturally perceive a new sense of social rejection from their adolescent. Security and understanding within the caregiver–child relationship serves as a safe base from which the early adolescent can explore their new social identity and can expend energy more fluidly on developmentally appropriate foci (e.g., social relationships, identity development, and academics) with fewer distractions from anxiety, worry, and uncertainty. Adolescents at age 13 need parental support in developing and supporting boundaries. Discussion and negotiation of rules that support adolescents' social interests while maintaining physical and emotional safety can be important at this age. Caregivers of 13-year-olds are learning alongside their teens, determining how to support their child's autonomy and ensure their child's safety while communicating in a responsive manner to their young teens. For example, when Gus arrived home late from playing football, they communicated their feelings of worry for his safety and brainstormed with Gus a plan for how he can communicate with them next time he may be late (e.g., phone call to let them know he is okay and on his way).

Thirteen-year-olds rely on models of early relationships as relational representations from which to generate expectations when initiating new relationships (Benson et al., 2006). Caregivers and other involved adult figures serve as natural role models for 13-year-olds to learn and practice social conduct, reasoning skills, and emotional regulation (Arzeen et al., 2012). From a study of 220 adolescents with an average age of 13.4, Johnson et al. (2016) reported that the teens nominated close family members as character role models most frequently, followed by friends and other adult figures. These 13-year-olds identified their role models based on how they treated other people and the quality of their relationships.

Having friends and family is important to 13-year-olds; family, friends, and school were noted by 13-year-olds in focus groups as being the ingredients for both happiness and unhappiness, regardless of gender (Johansson et al., 2007). In a longitudinal study of 497 13-year-olds, Spilt and colleagues (2015) compared youth perceptions of relationship quality to parent ratings of their child's relationships. Findings suggested that higher levels of perceived warmth or support in friend relationships were associated with fewer depressive symptoms in the 13-year-olds. Relatedly, when the 13-year-olds perceived low support from their identified best friends, this was a predictor of aggression. Thirteen-year-olds want to feel a sense of belonging at home, at school, and in friendships. Sense of belonging is associated with loneliness. When not with peers, 13-year-olds may express boredom and feel left out from peer groups. Regarding social preferences, research indicates that 13-year-olds, compared to 10-year-olds, may value leadership, ability, and influence as characteristics of social dominance as opposed to aggressive qualities (Wright et al., 1996). Young teens are likely experimenting with social relationships befriending peers with different levels of perceived social status and confidence. Perception of belonging may decrease as adolescents move into older teen years (Pretty et al., 1996).

Culture and Identity Development

Around the age of 13, adolescents develop a new specialization: self-reference processing, which gradually develops from 13 to 18 years old (Degeilh et al., 2015). Their sense of self develops as they integrate their experiences in an attempt to construct a unified, stable sense of identity, a process that continues into adulthood. Seeing themselves as products of previous experiences, adolescents during this stage are striving to achieve self-continuity with the goal of this psychosocial stage being fidelity, the ability to maintain loyalty to values and a sense of identity despite inconsistencies or conflicts (Adams et al., 2000; Seifert & Hoffnung, 2000).

According to Erikson's (1988) theory of identity development, at age 13 adolescents experience identity vs. role confusion. Young adolescents are continually constructing their emotional identities by distinguishing their own thoughts, feelings, and beliefs from those observed in relationships with others (Seifert & Hoffnung, 2000). Thirteen-year-olds can see themselves within social contexts and begin to develop a sense of themselves as belonging to various subgroups within society (Gemelli, 1996). Because of this, teens strive for the opportunity to take an active role in their families, schools, and peer groups while seeking acceptance and positive regard (Bronfenbrenner & Morris, 2006). Thirteen-year-olds can experience a sense of competence by completing household jobs; creating new ideas (such as artmaking or even replicating TikTok dances with friends); and being involved in social groups, band or choir, and sports activities. Adults can recognize 13-year-olds' efforts to contribute to the well-being of others and to succeed in new interests. Recognition of 13-year-old's efforts can bolster the young person's confidence to try new things despite the potential for perceived failure.

Modern social media consumption by adolescents indicates that 13-year-olds are updating social media profiles and developing online connections alongside a web of in-person social connections in their schools, clubs, and neighborhoods. Whitty and Young (2017) described online identity experimentation as a part of modern adolescence; 13-year-olds can use the internet as a resource for personal growth and social connection, which can aid in reaffirming their identity and self-perception.

Identity formation at the age of 13 is connected to gender and racial identity formation. Regarding sexual identity formation, adolescents at age 13 are influenced by cultural values, gender roles, language, family, peers, and religion when understanding their own gender identity and sexual orientation. Gender nonconforming youth may be more likely than their cisgender peers to experience bullying and to engage in substance use (Reisner et al., 2015). In one study by Legette (2018), Black pre-adolescents reported feeling proud of their Black identities, yet they reported concerns about how their academic performance and racial identity were perceived by classmates.

Socioeconomic status can impact perception of self at age 13. Levin et al. (2011) investigated international data of 58,352 13-year-olds from 35 countries and found a persistent association between family affluence (socioeconomic status relative to within-country variations) and life satisfaction ratings among 13-year-olds. Dronkers (2016) conducted a study of 13- and 14-year-olds across 22 different countries to examine the impact of parents' living arrangements (family structure) and the political and civic attitudes of adolescent participants. Dronkers reported differences, regardless of country, in civic attitudes between adolescents who lived in two-parent families and those who live in other family structures; no gender differences were found (Dronkers, 2016). The identity of 13-year-olds as they develop can be sustained to a greater degree by solidifying their sense of competence, belonging, and mattering rather than external factors such as socioeconomic status. Resources of a 13-year-old impact their developmental trajectory and life satisfaction into adulthood.

Resources and Protective Factors

Adolescents need protective factors and resources to thrive. This period of development presents tremendous opportunities for young people to establish new skills and values. An important resource for 13-year-olds is self-esteem, or feeling generally satisfied with oneself and perceiving oneself to be acceptable and capable at many things. Thirteen-year-olds can be encouraged to find interests and hobbies within and outside home and school. Parental warmth and stable caregiver relationships underlie 13-year-olds' resiliency as they traverse natural challenges and celebrations of their development.

Making friends and engaging in social relationships allow 13-year-olds to practice social skills and achieve social competency. Naturally motivated to seek out peer relationships, 13-year-olds can be supported by understanding the qualities they value in friends and discussing their inevitable impact on others. These adolescents can be empathic and aware of the emotions of others in a more advanced way than in childhood. Evie's best friend fell while they were running in physical education class one day. Evie quickly helped her friend up off the ground, locked elbows with her friend, and giggled with her about how embarrassing yet amusing the mishap had been. Evie sensed her friend's embarrassment and used humor and connection to provide her a welcomed refuge from her embarrassment.

At age 13, teens need environments that offer feedback to promote their competence and provide enough challenge that they must rely on their internal resources to problem-solve. Thirteen-year-olds are curious and creative when given environments to explore new ways of interacting, dressing, and expressing themselves. Thirteen-year-olds can develop a voice and stances on political and social phenomena. With access to internet material readily available, modern adolescents are primed for civic discussions and readily develop their own beliefs about current issues. At age 13, adolescents can be responsible and may value demonstrating their competence to others.

Notwithstanding the inherent challenges of development and personal life circumstances, 13-year-olds can be naturally resilient in sustaining onward development. Alessandri et al.'s (2017) research demonstrated that the relationship between family socioeconomic status at age 13 and school grades at end of senior year in high school was mediated by ego resiliency. Nutritious eating habits, realistic body image, role models, and sleep hygiene are additional factors that support healthy 13-year-old development. Although sleep duration decreases from infancy into adolescent years, 13-year-olds still need approximately 8–9 hours of sleep per night on average; not getting enough sleep may increase the risk of developing sleep-related problems (Schlarb et al., 2015). Caregivers may consider limiting nighttime screen and phone usage to encourage their pre-adolescents to naturally fall asleep without technological or social disruptions. Nutritionally, growth spurts, which occur during the onset of puberty, can require tissue expansion and specific nutrient requirements. For example, vitamin D and calcium are nutrients that promote bone growth (Das et al., 2017). Caregivers can support pre-adolescents to consume a range of foods with diverse nutrients and consult with their teen's physician for specific nutritional guidelines if needed. Eating meals together as a family at least three times per week is recommended (Hammons & Fiese, 2011).

Challenges and Risk Factors

At age 13, adolescents will embark on new challenges and risks to their developmental process. Depression and anxiety can develop in early adolescence. In a study of 1,942 13-year-olds, Kelly et al. (2016) reported associations between family conflict and adolescent depressed mood. Rice and Sher (2017) described that depression impacts male and female children at equal rates, whereas female adolescents report higher rates of depression than do male peers. Thirteen-year-olds may experience worry and stress, but due to their developing ability to reason through and name emotions, they may have difficulty reporting their concerns directly to others.

Bullying and unstable friendships may occur during age 13, as peers are navigating in and out of peer groups. Feeling left out or being excluded from social interactions and activities are influential on a 13-year-olds perception of self. In an effort to fit into social groups and/or to satisfy a personal curiosity, 13-year-olds might choose to endure the potential consequences of engaging in risky behaviors, such as experimenting with alcohol, drugs, or sex; creating new social media accounts without parental knowledge; or sneaking out of the house.

Physical body and hormone level changes can also impact self-esteem among 13-year-olds. Mixed results in research suggest a tentative connection between testosterone levels and suicidal behavior (Sher, 2014), underlining the hormonal impact on mood and behavior regulation. Gatta et al. (2017) conducted a study about adolescent alcohol consumption with a sample of 1,466 students (a mean age of 13.5 years) and reported an association between alcohol consumption and behavioral and/or psychological problems. The greatest increase in alcohol use in this study was between the ages of 13 and 14 for females and between the ages of 14 and 15 for males. Adversity during early adolescence can have a prolonged impact on lifelong health, resulting from adverse childhood experiences and elevated cortisol levels. Family disruption, particularly relationships with caregivers, can impact 13-year-olds in social-emotional as well as physical arenas. Early father absence in the home has been associated with earlier age at menarche (Webster et al., 2014). Similarly, earlier puberty was evident in cisgender girls who had family disruption (Ellis & Garber, 2000).

Adolescents at age 13 can experience sleep deprivation. Their growing bodies and active minds expend energy throughout the daytime hours; adequate sleep for 13-year-olds remains as important as during childhood. In a study of 1,101 participants ages 13 to 16 years, Vernon et al. (2018) found nighttime mobile phone usage and poor sleep increased over time, with connections to behavior, self-esteem, and coping.

Best Practices for Counseling and Therapy

Individual Counseling

In individual counseling, counselors can prepare for 13-year-olds to have options for verbal and nonverbal means of communication during session. Counselors can normalize for their teen clients that there may be times during counseling when the client cannot find the right words to portray or explain how they are feelings or what they are experiencing. In those moments, the client may benefit from expressing themselves through creative mediums such as art, dance, and music. Counselors can plan ahead to structure the counseling space for their 13-year-old clients to clearly offer options for nonverbal and creative expression such as artmaking materials (e.g., pencils, paint, canvas, paper, yarn, beads), sandtray and miniature figures, musical instruments and/or karaoke machine, open-ended toys (e.g., blocks, dolls, rope, puppets). Research shows positive outcomes from the incorporation of expressive arts, activity play therapy, and sandtray in counseling with pre-adolescent clients (e.g., Armstrong et al., 2015; Holliman & Foster, 2023; Ojiambo & Bratton, 2014).

Counselors can balance the use of nondirective and directive approaches during counseling with 13-year-olds. Teens need space to process their emotions without direction from or reliance on the therapist, and they also may desire support from the therapist through more concrete directed activities to learn new ways to process and organize their experiences.

Trust is important to 13-year-old clients, so counselors should be intentional in discussing confidentiality and privacy with them and their caregivers. In a similar respect, 13-year-old clients may be more careful in deciding if they can trust the clinician's intention and care during counseling sessions; clinicians can be genuine in their relationship with the teen so trust is gradually built. Counselors can do well not to expect or demand trust from 13-year-old clients; they are exercising their autonomy and decision-making skills in choosing what and to whom they share. When determining how to approach potentially sensitive conversations, such as conducting a risk assessment, it is important to be honest and straightforward. Thirteen-year-old clients might not readily verbalize their emotions or risk factors unless specifically asked to do so (e.g., about anxiety, suicidality, or alcohol use). Preventative assessment can support early identification of stressors and risks for 13-year-old clients to mitigate exacerbation of symptoms or factors if they have gone unidentified.

Counselors may observe that their 13-year-old clients initiate conversations about other people in their lives (e.g., friends, peers, teachers, family members) more readily than they initiate discussions about their own emotions and concerns. For example, Evie begins each counseling session by providing the counselor an overview of her friend group's recent dynamics, what they did in their classes that week, and what she thinks her sisters should be doing. Sometimes counselors can feel confused about the relevance of these seemingly surface level conversations with teen clients, desiring for the teen to talk about "why they are really there for counseling." As developmentally expected at this age, Evie is naturally interested in and influenced by the world around her and appreciates that her counselor shows sincere interest in her world too. The counselor can be mindful to connect Evie's sharing about others to Evie's internal experiences in those interpersonal interactions. For example, instead of asking follow-up questions about the other people, her counselor might reflect, "Sometimes you feel confident at school and sometimes you feel less confident at school," "Your friends' opinions are important to you," or "You wish you could have your mom all to yourself sometimes." Reflections that connect back to the teens' experiences can help bridge their internal and external worlds and communicate empathic understanding. Similarly, because a 13-year-old's view of self is influenced by perceptions of peer groups, the counselor may ask open-ended questions that support the 13-year-old's reflections about their own true feelings and experiences in contrast to the feelings and experiences of the other people in their lives, such as "So, your friends wanted you to do what they were doing. How did you feel in that situation?" Thirteen-year-olds are invested in how other people, such as peers and friends, view them. Depending on clinical needs and goals, group counseling can be a valuable counseling model for 13-year-old clients.

Group Counseling

Given an individual client's needs and goals, participating in group counseling with peers nearly their same age allows 13-year-old clients to practice interpersonal social skills and to be connected to a peer group. Thirteen-year-olds value the perceptions and opinions of their peers, so group counseling can be a valuable tool to encourage participation in the counseling process and to foster a sense of belonging among teen clients. Counselors can form adolescent counseling groups based on a common presenting concern (e.g., anxiety group, anger management group, group for children of alcoholics), a skill to be attained (e.g., mindfulness group, social skills group, psychoeducation group), a therapeutic modality (e.g., sandtray group, group activity play therapy), and/or a general counseling group. During the group counseling process, the counselor can use reflective listening skills and ask open-ended questions to build connections between group members, facilitate the group's process and interactions, and support individual members' processes.

At the onset of group and throughout the counseling process, the counselor needs to overtly discuss the limitations of confidentiality in the group setting, particularly that confidentiality and privacy are strongly encouraged to build trust and safety among participants but cannot be guaranteed in the group setting. The teens can choose what they do and do not verbally share with group members. Just as with individual counseling, it is developmentally responsive to provide opportunities for 13-year-olds to use creative and expressive media to express themselves nonverbally and verbally during group counseling sessions. When creating art as part of the therapeutic process, 13-year-olds benefit from being able to 1) nonverbally engage in their own creative process, which allows for the teen to internally process their thoughts, and, simultaneously, 2) choose when they verbally engage with peers and externally process their responses to prompts, feelings, and experiences in the group setting. Another creative group counseling approach for 13-year-olds is to invite clients to engage in group activities (e.g., Ashby et al., 2008; Swank & Shin, 2022), such as games, adventure play, nature-based play, and group tasks. Research demonstrates therapeutic effects of group play therapy for pre-adolescent clients, such as increased expression of feelings and self-awareness, reduction in behavior problems, and development of moral reasoning (e.g., Ojiambo & Bratton, 2014; Paone et al., 2008; Peryman et al., 2015).

Caregiver Involvement

Although a 13-year-old is a teenager, in many states, they are not above consenting age to ongoing counseling; caregiver involvement may be required and, regardless, strongly encouraged. It is important that clinicians directly discuss the confidentiality and rights of the 13-year-old (e.g., what are the limits of confidentiality in this setting, what will caregivers know from session, and how involved will caregivers be in the counseling process). If symptoms can be reduced or moderated by improving the quality of the parent–child relationship, the clinician can determine most clinically appropriate way(s) to support caregiver participation, such as parent consultation meeting, family counseling, filial therapy, family play therapy, and/or parenting groups. Practical goals of interventions with caregivers of 13-year-olds may include psychoeducation, learning and practicing communication skills, improving the quality and strength of the parent-teen relationship, and exploring the influence of attachment and attunement on their relationship with their child. Psychoeducation for 13-year-olds and their parents, separately or together, can focus on understanding of adolescent development, interpersonal neurobiology, conceptualization of adolescents' symptoms and parenting needs, and coping skills.

Additionally, caregivers may benefit from exploring how to engage in joint problem-solving with their teen. Thirteen-year-olds are learning to make decisions and perfection is not expected. Counselors can support caregivers in exploring how their teen's increasing sense of right and wrong as well as their budding capacity for complex thoughts and seeing different sides of situations opens the door for joint problem-solving. For example, Gus's counselor helped Gus and his parents to engage in joint problem-solving to negotiate Gus's bedtime and morning routines for school days. Gus reported feeling frustrated that he had to go to bed before his group of friends ended their virtual group video game, which he enjoyed being a part of. His parents reported feeling disrespected that Gus was not complying to their rules when they asked him to end his video game call. Gus and his parents brainstormed a list of all possible solutions to their impasse. Once their list of all possible choices was developed, they systematically crossed off items that were not adequately agreeable to both parties. At the end of this exercise, Gus and his parents agreed that Gus will have an extended bedtime on the weekend nights, during which he can complete the entire duration of the virtual video game calls with his friends, and he will maintain his normal bedtime on weekday nights.

Assessment and Systemic Collaboration

Counselors can incorporate inclusive language on assessment forms and during counseling sessions that reflect the nonbinary gender continuum, such as allowing their clients to self-identify on the intake form their preferred pronouns and a name they would like to be called by the counselor. Counselors can also assess for differences and similarities between how youth self-identify and how their parents identify them. In developing accurate conceptualization of 13-year-old clients' functioning, the counselor can attend to the many holistic factors that may impact the presentation of the client's clinical symptoms and presenting concerns, such as family; peers; physical, cognitive, and social development; substance use; sexuality/sexual development; interpersonal patterns; and background history. In written documentation and case development, rather than describe or consider a 13-year-old client, for example, as an "aggressive teen," the counselor can be more accurate and use unbiased and nonjudgmental language that recognizes the functionality and development of the teen's symptoms (e.g., aggressive behaviors). In this example, the counselor can be more accurate to report "this client appears to exhibit aggressive behaviors when they feel self-conscious or disappointed." Because 13-year-olds are keenly aware of their surroundings and perceptions of others, accuracy of language in formal and informal assessment is important to contextualize the young clients' experiences with validity and respect.

Thirteen-year-old clients are operating within their systems of care (e.g., at home, at school, in foster care placement) and coping with a range of stressors present in those systems. The counselor can support the 13-year-old client's systems to better understand the client's needs, perspectives, and frame of reference and to recognize when the client's symptoms are a result of their attempts to cope with dysfunction or discord present in their systems and/or interpersonal relationships. Regarding systemic advocacy and with signed releases of information, it can be imperative for counselors of 13-year-old clients to consult with and involve key people invested in a client's wellness and counseling process (e.g., foster parents, teachers, school staff, mentors, grandparents), to coordinate care with multidisciplinary providers (e.g., school personnel, medical providers, psychiatrists, care coordinator), and to advocate for clients' desired school interventions or care plan actions.

Conclusion

Thirteen-year-old clients are entering adolescence, a period of significant biological, social, and intrapersonal transitions. Thirteen-year-old clients are able to engage in verbal discussion of their concerns and experiences and also can benefit from opportunities to express their feelings and process their experiences nonverbally through creative media in the counseling process. Counselors need to understand how peer and parent relationships as well as identity development influence teens' development. In individual, group, and family counseling, counselors can support 13-year-old clients by respecting what is important to them, providing both structure and freedom in the counseling process, and supporting the teens' relationships in their systems.

References

Adams, G., Ryan, B., & Keating, L. (2000). Family relationships, academic environments, and psychosocial development during the university experience: A longitudinal investigation. *Journal of Adolescent Research*, *15*(1), 99–122. https://doi.org/10.1177/0743558400151006

Alessandri, G., Zuffiano, A., Eisenberg, N., & Pastorelli, C. (2017). The role of ego-resiliency as mediator of the longitudinal relationship between family socio-economic status and school grades. *Journal of Youth and Adolescence*, *46*, 2157–2168. https://doi.org/10.1007/s10964-017-0691-7

American Psychological Association. (2002). *Developing adolescents: A reference for professionals*. www.apa.org/pi/families/resources/develop.pdf

Armstrong, S. A., Brown, T., & Foster, R. D. (2015). Humanistic sandtray therapy with preadolescents. *Journal of Child and Adolescent Counseling*, *1*(1), 17–26. https://doi.org/10.1080/23727810.2015.1023167

Arzeen, S., Hassan, B., & Riaz, M. (2012). Perception of parental acceptance and rejection in emotionally empathic and non-empathic adolescents. *Pakistan Journal of Social and Clinical Psychology*, *9*(3), 60–69.

Ashby, J. S., Kottman, T., & DeGraaf, D. G. (2008). *Active interventions for kids and teens: Adding adventure and fun to counseling!* American Counseling Association.

Benson, M., McWey, L., & Ross, J. (2006). Parental attachment and peer relations in adolescence: A meta-analysis. *Research in Human Development*, *3*(1), 33–43. https://doi.org/10.1207/s15427617rhd0301_4

Biro, F. M., Galvez, M. P., Greenspan, L. C., Succop, P. A., Vangeepuram, N., Pinney, S. M., Teitelbaum, S., Windham, G. C., Kushi, L. H., & Wolff, M. S. (2010). Pubertal assessment method and baseline characteristics in a mixed longitudinal study of girls. *Pediatrics*, *126*(3), e583–e590. https://doi.org/10.1542/peds.2009-3079

Blakemore, S., Burnett, S., & Dahl, R. (2010). The role of puberty in the developing adolescent brain. *Human Brain Mapping*, *31*(6), 926–933. https://doi.org/10.1002/hbm.21052

Blanton, R., Cooney, R., Joorman, J., Eugene, F., Glover, G., & Gotlib, I. (2012). Pubertal stage and brain anatomy in girls. *Neuroscience*, *217*, 105–112. https://doi.org/10.1016/j.neuroscience.2012.04.059

Bronfenbrenner, U., & Morris, P. A. (2006). The bioecological model of human development. In W. Damon & R. M. Lerner (Eds.), *Handbook of child psychology* (pp. 793–828). Wiley.

Casey, B. J., Jones, R. M., & Hare, T. A. (2008). The adolescent brain. *Annals of the New York Academy of Sciences*, *1124*(1), 111–126. https://doi.org/10.1196/annals.1440.010

Centers for Disease Control and Protection. (2021). *Human papillomavirus (HPV)*. www.cdc.gov/hpv/parents/vaccine.html

Das, J. K., Salam, R. A., Thornburg, K. L., Prentice, A. M., Campisi, S., Lassi, Z. S., Koletzko, B., & Bhutta, Z. A. (2017). Nutrition in adolescents: Physiology, metabolism, and nutritional needs. *Annals of the New York Academy of Sciences*, *1393*(1), 21–33. https://doi.org/10.1111/nyas.13330

Degeilh, F., Guillery-Girard, B., Dayan, J., Gaubert, M., Chetelat, G., Egler, P., Baleyte, J., Eustache, F., & Viard, A. (2015). Neural correlates of self and its interaction with memory in healthy adolescents. *Child Development*, *86*(6), 1966–1983. https://doi.org/10.1111/cdev.12440

Dorn, L., Hostinar, C., Susman, E., & Pervanidou, P. (2019). Conceptualizing puberty as a window of opportunity for impacting health and well-being across the life span. *Journal of Research on Adolescents*, *29*(1), 155–176. https://doi.org/10.1111/jora.12431

Dronkers, J. (2016). Parents' living arrangement and the political and civic attitudes of 13- and 14-year-old children. *Journal of Family Research*, *28*, 381–397. https://doi.org/10.3224/zff.v28i3.26046

Ellis, B., & Garber, J. (2000). Psychosocial antecedents of variation in girls' pubertal timing: Maternal depression, stepfather presence, and marital and family stress. *Child Development*, *71*(2), 485–501. https://doi.org/10.1111/1467-8624.00159

Erikson, E. (1988). Youth: Fidelity and diversity. *Daedalus*, *117*(3), 1–24.

Galván, A. (2017). *The neuroscience of adolescence*. Cambridge University Press.

Gatta, M., Colombo, E., Penzo, M., & Battistella, P. (2017). The dysfunction of emotional expression as a related factor for alcohol misuse in young adolescents. *Journal of Child and Adolescent Substance Abuse*, *26*(1), 30–40. https://doi.org/10.1080/1067828X.2016.1184599

Gemelli, R. (1996). *Normal child and adolescent development* (1st ed.). American Psychiatric Publishing.

Hammons, A. J., & Fiese, B. H. (2011). Is frequency of shared family meals related to the nutritional health of children and adolescents? *Pediatrics*, *127*(6), e1565–e1574. https://doi.org/10.1542/peds.2010-1440

Harter, S. (1983). Developmental perspectives on the self-system. In E. M. Hetherington (Ed.), *Handbook of child psychology* (pp. 275–385). John Wiley.

Hemberg, J., Korzhina, Y., Groundstroem, H., Ostman, L., Nystrom, L., & Nyman-Kurkiala, P. (2021). Loneliness – two sides to the story: Adolescents' lived experiences. *International Journal of Adolescence and Youth*, *26*(1), 41–56. https://doi.org/10.1080/02673843.2021.1883075

Herman-Giddens, M. E., Steffes, J., Harris, D., Slora, E., Hussey, M., Dowshen, S. A., Wasserman, R., Serwint, J. R., Smitherman, L., & Reiter, E. O. (2012). Secondary sexual characteristics in boys: Data from the Pediatric Research in Office Settings Network. *Pediatrics*, *130*(5), e1058–e1068. https://doi.org/10.1542/peds.2011-3291

Hewlett, B. (2013). *Adolescent identity: Evolutionary, cultural, and developmental perspectives* (1st ed.). Routledge.

Holliman, R., & Foster, R. D. (2023). The way we play in the sand: A meta-analytic investigation of sand therapy, its formats, and presenting problems. *Journal of Child and Adolescent Counseling*, *9*(2), 205–221. https://doi.org/10.1080/23727810.2023.2232142

Johansson, A., Brunnberg, E., & Eriksson, C. (2007). Adolescent girls' and boys' perceptions of mental health. *Journal of Youth Studies*, *10*(2), 183–202. https://doi.org/10.1080/13676260601055409

Johnson, S., Buckingham, M., Morris, S., Suzuki, S., Weiner, M., Hershberg, R., & Fremont, E. (2016). Adolescents' character role models: Exploring who young people look up to as examples of how to be a good person. *Research in Human Development*, *13*, 126–141. https://doi.org/10.1080/15427609.2016.1164552

Kelly, A. B., Mason, W. A., Chmelka, M. B., Herrenkohl, T. I., Kim, M. J., Patton, G. C., Hemphill, S. A., Toumbourou, J. W., & Catalano, R. F. (2016). Depressed mood during early to middle adolescence: A bi-national longitudinal study of the unique impact of family conflict. *Journal of Youth and Adolescence*, *45*(8), 1604–1613. https://doi.org/10.1007/s10964-016-0433-2

Kunnen, S. (2012). *A dynamic systems approach to adolescent development*. Psychology Press.

Lee, Y., & Styne, D. (2013). Influences on the onset and tempo of puberty in human beings and implications for adolescent psychological development. *Hormonal Behavior*, *64*(2), 250–261. https://doi.org/10.1016/j.yhbeh.2013.03.014

Legette, K. (2018). School tracking and youth self-perceptions: Implications for academic and racial identity. *Child Development*, *89*(4), 1311–1327. https://doi.org/10.1111/cdev.12748

Levin, K., Torsheim, T., Vollebergh, W., Richter, M., Davies, C., Schnohr, C., Due, P., & Currie, C. (2011). National income and income inequality, family affluence and life satisfaction among 13-year-old boys and girls: A multilevel study in 35 countries. *Social Indices Research*, *104*, 179–194. https://doi.org/10.1007/s11205-010-9747-8

Meschke, L., Zweig, J., Barber, B., & Eccles, J. (2000). Demographic, biological, psychological, and social predictors of the timing of first intercourse. *Journal of Research on Adolescence*, *10*(3), 315–338.

Ojiambo, D., & Bratton, S. C. (2014). Effects of group activity play therapy on problem behaviors of preadolescent Ugandan orphans. *Journal of Counseling & Development*, *92*(3), 355–365. https://doi.org/10.1002/j.1556-6676.2014.00163.x

Paone, T. R., Packman, J., Cleborne, M., & Rothman, T. (2008). A school-based group activity therapy intervention with at-risk high school students as it relates to their moral reasoning. *International Journal of Play Therapy*, *17*(2), 122–137. https://doi.org/10.1037/a0012582

Perryman, K. L., Moss, R., & Cochran, K. (2015). Child-centered expressive arts and play therapy: School groups for at-risk adolescent girls. *International Journal of Play Therapy*, *24*(4), 205–220. https://doi.org/10.1037/a0039764

Pretty, G., Conroy, C., Dugay, J., Fowler, K., & Williams, D. (1996). Sense of community and its relevance to adolescents of all ages. *Journal of Community Psychology*, *24*(4), 365–379. https://doi.org/10.1002/(SICI)1520-6629(199610)24:4<365::AID-JCOP6>3.0.CO;2-T

Pullen Sansfaçon, A., Medico, D., Suerich-Gulick, F., & Temple Newhook, J. (2020). "I knew that I wasn't cis, I knew that, but I didn't know exactly": Gender identity development, expression and affirmation in youth who access gender affirming medical care. *International Journal of Transgender Health*, *21*(3), 307–320. https://doi.org/10.1080/26895269.2020.1756551

Reisner, S., Greytak, E., Parsons, J., & Ybarra, M. (2015). Gender minority social stress in adolescence: Disparities in adolescent bullying and substance use by gender identity. *Journal of Sex Research*, *52*(3), 243–256. https://doi.org/10.1080/00224499.2014.886321

Rice, T., & Sher, L. (2017). Adolescent suicide and testosterone. *International Journal of Adolescent Medicine and Health*, *29*(4). https://doi.org/10.1515/ijamh-2015-0058

Schlarb, A. A., Gulewitsch, M. D., Weltzer, V., Ellert, U., & Enck, P. (2015). Sleep duration and sleep problems in a representative sample of German children and adolescents. *Health*, *7*(11), 1397. https://doi.org/10.4236/health.2015.711154

Schlegel, A. (2015). The cultural context of adolescent self-regulation. In G. Oettingen & P. Gollwitzer (Eds.), *Self-regulation in adolescence*. Cambridge University Press.

Seifert, K., & Hoffnung, R. (2000). *Child and adolescent development* (5th ed.). Wadsworth Publishing.

Sher, L. (2014). Testosterone and suicidal behavior. *Expert Review of Neurotherapeutics*, *3*, 257–259. https://doi.org/10.1586/ern.12.6

Spilt, J., Van Lier, P., Branje, S., Meeus, W., & Koot, H. (2015). Discrepancies in perceptions of close relationships of young adolescents: A risk for psychology? *Journal of Youth and Adolescence*, *44*, 910–921. https://doi.org/10.1007/s10964-014-0234-4

Steinberg, L. (2017). *Adolescence* (12th ed.). McGraw Hill Education.

Swank, J. M., & Shin, S. M. (2022). Nature-based child-centered play therapy: Taking the playroom outside. In J. A. Courtney, J. L., Langly, L. L. Wonders, R. Heiko, & R. LaPierre (Eds.), *Nature based play and expressive therapies: Interventions for working with children, teens, and families* (pp. 127–135). Routledge. https://doi.org/10.4324/9781003152767-14

Tomova, A., Robeva, R., & Kumanov, P. (2011). Timing of pubertal maturation according to the age at first conscious ejaculation. *Andrologia*, *43*, 63–166. https://doi.org/10.1111/j.1439-0272.2009.01037.x

Vernon, L., Modecki, K., & Barber, B. (2018). Mobile phones in the bedroom: Trajectories of sleep habits and subsequent adolescent psychosocial development. *Child Development*, *89*(1), 66–77. https://doi.org/10.1111/cdev.12836

Webster, G., Graber, J., Gesselman, A., Crosier, B., & Schember, T. (2014). A life history theory of father absence and menarche: A meta-analysis. *Evolutionary Psychology*, *12*(2), 273–294. https://doi.org/10.1177/147470491401200202

Wendelken, C., Ferrer, E., Ghetti, S., Bailey, S., Cutting, L., & Bunge, S. (2016). Frontoparietal structural connectivity in childhood predicts development of functional connectivity and reasoning ability: A large-scale longitudinal investigation. *The Journal of Neuroscience*, *37*(35), 1–19. https://doi.org/10.1523/JNEUROSCI.3726-16.2017

Whittle, S., Yap, M., Fornito, A., Simmons, J., Barrett, A., Sheeber, L., & Allen, N. (2008). Prefrontal and amygdala volumes are related to adolescents' affective behaviors during parent–adolescent interactions. *PNAS*, *105*(9), 3652–3657. https://doi.org/10.1073/pnas.0709815105

Whitty, M., & Young, G. (2017). *Cyberpsychology: The study of individuals, society and digital technologies*. John Wiley & Sons.

Wright, J., Zakriski, A., & Fisher, P. (1996). Age differences in correlates of perceived dominance. *Social Development*, *5*, 24–40. https://doi.org/10.1111/j.1467-9507.1996.tb00070.x

Chapter 4

The 14-Year-Old

Ali Hamilton-Fay

Dillion is a biracial, 14-year-old, cisgender boy whose parents have brought him for counseling due to increasing anxiety and fighting about getting to school. Dillion's parents report he is more withdrawn, retreating to his electronics and less willing to engage with the family. During the intake, Dillion reports difficulty sleeping, feeling overwhelmed by worries about school shootings, getting cut from a sports team due to the number of available roster spots, and navigating the demands of high school. While in previous years he had been average height and weight as compared to his peers, since beginning the school year, he has noticed that he is now is physically smaller than others his age. Dillion reports feeling most comfortable interacting with others virtually and that he spends most of his time online, using social media and playing video games.

In comparison, 14-year-old Kimberly is a White ninth grader from a blended family who presented for counseling due to increasing sadness, low mood, and low motivation. Kimberly's family reports slipping grades and increasing withdrawal from the family. She reports wanting to be social but feels like she does not fit in at school, struggles to keep or make friends, and is having trouble maintaining interests. Kimberly has disclosed feeling generally uncomfortable about her appearance and body and concerned about social standing and that she tried hard to be interested in the same things girls her age like, but it doesn't feel right. Kimberly states she feels alone because everyone seems to know what they want, who they are, and what they like to do while she's just treading water.

Stephanie is a 14-year-old, cisgender, Latina girl, beginning her first year of local, public high school after attending a small, private K–8 school in a nearby suburb. Prior to this school year, Stephanie's family reports she had been an above-average student, had a small group of friends, and was generally compliant with family expectations. Since transitioning to a new school, her family has noticed an increase in frustration, anger, and hostility and constant fighting with parents about rules related to curfew, acceptable activities, and attitude during family activities.

These are all 14-year-olds experiencing distressing yet developmentally common difficulties. While age may not fully account for the root of their struggles, understanding the complexity of 14-year-old's developmental process and conceptualizing them through a developmental lens can help counselors identify interventions that will support them and facilitate growth and development. The developmental trajectory of 14-year-olds is impacted by their biology, life experiences, and interactions. Fourteen-year-olds are

DOI: 10.4324/9781003196297-6

physically, cognitively, emotionally, and socially maturing at varying rates and are constantly negotiating how to present themselves and move through the world. These variations in presentation are a critical part of their identity development process and may create friction when they are at odds with societal and familial expectations. This chapter will explore a variety of factors that influence development, identify protective and risk factors, and outline best practices for consideration when working with 14-year-olds.

Physical Development

Due to the differences in pubertal status and pubertal tempo, 14-year-olds will not experience the same changes at the same time (National Academies of Sciences, Engineering and Medicine [NASEM], 2019). Pubertal timing and tempo are influenced by genetics, environmental exposures, maltreatment, and stressors. According to McNeely and Blanchard (2011), the changes that may be experienced by 14-year-olds during puberty include changes in height, weight, appetite, skin, and body hair appearance. Breast tissue changes, initiation of spermarche and menarche, development of body odor, vocal changes, and variations in hormone levels also occur during puberty. Medical evaluation is recommended for adolescents if physical changes have not begun by age 13–13.5 to rule out concerns associated with delayed puberty.

These physical changes may impact the self-image of 14-year-olds if development occurs significantly earlier or later than peers or if physical changes are not in line with social ideals (McNeely & Blanchard, 2011). Early pubertal development can reinforce inappropriate assumptions of maturity. Fourteen-year-olds who develop early may be pressured into or provided with opportunities to engage in risky activities and may experience inappropriate and unwanted attention from older persons. They may also be judged more harshly or afforded less protection, empathy, or support than their same age, lesser developed peers (Epstein et al., 2017). Black and African American children may enter puberty at a younger chronological age than their White peers (Ramnitz & Lodish, 2013), increasing the risk of being perceived and treated as older or more mature. Black and African American children are often held to adult standards and disciplined like adults due to the misperception that they are older and more mature than their same-age White peers (Epstein et al., 2017; Goff et al., 2014; Nanda, 2012). Later development can lead to assumptions of childlike status resulting in exclusion from social experiences or physical activities where size or maturity is a factor.

Helping 14-year-olds understand the individuality of pubertal timelines, hearing their concerns about puberty, and providing them with age-appropriate experiences and expectations that align with their development (increased social activities, responsibilities, and autonomy) are important ways to support 14-year-olds during this period.

Brain Development

Pubertal hormones influence brain development. Since pubertal changes happen at a varying pace, brain development will also occur at an individual rate. Neural "plasticity" increases during early adolescence, which allows for more flexibility in thinking, growth in learning and skills, and adaptability (Arain et al., 2013).

The hippocampus, amygdala, and prefrontal cortex are sections of the brain influenced by pubertal development (NASEM, 2019). During adolescence, the hippocampus increases in size, supporting greater capacity for memory retrieval and retention. The combination of increased retention and recall and neural plasticity allows 14-year-olds to use past experiences to influence present behavior and choices.

The amygdala monitors our environment, recognizes threats, attends to the mood and affect of others, and is highly responsive to stimuli at this age (Galván, 2017). This heightened sensitivity and responsiveness can explain a 14-year-old's seemingly out of proportion emotional responses to common situations and their difficulty accurately assessing the impact of challenges, by misestimating the consequences or outcomes.

The prefrontal cortex obtains information from the amygdala, hippocampus, and other areas of the brain and processes this information by assessing its validity to makes choices, decisions, or judgments (Arain et al., 2013). The prefrontal cortex finishes developing around age 25; therefore, adolescent brains tend to operate from their amygdala (Arain et al., 2013) and respond with greater emotional reactivity.

Fourteen-year-old brains tend toward reward-motivated behaviors (socializing over studying) that provide immediate positive impacts (Galván, 2017, p. 11). They may engage in longer-term, reward-motivated behaviors; however, the duration of their focus will be based on the personal value of the goal. Due to the developmental process of the brain, a 14-year-old's maturity, logic, reasoning, and emotionality can fluctuate wildly (Arain et al., 2013). Fourteen-year-olds may be able to discuss and evaluate options when not immediately pressed to make a decision, but when under pressure, they may default to an emotional response rather than a thoughtful or logical one (Galván, 2017). While it may seem they aren't thinking before they act, 14-year-olds *are* thinking; they are using their emotional brains.

Cognitive Development

Piaget's cognitive development theory (Inhelder & Piaget, 2013) coupled with the neurobiological research mentioned previously, support the idea that there is a substantial shift in thinking during the adolescent years (Arain et al., 2013; Galván, 2017; NASEM, 2019). Piaget asserts that children in early adolescence move from concrete thinking into the formal operations stage, where they begin to use deductive thought to apply logic and reasoning to abstract concepts, solve problems, and make decisions (Inhelder & Piaget, 2013). Fourteen-year-olds may show a new eagerness to learn more advanced material or to understand concepts on a deeper level (Galván, 2017). Despite this growth, 14-year-olds still struggle with thinking beyond the present or immediate future, resulting in organizational or executive functioning difficulties (Galván, 2017).

Cognitive changes influence how 14-year-olds view their world. They are becoming more aware of the perspectives of others and more concerned with their future and long-term goals and are beginning to think about ethics, morals, and identity (Galván, 2017). These new capabilities are often used inconsistently and ineffectively but will continue to develop over time. It is important to recognize and celebrate these sparks of growth while holding age-appropriate and individual expectations.

Emotional Development

In early adolescence, hormonal changes may contribute to 14-year-olds' emotional volatility and negativity (Gianine & Lewis, 2003). Fourteen-year-olds are also presented with life events and increased challenges that may overwhelm their ability to successfully navigate these new, often co-occurring circumstances. If their ability to cope is overwhelmed (Gianine & Lewis, 2003), they may need more support to access and expand current coping skills and emotional competencies to effectively respond to these situations.

Gains in cognitive development change the way 14-year-olds interact with, respond to, and view the world (Gianine & Lewis, 2003). As 14-year-olds develop a deeper understanding of people, actions, and experiences, they need to make emotional adjustments to cope and respond to this new level of understanding. Fourteen-year-olds are more likely to express their emotions verbally (e.g., yelling or arguments) or physically (e.g., smiles, hugs, stomping, door-slamming) and may seem regularly annoyed or moody (Ames et al., 1988). This behavior is inconsistent and can be just as confounding to adults as it is to the 14-year-old (Ames et al., 1988).

While 14-year-olds can recognize more complex emotions in themselves, they have difficulty identifying the intensity and nuance of emotions in others (Rutter et al., 2019). Emotional responses from others may be miscategorized and interpreted as more intense or threatening, resulting in defensive responses. For example, teens may misjudge fear or disappointment from adults as anger and, therefore, respond in kind. Misreading emotional responses from others can negatively impact experiences, self-esteem, and interpersonal relationships. Counselors working with 14-year-olds often partner with parents/caregivers in learning how to respond to the unpredictable emotional ups and downs and intense interactions with their teen.

Social and Relationship Development

Social Acceptance and Peers

Feeling significant or important to others is a vital part of belonging (Harms, 2021). It is normal for 14-year-olds to strive for belonging with peers and move emotionally and socially away from family to explore their own identity. Feeling like they do not fit in at home can increase their motivation to seek out belonging and acceptance elsewhere (Eckstein et al., 1999). Being a part of a group can bolster self-esteem and increase their sense of worth, even if the group does not align with their personal or family beliefs. Fourteen-year-olds' drive for belonging and sensitivity to criticism can be intense enough that peer pressure may override their better judgment and values (Harms, 2021) and lead to engagement in harmful behaviors.

Peer pressure is not always negative and can foster prosocial, constructive behaviors, choices, and experiences (Harms, 2021) and be a source of emotional support (Nawaz, 2011). Positive peer groups can provide opportunities for teens to evaluate their own thoughts, values, and beliefs in a supportive environment (Pugh & Hart, 1999). Peers can also serve as role models for behavior and provide new information, perspectives, feedback, and alternative solutions for navigating new situations (Ragelienė, 2016).

Fourteen-year-olds may have exposure to different peer groups depending on the structure and number of activities in which they participate. The more diverse the peer engagement is, the more likely 14-year-olds will be exposed to a wider variety of people and experiences to support positive social and identity development (Pugh & Hart, 1999).

Negative peer interactions such as relational victimization (e.g., rumor spreading, friendship withdrawal, and social exclusion) can significantly contribute to feelings of social anxiety and depression in adolescence (La Greca & Harrison, 2005). Having quality, close, or "best" friendships demonstrating companionship, nurturance, approval, support, and reliable alliance may serve a protective function against social anxiety, but close friendships are not immune to relational victimization. Given the covert nature of relational victimization and the tendency for 14-year-olds to confide in each other over adults, it may be hard to correct or prevent these behaviors. The use of social media may also present a vehicle for relational victimization of which adults may be unaware. Adults can provide support to 14-year-olds navigating peer conflict by validating their feelings and experiences, allowing autonomy in how to handle the issue (provided safety is not a concern), being present with them in their hard and painful feelings, and providing reassurance of their worth and value.

Parents/Caregivers Relationship

As they strive for more autonomy and engage more with peers, 14-year-olds may change how they relate to the family unit and often shift their behavior depending on the presence of peers or in public settings (Eckstein et al., 1999). For example, when peers/others are assumed to be "watching," a 14-year-old may refuse to acknowledge their parents/caregivers at public places or ask to be dropped off out of view of their peers.

With increased sensitivity to the opinions and feedback of peers, 14-year-olds may prioritize values, decisions, and actions that may conflict with family values or seem out of character (Eckstein et al., 1999). A central task of adolescence is moving toward greater independence from families (Erikson, 1968); however, 14-year-olds still need close and supportive relationships with parents/caregivers (Salgado et al., 2021). While it can be difficult for adults to strike a balance between setting expectations and allowing for independent decision-making and providing information while making space for open discussions, it is beneficial for skill-building and fostering relationships between teens and their adults.

Dating/Romantic Relationships

In conversations between adults and 14-year-olds about dating, the topic of sexual activity often arises, but characteristics of healthy and unhealthy relationships are often not discussed (Power to Decide, 2016). More than 70% of cisgender women and 60% of cisgender men reported their first experience with interpersonal violence occurred prior to age 25 and many occurring before age 18 (Leemis et al., 2022). Considering these statistics and the developmental movement toward intimate relationships, consent and healthy relationships need to be discussed.

Ideally, conversations would begin in younger years and continue throughout adolescence and into adulthood. To spark conversation about healthy relationships, adults can initiate dialogue about character relationships/actions in music, books, tv or movies, or people in real life, naming positive and negative relationship attributes and their impact. Modeling consent (e.g., asking permission before physical contact) and healthy relationship actions (e.g., disagreeing respectfully, verbalizing and respecting wants and needs) can provide tangible examples of healthy relationships as teens are developing their relationship skills.

Relationships With Other Trusted Adults

Supportive non-parental/caregiver figures can facilitate positive development in early adolescents by providing different types of support, connection, and role modeling (Yu & Deutsch, 2019). These relationships provide the best combination of parental/caregiver and peer qualities. Having a trusted adult who is accessible and can provide nonjudgmental support, validation, and perspective can help 14-year-olds feel heard and seen (Yu & Deutsch, 2019). Bridging the gap between parents/caregivers and peers, trusted adults can help adolescents improve information-processing and problem-solving skills (Yu & Deutsch, 2019). These relationships can complement positive parent/caregiver–child relationships or serve as a support for those in strained or unsupportive family relationships (Yu & Deutsch, 2019).

Cultural and Identity Development

Sense of Self

Erikson (1968) identified exploration and determination of personal identity as the most important tasks of adolescence (Erikson, 1968). Exposure to new experiences, people, concepts, and information, with their growing cognitive and emotional capacity and opportunities to explore different ways of being, provide 14-year-olds with the building blocks needed to begin figuring out their place in the world, who they want to be, and how they want to live.

Identity is shaped by family, cultural, and societal expectations; by the media, peers, and experiences out in the world; and within the institutions they belong (NASEM, 2019). Life circumstances such as changing family constellations (e.g., divorce, marriage, dating, births, deaths), moving, changing schools, or beginning new school years can motivate 14-year-olds to reinvent themselves.

The 14-year-old's identity may seem fluid or inauthentic due to rapid changes in music preferences, clothing/hair styles, language/slang usage, new or declining interests, and/or varying friend groups. Adults and environments that encourage self-expression and promote acceptance of, and respect for, different viewpoints and perspectives can enhance their confidence and identity development (Nawaz, 2011). Peers also play an important role in identity development. Being part of a peer group that demonstrates mutual respect, acceptance, and communication can provide a space for 14-year-olds to explore different identities with less risk to their self-image (Salgado et al., 2021).

A primary goal of adolescence is to develop a meaningful sense of self. To do this, adolescents must integrate multiple identities to create a consistent and unique understanding of who they are (Branje, 2022). Imagine a "dressing room" of sorts where the clothing options represent identities. Fourteen-year-olds have just entered this room, arms filled with various articles of clothing (identities), hoping to put together a unique "outfit" that fits them and shows the world who they are.

Gender Identity

Fourteen-year-olds will continue to explore and express their gender identity and often have a more fluid and flexible understanding of gender identity and gender expression. They may express and explore their gender identity in different ways, at different times, and with different levels of significance (perhaps through their physical appearance, pronouns, or name). Fourteen-year-olds who are experiencing psychological distress due to the discrepancy between biological sex and gender identity may seek medications that delay the onset of puberty or suppress the development of secondary sex characteristics to reduce distress and continue exploring their gender identity (Montemayor, 2019).

Nonjudgmental support of identity exploration can reduce stigma and shame and promote resilience (Janssen & Leibowitz, 2018). Family/caregiver rejection or negative responses to gender identity expression can result in negative psychological consequences, such as increased risk of mental health concerns, suicide, self-harm, and substance use (Montemayor, 2019; Janssen & Leibowitz, 2018). Professional support for family/caregivers can be helpful for reducing negative reactions toward the adolescent when families struggle to understand or accept their child's gender identity.

Sexual Identity

LGBTQ+ youth are "coming out," or affirming a sexual orientation other than heterosexual, at younger ages (Trevor Project, 2022). Coming out is a nuanced and individual process that may be gradual for some and more abrupt for others (Montemayor, 2019). Recognizing attractions, experimentation, and naming one's experience occurs at varying rates and, for some, can be fluid (Stewart et al., 2019). Both other-sex and same-sex crushes and sexual experiences are normal during adolescence and do not necessarily define sexual identity, as sexuality often develops along a continuum, and each person's sexual identity has individual nuances (Montemayor, 2019).

Social assumptions of heteronormativity can make coming out a necessary and repeated process. Coming out to affirming people can have a positive impact on mental health. According to the Trevor Project (2019), having just one affirming adult can reduce the risk of suicide for LGBTQ teens by 40%. Living authentically can bolster mental health. Teens may also find additional affirming support within their communities such as school programs (Gender and Sexuality Alliances), affirming community organizations, and affirming social media groups.

While coming out and living authentically can be beneficial, it is not without risks. Fourteen-year-olds who do not identify as heterosexual may face rejection by peers, parents/

caregivers, family members, and institutions, which can result in negative consequences. Rejection and discrimination can increase the risk of mental health concerns, suicide, and substance use (Byrd & Luke, 2021; Montemayor, 2019). Safety assessment and safety planning are encouraged when supporting anyone working through their coming out process.

Racial, Ethnic, and Cultural Identity

For early adolescents, racial and ethnic identity development is marked by a shift from being aware of labels used to identify differences to understanding what it means to be a part of these groups (Spencer et al., 2000). The importance of racial, ethnic, and cultural identity for a 14-year-old depends on their level of self-awareness, degree of identification with those groups, and readiness and desire for self-exploration and social experiences (Whaley, 1993).

As 14-year-olds strive for belonging and peer acceptance, differences in race, ethnicity, and culture may become more salient (Holcomb-McCoy, 2005). Fourteen-year-olds are typically aware of stereotypes associated with races, ethnicities, and cultures and can recognize the benefits and risks associated with different group memberships (Cheon et al., 2020). For children of multiple or nondominant identity groups, attachment to a particular group identity may vary depending on circumstances and social influences (Spencer et al., 2000). Fluidity in identity may be a function of exploration as teens find a way to bring together coexisting identities and integrate aspects of their different cultural systems to achieve a template for their own attitudes, values, and behavior (Barbarin, 1993).

Increased access to information, growing cognitive skills, and increased social interactions can bring more awareness of the social injustices associated with the treatment of nondominant groups (Holcomb-McCoy, 2005). Fourteen-year-olds from nondominant groups may start to recognize the marginalization of their own group, while members of the dominant group may question the historical and present-day inequities and injustices that have been perpetrated (Holcomb-McCoy, 2005). Increased awareness of discrimination and oppression may negatively impact the self-esteem and identity development of youth with marginalized identities even if they have not personally experienced such treatment (Whaley, 1993).

Fourteen-year-olds may spend considerable time thinking about who they are and where they come from working toward a state of confidence in their racial, ethnic, and cultural identities and trying to find balance between these identities and their national culture (Cheon et al., 2020). Individual differences in development and experiences influence when and how adolescents move through this process (Spencer et al., 2000).

Religious, Spiritual, and Moral Identity

Early adolescence may mark the end of passive agreement with family beliefs and values (Ream & Savin-Williams, 2003). Growing cognitive complexity and greater personal and social awareness allow for a deeper and more nuanced understanding of family religious/spiritual/moral beliefs and practices, which may invite questions or challenges to previous teaching (Quagliana et al., 2013). Fourteen-year-olds may choose to abstain from religious traditions or explore new beliefs and practices that differ from those of their family.

While families are often the primary influence on a young adolescent's belief systems, peers, media, and exposure to information about other belief systems factor into a teen's exploration and identity formation (Ream & Savin-Williams, 2003). Making sense of themselves and the world around them and a growing awareness of the more unexplainable events in life (tragedies and death) may influence a 14-year-old's belief system. Questioning one's religious, spiritual, or moral identity can be an opportunity for teens to engage in dialogue with trusted adults and peers to help solidify their core beliefs (Mahoney et al., 2013).

Fourteen-year-olds may be reluctant to participate in organized spiritual practices outside the home if beliefs conflict with emerging identities or beliefs of peer groups (Eckstein et al., 1999). When spiritual messages conflict with their burgeoning sense of self, teens may have internal and relational conflict as they struggle to reconcile these differences. If the messages and beliefs align positively, spirituality and participation in religious practices can increase self-esteem, promote prosocial activities, and build a sense of security (Ream & Savin-Williams, 2003).

Disability Identity

Disability identity development will vary individually for 14-year-olds depending on the type of disability, the degree to which the disability impacts functioning, the attitude of society/community, the structure of the environment, and access to resources. Unsupportive environmental structures or attitudes of society/community can negatively impact disability identity development if they limit movement toward autonomy, independence, or engagement. When others hold negative assumption/biases and/or view the disability as a problem with the individual rather than a lack of accessibility within the environment, it can be detrimental to an adolescent's identity development. When adolescents with disabilities experience positive, inclusive relationships and accessible environments and are provided sufficient accommodations, they are able to grow and thrive (Buder & Perry, 2023; Olkin, 2022).

According to Maxey and Beckert (2016), 14-year-olds' increasing awareness of differences and negative assumptions about disabilities may result in vulnerability to stigma, bullying, and isolation from peers. Fourteen-year-olds with disabilities largely have the same desires for friendship, belonging, and independence as their peers living without disabilities. Fulfilling these desires requires access to social activities and experiences that value the contributions of all people and opportunities for adolescents with disabilities to build autonomy and independence (Maxey & Beckert, 2016). Disability identity formation is a combination of life experiences, internal perception of disability, and how one's disability is perceived by others (Johnstone, 2004). Support and access can help 14-year-olds develop a positive self-identity that includes disability pride (Olkin, 2022).

Socioeconomic Status and Impact on Identity

Socioeconomic status (SES) can impact all areas of identity and adolescent development. Fourteen-year-olds with high SES have more access to resources for support and exploration as well as greater security in meeting basic needs (Phillips & Pittman, 2003). Fourteen-year-olds with lower SES may have reduced access to quality healthcare, nutrition, education, and time with parents/caregivers due to financial strain, which can contribute to negative physical, emotional, and mental health outcomes (Bradley & Corwyn, 2002). Teens with lower SES may not be able to participate in as many activities or with the same frequency as peers with higher SES backgrounds, which may impact social belonging and self-esteem (Phillips & Pittman, 2003). If their peers and communities hold negative views about persons of lower SES or perpetuate stereotypes related to class and status, 14-year-olds may develop a negative self-image or abandon their aspirations (Phillips & Pittman, 2003). Lower SES is not an automatic predictor of unhealthy development but should be considered when appraising 14-year-old development across all domains (Bradley & Corwyn, 2002).

Resources and Protective Factors

Fourteen-year-olds' levels of resilience are influenced by their internal predispositions, experiences, and relationships. No single factor determines how successfully an adolescent will navigate stress and challenges. At 14, most of a teen's internal resources are still developing including their positive coping, self-regulation, and communication skills. Positive connection to others, community, and institutions; sense of physical and psychological safety and belonging; having developmentally appropriate expectations; and opportunities for skill development are some external factors that promote resilience (Youth.gov, n.d.). Recognizing the complex, dynamic nature of resilience (Windle, 2010) and the interactive relationship between resilience and development (Ahern, 2006) help to clarify the variation in resilience among 14-year-olds.

Challenges and Risk Factors

Self-Esteem

A characteristic of adolescence is self-consciousness (Harms, 2021). This may be a consequence of teen's cognitive growth and increased abilities to evaluate, compare, and hypothesize (Inhelder & Piaget, 2013). Their developing critical eye can turn inwards resulting in a newly intense focus on how they are perceived by others. Fourteen-year-olds may often feel like everyone is watching, judging, and evaluating every move, decision, action, or inaction. This can cause great fluctuations in their self-esteem.

A 14-year-old's preoccupation with evaluation is not limited to social interactions. They are frequently evaluated by peers, adults, and the systems in which they grow and live. Judgments from others may be based on appearance; social group standing; intellectual, athletic, or artistic abilities; and/or future aspirations. The constant appraisal can create hyperfocus on evaluation from others, making it difficult to meet conflicting perceived expectations.

Decision-Making

Decisions are made by weighing the options of competing and complex motivations of varying importance and discernment – taking in information, evaluating options, and choosing a path of action – is a learned skill (Hartley & Somerville, 2015). Fourteen-year-olds have made large gains in their ability to think logically and systematically; however, they may underestimate or overestimate the consequences of their actions (Eckstein et al., 1999), making it difficult to use predicted outcomes as a determining factor when faced with a choice.

Limited critical thinking abilities can lead 14-year-olds to focus on a narrow range of options when faced with a problem, which can result in oversimplification of the actual issue (Eckstein et al., 1999). Adults can support 14-year-olds in developing their decision-making skills by providing opportunities for them to practice solving problems in low-risk situations and allowing them to experience the consequences of their actions/inaction. These lower stake situations can help teens develop their ability to anticipate consequences and make positive choices (Arain et al., 2013; Hartley & Somerville, 2015).

Social Media/Media Use

Social media and media use can be very beneficial for 14-year-olds, but it is not without risks. Social media can provide positive exposure to new ideas, increase awareness of current events, and provide greater access to support networks, creative outlets, and learning opportunities (Council on Communications and Media, 2016). Social media can also be an important source of social connection and support (OSG, 2023). Access to media can provide opportunities for 14-year-olds to witness people authentically living identities that may not be represented in their communities or families. Positive representation of multiple and intersecting identities in media can provide support for identity exploration and development (NASEM, 2019). However, limited, negative, or inappropriate representation in the media of specific identities can be harmful to identity development (American Psychological Association, 2002).

The Surgeon General of the United States (2023) identified several positive aspects of social media use while calling attention to many risks including increase in depression and anxiety for teens who use social media greater than three hours per day (OSG, 2023). Excessive social media use can negatively impact health by limiting in-person social interaction, creating unrealistic expectations related to body image and achievement, increasing opportunities for cyberbullying, and normalizing risky or unhealthy behaviors (Council on Communications and Media, 2016). Helping teens understand the consequences of an online presence and media consumption is important to help them reap the benefits of the digital age and be protected from many of the risks of time spent online.

Sexual Activity

Beginning to explore and understand sexual activity is a natural part of adolescence. Although younger adolescents tend to experiment with their sexuality through sexual fantasy and/or masturbation, sexual intercourse is less common (Tulloch & Kaufman, 2013). Fourteen-year-olds who experiment with sexual activity may not be equipped to handle the consequences (Doskoch, 2007). Developmentally appropriate, evidence-based education can help 14-year-olds make informed choices about sexual activity and their reproductive health (Breuner et al., 2016). When adolescents have discussions about dating, pregnancy, contraception, and STIs with parents/caregivers, they are more likely to delay sexual activity, have fewer sexual partners and engage in safe sex practices (Holman & Koenig Kellas, 2018; Power to Decide, 2016). Fourteen-year-olds of all genders and sexual orientations need consistent messaging about sexual health, potential consequences of sexual activity, safer sex practices, values, and expectations to ensure that they are educated and empowered to share responsibility for their sexual behavior and relationships (Widman et al., 2016).

Substance Use and Experimentation

Experimentation with substances including alcohol and legal and illegal drugs is not uncommon for adolescents between 12–16 years of age. Fourteen is the average age of first marijuana use (AACP, 2018). Early experimentation with substances is a significant predictor of later substance use disorders (Glowiak, 2019); however, experimentation may not necessarily lead to a disorder. Substance use in early adolescence can negatively impact brain development and functioning, emotional development, and decision-making and contribute to poor physical health outcomes in adulthood (Centers for Disease Control and Prevention [CDC], 2020). Adults can support 14-year-olds through frequent, open-ended conversations about substance use that allow space for questions without negative repercussions or punishment and consideration for how to respond and intervene when 14-year-olds are actively using substances. Because of the potential risks related to early experimentation and use, substance use in 14-year-olds should be taken seriously and addressed with care and support (Glowiak, 2019).

Impact of Risk Factors

Risk factors that may negatively influence the development of 14-year-olds are related to their unique predispositions, experiences, and relationships. The World Health Organization (WHO; 2020) reports that half of all mental health conditions begin by age 14 but often go undiagnosed. Navigating the world with less supervision, social struggles, self-esteem issues, and a greater ability to project and wonder about hypothetical situations can influence mental health and lead to rumination and anxiety (Galván, 2017). Fourteen-year-olds may also experience increased stressors within their educational environments including amount and intensity of academics, navigating the physical building/school, and adapting to multiple teachers, classrooms, and peer groups.

Ineffective coping skills, emotional expression and regulation coupled with negative or unsupportive family and/or peer relationships, negative peer pressure, negative media influences, unsupported identity exploration, exposure to violence, low SES, discrimination, or lack of access to quality, competent support services also contribute to poor adolescent mental health (WHO, 2020).

Best Practices for Counseling and Therapy

Modality

Therapeutic modalities need to be adapted to the unique developmental space of the 14-year-old. As 14-year-olds do not have the same capacity for logical thought, introspection, and decision-making, attempting to use a modality created for adults with 14-year-olds will be ineffective. Conversely, attempting to engage them in a modality intended for young children without adaptation will fall flat, and they will likely disengage from counseling. At 14, teens often benefit from an integration of activities, creativity, and talk in counseling sessions. Expressive therapies such as creative arts, movement, storytelling, and sandtray can remove barriers that may inhibit progress with traditional talk therapy alone. Providing space and choice to project internal thoughts, experiences, and feelings onto external items, as in sandtray or expressive art therapies, can create a sense of safety and distance from difficult topics, allowing for deeper engagement and processing. Adapting the presentation of therapy by offering opportunities to "do something" (e.g., games, art, physical activity, music) can encourage expression in a way that is non-threatening. Providing flexibility and choices (e.g., seating, lighting, topics of discussion, activities) can increase engagement by developing a partnering relationship where 14-year-olds feel respected and valued.

Group therapy can be an effective treatment option due to the influence of peer relationships on adolescents. Groups can provide a safe environment for self-expression, opportunities for learning and finding commonality of experience, developing social skills, and increasing social support. Additionally, group therapy can promote identity development, providing an opportunity to witness and try out new behaviors in relationships and provide corrective emotional and relational experiences (Leader, 1991). Knowing they are not alone in their struggles can alleviate some of the isolation that comes with the adolescent experience.

Assessment

Gathering information about presenting concerns should be a collaborative effort between the therapist, the 14-year-old, and the caregivers/parents. When completing intakes or using assessment instruments, it is necessary for counselors to honor both the caregivers/parents' and 14-year-old's perspective. Caregivers/parents may not have all of the information a clinician needs to properly determine the primary problems/concerns, treatment goals, interventions, or diagnosis. Assessments that allow for both adolescent and parent/caregiver perspectives to inform treatment are valuable tools. Counselors can complete the intake in two parts – spending time with just caregivers/parents and time with just the 14-year-old. This allows everyone to speak openly, without influence of the other. Providing the opportunity for the 14-year-old to give their own input on how and why they may be struggling, what they feel is the most pressing concern, and the impact of their relationships and environments on them will help create trust, buy-in, and build the therapeutic relationship.

Therapeutic Relationship

Establishing an honest and genuine relationship is vital to counseling 14-year-olds. If counseling is initiated by caregivers/parents without the agreement of the 14-year-old, the teen may feel pathologized (Edgette, 2006), criticized, or punished and may present as hostile/defensive in therapy. Therapists can become a genuine support if they can establish a meaningful, authentic relationship by presenting in a genuine way, meeting adolescents where they are developmentally, and prioritizing their needs. Counselors can engage

14-year-olds in supportive dialogue and psychoeducation around topics they may find difficult to discuss with other adults while supporting their physical, emotional, and identity development. Therapists can build strong relationships with 14-year-olds by being honest, interested in their lives and who they are, and appreciative that they choose to share their thoughts, perspectives, and ideas through the counseling process (Edgette, 2006).

Working With Families

Families play important roles in supporting and influencing development, and teens benefit from familial engagement and support in the therapeutic process. Families can provide insight into the environments and systems in which the 14-year-old is living and how they are impacting their development and progress. Families can offer support and encouragement by making appropriate adjustments to the environment or family system to support the child. Holding regular caregiver/parent consultations and/or family sessions where feedback from the adults can be provided, progress at home and in therapy can be reviewed, and psychoeducation and recommendations can be provided is often highly beneficial for 14-year-olds and their families. Parent/caregiver psychoeducation should include information about the 14-year-old's current level of development to inform appropriate expectations and boundaries, guidance on how to provide opportunities for autonomy and decision-making, skills to improve relational patterns and create open and supportive communication, and information on how skills and interventions can help resolve presenting concerns.

Depending upon family dynamics, consideration should be given to holding caregiver/parent sessions with or without the client present, or if a combination of both is appropriate. Sessions without the client present may allow for caregivers/parents to speak more freely and be more open to recommendations while protecting the client from unhelpful evaluations or negative feedback from the parents/caregivers. Holding sessions with the client present allows for all family members to receive the same information at the same time and practice communication skills. Either way, the therapist should include the 14-year-old in discussion about which session format is the most appropriate, discuss confidentiality, and collaborate with the 14-year-old about discussion topics prior to the caregiver/parent session so that the client is comfortable with the scope of the upcoming session. Following caregiver/parent and/or family sessions, the therapist and client should debrief and discuss client's thoughts, feelings, and experiences during or about the caregiver/parent session.

It is possible families will not be supportive of therapy or unable or unwilling to implement clinical recommendations. In these cases, the focus of therapy may include seeking supportive adults outside the family and management of stressors related to unsupportive family systems in addition to the original presenting concern.

Working Within Educational Systems

Understanding the elements of the client's educational environment and how they impact client functioning and well-being is important when assessing presenting concerns.

Academic/educational expectations may not align with the teen's development, contribute to presenting concerns, and/or inhibit positive growth and development. After obtaining appropriate consent, therapists may find it beneficial to consult and collaborate with teachers and school staff to support 14-year-olds in counseling. Psychoeducation about typical development and the client's individual development can help school personnel have greater understanding and empathy for the client. Working with school personnel to explore and understand the impact of the school environment, structure, and culture on the teen and to identify typical and creative accommodation options and structural and environmental shifts to support 14-year-olds within school settings can be instrumental for their health and development.

Conclusion

Fourteen is a dynamic age, where development is occurring at a unique pace and varying rates across many domains. A 14-year-old's development is dependent on pubertal timing and tempo and the influence of heredity, life experiences, and relationships. This comes at a time when self-esteem is fragile, belonging and acceptance of peers are most desired, and finding one's fit involves exploration of the new and differentiation from what is known. Fourteen-year-olds are navigating big life events, changing social dynamics, and increasing expectations with significantly less supervision and guidance but greater consequences. For counselors working with 14-year-olds, recognizing the complexity and nuances of their developmental experience is crucial to understanding and supporting their growth.

References

Ahern, N. R. (2006). Adolescent resilience: An evolutionary concept analysis. *Journal of Pediatric Nursing*, *21*(3), 175–185. https://doi.org/10.1016/j.pedn.2005.07.009

American Psychological Association. (2002). *Developing adolescents: A reference for professionals* [Brochure]. www.apa.org/pi/families/resources/develop.pdf

Ames, L. B., Baker, S. M., & Ilg, F. L. (1988). *Your ten- to fourteen-year-old*. Delacorte Press.

Arain, M., Haque, M., Johal, L., Mathur, P., Nel, W., Rais, A., Sandhu, R., & Sharma, S. (2013). Maturation of the adolescent brain. *Neuropsychiatric Disease and Treatment*, *9*, 449–461. https://doi.org/10.2147/ndt.s39776

Barbarin, O. A. (1993). Emotional and social development of African American children. *Journal of Black Psychology*, *19*(4), 381–390. https://doi.org/10.1177/00957984930194001

Bradley, R. H., & Corwyn, R. F. (2002). Socioeconomic status and child development. *Annual Review of Psychology*, *53*, 371–399. https://doi.org/10.1146/annurev.psych.53.100901.135233

Branje, S. (2022). Adolescent identity development in context. *Current Opinion in Psychology*, *45*, 101–286. https://doi.org/10.1016/j.copsyc.2021.11.006

Breuner, C. C., Mattson, G., Committee on Adolescence, & Committee on Psychosocial Aspects of Child and Family Health. (2016). Sexuality education for children and adolescents. *Pediatrics*, *138*(2), e1–e11. https://doi.org/10.1542/peds.2016-1348

Buder, S., & Perry, R. (2023, April 12). The social model of disability explained. *The Creature Times*. www.thesocialcreatures.org/thecreaturetimes/the-social-model-of-disability

Byrd, R., & Luke, C. (2021). *Counseling children and adolescents: Cultivating empathic connection*. Routledge.

Centers for Disease Control and Prevention. (2020, February 10). Teen substance use & risks. https://www.cdc.gov/ncbddd/fasd/features/teen-substance-use.html

Cheon, Y. M., Ip, P. S., Haskin, M., & Yip, T. (2020). Profiles of adolescent identity at the intersection of ethnic/racial identity, American identity, and subjective social status. *Frontiers in Psychology*, *11*, 1–13. https://doi.org/10.3389/fpsyg.2020.00959

Council on Communications and Media. (2016). Media use in school-aged children and adolescents. *Pediatrics*, *138*(5), 1–6. https://doi.org/10.1542/peds.2016-2592

Doskoch, P. (2007). Teenagers report both positive and negative consequences from sex. *Perspectives on Sexual and Reproductive Health*, *39*(2), 120–121. https://doi.org/10.1363/3912007b

Eckstein, D. G., Rasmussen, P. R., & Wittschen, L. (1999). Understanding and dealing with adolescents. *Individual Psychology*, *55*(1), 31–50.

Edgette, J. S. (2006). *Adolescent therapy that really works: Helping kids who never asked for help in the first place*. W.W. Norton & Company, Inc.

Epstein, R., Blake, J. J., & González, T. (2017). *Girlhood interrupted: The erasure of Black girls' childhood*. Social Science Research Network.

Erikson, E. H. (1968). *Identity, youth and crisis*. W.W. Norton & Company, Inc.

Galván, A. (2017). *The neuroscience of adolescence*. Cambridge University Press.

Gianine, R. D., & Lewis, M. (2003). Emotional development in adolescence. In G. R. Adams & M. D. Berzonky (Eds.), *Blackwell handbook of adolescence* (pp. 269–289). Blackwell.

Glowiak, M. V. (2019). "Escaping reality": Adolescent substance abuse. In D. Capuzzi & D. R. Gross (Eds.), *Youth at risk: A prevention resource for counselors, teachers, and parents* (pp. 349–371). American Counseling Association.

Goff, P. A., Jackson, M. C., Di Leone, B. A. L., Culotta, C. M., & DiTomasso, N. A. (2014). The essence of innocence: Consequences of dehumanizing Black children. *Journal of Personality and Social Psychology*, *106*(4), 526–545. https://doi.org/10.1037/a0035663

Harms, L. (2021). *Understanding human development* (3rd ed.). Oxford University Press.

Hartley, C. A., & Somerville, L. H. (2015). The neuroscience of adolescent decision-making. *Current Opinion in Behavioral Sciences*, *5*, 108–115. https://doi.org/10.1016/j.cobeha.2015.09.004

Holcomb-McCoy, C. (2005). Ethnic identity development in early adolescence: Implications and recommendations for middle school counselors. *Professional School Counseling*, *9*(2), 120–127. https://doi.org/10.5330/prsc.9.2.21q8m2724r545414

Holman, A., & Koenig Kellas, J. (2018). "Say something instead of nothing": Adolescents' perceptions of memorable conversations about sex-related topics with their parents. *Communication Monographs*, *85*(3), 357–379. https://doi.org/10.1080/03637751.2018.1426870

Inhelder, B., & Piaget, J. (2013). *The growth of logical thinking from childhood to adolescence: An essay on the construction of formal operational structures*. Routledge.

Janssen, A., & Leibowitz, S. (Eds.). (2018). *Affirmative mental health care for transgender and gender diverse youth: A clinical guide*. Springer.

Johnstone, C. (2004). Disability and identity: Personal constructions and formalized supports. *Disability Studies Quarterly*, *24*(4). https://doi.org/10.18061/dsq.v24i4.880

La Greca, A. M., & Harrison, H. M. (2005). Adolescent peer relations, friendships, and romantic relationships: Do they predict social anxiety and depression? *Journal of Clinical Child & Adolescent Psychology*, *34*(1), 49–61. https://doi.org/10.1207/s15374424jccp3401_5

Leader, E. (1991). Why adolescent group therapy? *Journal of Child and Adolescent Group Therapy*, *1*(2), 81–93. https://doi.org/10.1007/BF00972968

Leemis, R. W., Friar, N., Khatiwada, S., Chen, M. S., Kresnow, M., Smith, S. G., Caslin, S., & Basile, K. C. (2022). *The national intimate partner and sexual violence survey: 2016/2017 report on intimate partner violence*. National Center for Injury Prevention and Control, Centers for Disease Control and Prevention.

Mahoney, A., Leroy, M., Kusner, K., Padgett, E., & Grimes, L. (2013). Addressing parental spirituality as part of the problem and solution in family psychotherapy. In D. F. Walker & W. L. Hathaway (Eds.), *Spiritual interventions in child and adolescent psychotherapy* (pp. 65–88). American Psychological Association.

Maxey, M., & Beckert, T. E. (2016). Adolescents with disabilities. *Adolescent Research Review*, *2*(2), 59–75. https://doi.org/10.1007/s40894-016-0043-y

McNeely, C., & Blanchard, J. (2011). *The teen years explained: A guide to healthy adolescent development*. Center for Adolescent Health at Johns Hopkins Bloomberg School of Public Health.

Montemayor, R. (2019). *Sexuality in adolescence and emerging adulthood*. The Guilford Press.

Nanda, J. (2012). Blind discretion: Girls of color & delinquency in the juvenile justice system. *University of California Los Angeles Law Review*, *59*, 1502.

National Academies of Sciences, Engineering, and Medicine. (2019). *The promise of adolescence: Realizing opportunity for all youth* (R. J. Bonnie & E. P. Backes, Eds.). The National Academies Press. https://doi.org/10.17226/25388

Nawaz, S. (2011). The relationship of parental and peer attachment bonds with the identity development during adolescence. *FWU Journal of Social Sciences*, *5*(1), 104–119.

Office of the Surgeon General (OSG), United States, Public Health Service. (2023). *Social media and youth mental health: The Surgeon General's advisory*. U.S. Department of Health and Human Services, Public Health Service, Office of the Surgeon General. www.hhs.gov/sites/default/files/sg-youth-mental-health-social-media-advisory.pdf

Olkin, R. (2022, March 29). *Conceptualizing disability: Three models of disability*. American Psychological Association. www.apa.org/ed/precollege/psychology-teacher-network/introductory-psychology/disability-models

Phillips, T. M., & Pittman, J. F. (2003). Identity processes in poor adolescents: Exploring the linkages between economic disadvantage and the primary task of adolescence. *Identity*, *3*(2), 115–129. https://doi.org/10.1207/s1532706xid030202

Power to Decide (formerly The National Campaign to Prevent Teen and Unplanned Pregnancy). (2016). *Survey says: Parent power*. https://powertodecide.org/what-we-do/information/resource-library/parent-power-october-2016-survey-says

Pugh, M. J. V., & Hart, D. (1999). Identity development and peer group participation. *New Directions for Child and Adolescent Development*, *1999*(84), 55–70. https://doi.org/10.1002/cd.23219998406

Quagliana, L. H., Ebstyne, K. P., Quagliana, D. P., & Mans Wagner, L. (2013). Spiritually oriented interventions in developmental context. In D. F. Walker & W. L. Hathaway (Eds.), *Spiritual interventions in child and adolescent psychotherapy* (pp. 89–110). American Psychological Association.

Rageliené, T. (2016). Links of adolescents identity development and relationship with peers: A systematic literature review. *Journal of the Canadian Academy of Child and Adolescent Psychiatry*, *25*(2), 97–105.

Ramnitz, M. S., & Lodish, M. B. (2013). Racial disparities in pubertal development. *Seminars in Reproductive Medicine*, *31*(5), 333–339. https://doi.org/10.1055/s-0033-1348891

Ream, G. L., & Savin-Williams, R. C. (2003). Religious development in adolescence. In G. R. Adams & M. D. Berzonky (Eds.), *Blackwell handbook of adolescence* (pp. 51–59). Blackwell.

Rutter, L. A., Dodell-Feder, D., Vahia, I. V., Forester, B. P., Ressler, K. J., Wilmer, J. B., & Germine, L. (2019). Emotion sensitivity across the lifespan: Mapping clinical risk periods to sensitivity to facial emotion intensity. *Journal of Experimental Psychology: General*, *148*(11), 1993–2005. https://doi.org/10.1037/xge0000559

Salgado, M., González, L., & Yáñez, A. (2021). Parental involvement and life satisfaction in early adolescence. *Frontiers in Psychology*, *12*. https://doi.org/10.3389/fpsyg.2021.628720

Spencer, M. S., Icard, L. D., Harachi, T. W., Catalano, R. F., & Oxford, M. (2000). Ethnic identity among monoracial and multiracial early adolescents. *The Journal of Early Adolescence*, *20*(4), 365–387. https://doi.org/10.1177/0272431600020004001

Stewart, J. L., Spivey, L. A., Widman, L., Choukas-Bradley, S., & Prinstein, M. J. (2019). Developmental patterns of sexual identity, romantic attraction, and sexual behavior among adolescents over three years. *Journal of Adolescence*, *77*, 90–97. https://doi.org/10.1016/j.adolescence.2019.10.006

The American Academy of Child and Adolescent Psychiatry. (2018). *Teens: Alcohol and other drugs* [Fact Sheet]. www.aacap.org/AACAP/Families_and_Youth/Facts_for_Families/FFF-Guide/Teens-Alcohol-And-Other-Drugs-003.aspx

The Trevor Project. (2019, June). *Accepting adults reduce suicide attempts among LGBTQ youth*. www.thetrevorproject.org/wp-content/uploads/2019/06/Trevor-Project-Accepting-Adult-Research-Brief_June-2019.pdf

The Trevor Project. (2022, October). *Age of sexual orientation outness and suicide risk*. www.thetrevorproject.org/wp-content/uploads/2022/10/October-2022-Research-Brief-Final.pdf

The World Health Organization. (2020). *Adolescent mental health* [Fact Sheet]. www.who.int/news-room/fact-sheets/detail/adolescent-mental-health

Tulloch, T., & Kaufman, M. (2013). Adolescent sexuality. *Pediatrics in Review*, *34*(1), 29–38. https://doi.org/10.1542/pir.34-1-29

Whaley, A. L. (1993). Self-esteem, cultural identity, and psychosocial adjustment in African American children. *Journal of Black Psychology*, *19*(4), 406–422. https://doi.org/10.1177/00957984930194003

Widman, L., Choukas-Bradley, S., Noar, S. M., Nesi, J., & Garrett, K. (2016). Parent-adolescent sexual communication and adolescent safer sex behavior: A meta-analysis. *JAMA Pediatrics*, *170*(1), 52–61. https://doi.org/10.1001/jamapediatrics.2015.2731

Windle, G. (2010). What is resilience? A review and concept analysis. *Reviews in Clinical Gerontology*, *21*(2), 152–169. https://doi.org/10.1017/s0959259810000420

Youth.gov. (n.d.). *Risk & protective factors*. https://youth.gov/youth-topics/youth-mental-health/risk-and-protective-factors-youth

Yu, M. V., & Deutsch, N. L. (2019). Aligning social support to youth's developmental needs: The role of nonparental youth–adult relationships in early and late adolescence. *Applied Developmental Science*, *25*(2), 133–149. https://doi.org/10.1080/10888691.2018.1548940

Part III

Middle Adolescence

Chapter 5

The 15-Year-Old

Emily Michero

Tatiana, an insightful and high-achieving 15-year-old Latina client, plopped down in my office with an audible sigh and launched into a story about her weekend that included an argument with her mother, Crystal, about time management. Previously, academics were here primary focus, but now in high school, she reported more interest in theater, friends, and dating than homework. She expressed feeling conflicted by seemingly opposing feelings and pieces of herself.

"It's just so hard to grow into yourself!," she exclaimed. As she described juggling her multiple identities and interests, she continued, "It's not that all the parts of me aren't there, it's hard getting them sorted out." Similarly, Tatiana's mother Crystal reported, "I admire who she is, but I am slowly mourning the loss of Tatiana's childhood and innocence. She is on her journey of becoming her adult self and I don't want to get in the way." I was struck by both of their insight about the emotional growing pains happening at 15 and how these changes may challenge existing relationships and existing sense of self.

When I meet a new 15-year-old client, I am curious to discover what their worldview and presentation will be. I wonder if I will meet a seemingly mature adolescent who is struggling to navigate complex social or romantic relationships. I wonder if I will meet an adolescent who presents similarly to a much younger preteen, struggling to complete homework assignments and primarily motivated by television or video games. Fifteen is a fascinatingly diverse age of development. Regardless of the difference in presentation, 15-year-old brains, bodies, and social lives are changing at a rapid rate – many believe the most rapid rate since toddlerhood (Siegel, 2014). In this chapter, we will explore the many facets of the 15-year-old and helpful tips for counselors lucky enough to work with this transitional age group.

Physical Development

Fifteen sits between early and late adolescence according to most adolescent development models (Berk, 2017). By late adolescence, puberty (changes in primary and secondary sex characteristics) is underway and likely close to completion. Primary sex characteristics include the reproductive organs, ovaries for people assigned female at birth (AFAB) and testes for teens assigned male at birth (AMAB). Secondary sex characteristics include the visible characteristics of sexual development, breast development for AFAB teens and pubic hair growth for all sexes. Hormones also play a large role in adolescent pubertal

DOI: 10.4324/9781003196297-8

development. Sex hormones (produced from testes or ovaries) are produced throughout life yet begin to increase significantly at the onset of puberty (Berk, 2017). By 15, most AFAB adolescents have had menarche, breast development is likely complete, and full height has been reached (Berk, 2017). With puberty blockers or other hormonal interventions, developmental outcomes may differ.

Having one's body dramatically change, especially during a vulnerable developmental stage, is challenging for teens. I recently discussed the simultaneous occurrence of increased insecurity and puberty with a 15-year-old client who reported, "It's like the fire station is on fire." That clearly illustrated their experience! Beyond embarrassment about cracking voices, managing menstruation, and getting acquainted with a new body, puberty can be especially hard for some adolescents. Cultural responses to puberty, social norms, and peer comparison impact the way adolescents respond to puberty. Puberty can be especially stressful for those who identify as transgender or nonbinary as these changes further highlight the incongruence with their gender assigned at birth. The fear surrounding the development of secondary sex characteristics can be overwhelming and can highly impact many 15-year-old transgender or nonbinary clients. The phrase "growing pains" applies quite literally and figuratively to puberty.

Brain Development

An increase in neuroplasticity, along with a transformational pruning process, rewiring of the prefrontal cortex, and shifts in dopamine receptors are only some of the changes happening in a 15-year-old brain (Siegel, 2014). Additionally, adolescents are more sensitive to rewards than ever before or after due to an increase in dopamine receptors (Steinberg, 2014). Conversely, an adolescent's baseline level of dopamine is lower than in adulthood, which can lead to increased levels of boredom and lead adolescents to seek exciting experiences (Siegel, 2014). Therefore, adolescent brains experience a heightened level of dopamine from pleasurable experiences while simultaneously having a lower baseline of dopamine that can lead to boredom (Siegel, 2014). As we can imagine, this combination can be one of the driving forces for adolescent risk-taking behavior, which will be presented in a subsequent section. In addition, the prefrontal cortex is continuing to mature; therefore, the ability to perform tasks that require planning and delayed gratification continues to develop throughout adolescence (Berk, 2017).

The "use it or lose it" process of adolescent pruning is in full force at 15. During this process, neural pathways that are being used are reinforced through myelination while connections that are not used eventually decay. Consider an adolescent who plays piano or baseball during the pruning process. Their talents will be reinforced and enhance their performance. Similarly, this principle can be applied to substance misuse or other problematic behaviors that will also be reinforced.

Cognitive Development

I have come to recognize that clients may reappear around 15. Recently a mom of a now 15-year-old client, Kara, called and began with, "Well, you said we might be back at 15 and here we are." I saw Kara, a friendly but impulsive Latinx female, when she was 12 and navigating peer relational difficulties. She had a loving adoptive family and was aware of some of the traumatic circumstances that led to her being removed from her biological parents. At 12, she talked about her biological family with factual statements but was focused on the goings-on of fifth-grade social dynamics in her middle school. Her mom and I discussed the impact of Kara's early childhood through the lens of attachment and trauma during parent consultations, but Kara and I only talked about her biological family experiences in a concrete manner. Fast forward to 15, and Kara returns to my office as a full-blown teenager. She begins to tell me about her dating life, which was full of intensity and attachment, yet those relationships seem to burn out quickly. With little prompting from me, she seamlessly connected her fear of rejection, clinginess to boyfriends, and need for approval to her early childhood. Her ability to reflect upon her early experiences and recognize the impact on her relational patterns was profound and mature. Yet despite all her maturity, she continued to struggle with impulse control, peer pressure, and resisting the urge to seek validation from romantic relationships. While understanding the impact of her childhood increased self-compassion in the face of current struggles, she needed to foster mindfulness and self-esteem to create a shift in behavior.

The formal operations stage is marked by one's ability to utilize abstract thought and hypotheticals. No longer does a 15-year-old need to experience something to understand it; they can imagine and hypothesize about the unknown. While this is a remarkable skill for problem-solving, it also opens many scenarios for worry and anxiety due to two hallmarks of adolescent cognitive development: the personal fable and the imaginary audience. These aspects of adolescent development are very present for most 15-year-olds. Due to inherent egocentrism and a belief that others are interested in them; adolescents develop a personal fable that enhances their importance. At first thought, this egocentrism can be interpreted as an inflated sense of self and self-esteem. Instead, I often see 15-year-olds' personal fables center around a negative view of self and an inflated view of how others must be interested in or perseverating on their shortcomings. Similarly, the imaginary audience of adolescence adds to anxiety and negative self-talk rather than increasing confidence.

Adolescent decision-making is an essential consideration for counselors as it impacts informed consent, treatment planning, and confidentiality. Without pressure to act quickly or peer influence, 15-year-olds have the cognitive capacity to make decisions like adults (Icenogle et al., 2019). For decades researchers have discovered adolescents, around age 15, demonstrate the ability to engage in decision-making comparable to adults (Grisso & Vierling, 1978; Belter & Grisso, 1984; Moyer & Sullivan, 2008). Recent research reaffirms this assertion along with concluding that adolescent cognitive capacity rivals adult levels years before their psychological maturity catches up, terming this phenomenon the "maturity gap" (Icenogle et al., 2019). While these researchers highlight the impressive cognitive capacity of the 15-year-old, these findings may not translate to mature decision-making in all situations, especially those charged with emotion. Many real-life decisions include two of the biggest threats to 15-year-old decision-making: psychosocial stressors and peers (Moyer & Sullivan, 2008; Moyer & Yu, 2012). Icenogle and Cauffman (2021) describe adolescents as possessing the capacity for competent decision-making while acknowledging the impact this "maturity gap" has on their situational decision-making.

Emotional Development

Discerning what is "normal" emotional development for 15 is complicated. The 15-year-old is often labeled as moody or angsty. While this may be true, it is hard to see the complexity of their emotional development through the lens of teen angst. Intense emotions are normal at 15, yet without support, coping skills, or resiliency, intense emotions can develop into additional struggles.

Erik Erikson's theory of psychosocial development places 15-year-olds in the identity vs. role confusion stage of development and purports adolescence is one of the most formative stages of one's development (Erikson, 1994). In this stage, an adolescent may experience conflict between growing into their identity and juggling worry about what others think of them, resulting in role confusion. Recently a 15-year-old client discussed dating in high school. They said, "I don't know who I am well enough to attach myself to another person. I'm a different person almost every day." This client seemed at peace with their identity development and the ambiguity of not knowing who they are quite yet. Unfortunately, other 15-year-old clients feel lost without the security of a known role in peer groups and force themselves into potentially incongruent identities. According to Erikson (1994), a secure adolescent experiences "fidelity" with their identity: the ability to sustain a sense of self despite contradiction and value systems. In essence, the question is if they can remain true to their values, beliefs, and sense of self in the face of contradictory stimuli and environments. This is aspirational for all but an especially hard ask at 15, partially due to the emphasis 15-year-olds place on peer relationships.

Social and Relationship Development

Fifteen-year-old adolescents experience increased independence from parents and yet an increased interdependence with peers. They yearn for social connection, and it is easy to see the positive impact of healthy friendships. Adolescents who have positive peer relationships are more likely to succeed in school and less likely to report isolation, depression, or emotional distress (Flook et al., 2005).

Fifteen-year-old adolescents have often learned a lot about social relationships through trial and error during early adolescence. Although 15-year-olds often present with an air of confidence about social relationships, especially to peers, they are still in the process of developing their social and relational skills. This acquisition of social skills is a vital part of relational development and is missed by those adolescents who are isolated and do not have the opportunity to learn these important relational skills.

Romantic relationships may be at the forefront of many 15-year-old's minds, yet others may recoil at the thought of romance. With the never-ending influence of media and the internet, 15-year-olds are susceptible to losing sight of what they want from a romantic relationship and instead try to emulate what they have been exposed to, including gender stereotypes and sexual behavior. Given approximately 43% of adolescents reported pornography use; pornography may be 15-year-olds' introduction to sex, leading to misguided sex education (Farré et al., 2020).

Culture and Identity Development

Culture

A strong racial identity can provide protective factors against the negative effects of racism for adolescents (Sellers & Shelton, 2003). Ethnic racial identity (ERI) has been defined as the beliefs and ideas one has about their ethnic and racial identity and the significance they place upon those memberships (Umaña-Taylor et al., 2014). Adolescents who reflect upon their ERI may have an increased ability to cope with ethnic-racial stressors (Neblett et al., 2012). We also know a strong tie to culture, including ethnic and racial identity, increases adolescents' resiliency (Zimmerman et al., 2013). The research is clear that a strong ERI helps moderate the negative impact of racism and discrimination, yet these factors are not enough to mediate the added struggles for adolescents of color. Quinceañeras, the celebration of female 15-year-olds' transition from childhood to adulthood in many Latinx cultures, are a beautiful example of how a cultural tradition can strengthen adolescents' ERI through community and tradition.

Unfortunately, there is a great disparity in adolescent outcomes that highlights the inequity of resources for adolescents (National Academies Press, 2019). Academic achievement, high school graduation rates, suspension rates, and arrest rates illustrate the racial distributions between White adolescents and Black, Hispanic, Indigenous, and other minoritized students.

Additionally, tension may exist between a cultural emphasis on interdependence and the Western emphasis on independence. This tension may be especially high for adolescents and their families who have recently immigrated to the United States. The contrast in expectations for adolescence, the normalizing of adolescent acting out behavior, and different cultural beliefs about interdependence may cause immigrant families to tightly restrict their adolescent. Adolescents respond to this restriction in a variety of ways, some of which include rebellion. It is important for counselors to be knowledgeable about clients' cultural backgrounds while remaining culturally humble. Clients and their families are the experts on their unique family values and beliefs about the role of adolescents.

Identity

Identity is the "fundamental organizing principle that develops throughout the lifespan" according to Erik Erikson (1994) and is one's subjective sense of self. We all possess horizontal and vertical identities (Solomon, 2012). One's vertical identity is a direct link to our parents, such as race, ethnicity, country, and often religion. Horizontal identities ties one to a group that may or may not be associated with one's family of origin. Often vertical identities inherently come with a level of familial or parental support, while horizontal identities can leave adolescents feeling different than their family of origin (Solomon, 2012). Many horizontal identities, such as sexual orientations, gender identities, and disabilities can lead to feelings of isolation from culture and family. Adolescents may have minoritized identities in common with their families in areas such as race, ethnicity, socioeconomic status, and religion. These teens may feel less isolated within their families while also experiencing discrimination from dominant groups.

This experience of isolation and cultural biases often leaves our LGBTQI youth in a vulnerable position. LGBTQI adolescents are more likely to misuse substances, self-harm, and attempt suicide (CDC) due to the discrimination and oppression these youth experience.

Spiritual Development

While research indicates religion and spirituality are declining in the United States, Christianity remains the dominant religion. Adolescents whose familial or personal religious beliefs contrast with the dominant religion may experience discrimination and prejudice.

For 15-year-olds, as cognitive abilities increase so does their ability to think abstractly about religion or spirituality. According to Fowler's *Stages of Faith*, adolescents are typically in a time of "synthetic-conventional faith" (Fowler, 2006). In the synthetic-conventional faith stage, typically from ages 13–18, adolescents can see from another's perspective, including what one might think about their faith. There continues to be a reliance on authority figures, and during this stage authority, figures often shift away from parents and toward spiritual leaders and peers. While counselors do not promote any religious or spiritual practice, they may have the opportunity to educate parents about the impact of 15-year-olds' cognitive, social, and emotional development on religion and spirituality.

Resources and Protective Factors

Fifteen-year-olds are most often amazingly resilient, creative, and resourceful (Siegel, 2014) despite the myriad of risk factors for this age. This resilience is at the heart of 15-year-olds' resources and protective factors.

Resiliency

Resiliency may be one of the key aspects of healthy adolescent development. Resiliency is often defined as one's ability to adapt and cope well with stressors or to "bounce back" from adversity or trauma. Zimmerman and colleagues (2013) identified three protective factors that foster resiliency in adolescents: positive racial identity, relationships with adults, and prosocial behavior. Combined, these factors increase 15-year-olds' ability to tolerate and cope with distress. Assets such as efficacy, identity, and orientation toward the future also positively impact resiliency (Zimmerman et al., 2013). If adolescents experience a sense of efficacy (the ability to produce a desired result), they feel empowered. These teens are more likely to put in effort to overcome challenges and seek support when necessary.

One's ability to look toward the future fosters hope and the opportunity for things to be better and increases patience for delayed gratification. A major shift in adolescent depression occurs when clients can see beyond their current pain and into a more hopeful future. When I hear adolescent clients speak of the future with hope, I feel encouraged and know they are tapping into their resilience.

Adult Relationships

Many counselors are introduced to attachment theory and the impact the first years of life have on our attachment structure (Bowlby, 1969). While this early influence on attachment is true, we sometimes lose sight of the profound impact caring adults can have on adolescents' attachment style and general well-being. As noted earlier, adolescence is a time of vastly increased neuroplasticity, second only to those first few years of life, so it makes sense that the impact of a caring and trusted adult at this age has the potential to make a profound impact on their development. A strong relationship with a parent or a mentor has a cascading impact on adolescent risk factors, such as violence, depression, and suicide (Zimmerman et al., 2013). Counselors are wise to not underestimate the impact positive caring adults can have on a 15-year-old's life, including the client–counselor relationship.

Challenges and Risk Factors

Risk-taking is a normative part of adolescence. We want teenagers to engage in healthy risk-taking behaviors as part of the developmental process of defining boundaries, and it can serve to test the boundaries of independent decision-making. Without some level of risk-taking, adolescents would never drive a car, go on a date, or leave home. Unfortunately, a common yet dangerous aspect of adolescent risk-taking is that it can result in tragic consequences. In 2021, the primary cause of death for 15–24 was accidents (15,792), followed by homicide (6,635) and suicide (6,528) (Centers for Disease Control and Prevention [CDC], 2021). Between 14 and 15, there is the highest intersection between lack of impulse control and sensation-seeking (Harden & Tucker-Drob, 2011). One way adolescents pursue sensations is through the use of mind-altering substances.

Alcohol and Drug Use

Alcohol and substance use is enticing to some 15-year-olds because it provides an element of risk, a behavior often associated with being "cool" or "mature," along with reduced social inhibition for teens, who are often achingly self-conscious. Another, potentially larger, problem is that drugs/alcohol can provide a sense of escape and numbing relief for some teens. While the motivating factors toward substance use do not differ much from the motivating factors for adults, the impact on the 15-year-old brain is more consequential.

Adolescents who drink at 15 are significantly more likely to binge drink as adolescents and develop substance abuse problems as adults (Steinberg, 2014). As with all pleasurable experiences, alcohol releases more dopamine in adolescents than in adults. Recalling the convergence of impulse control and sensation-seeking along with the neurological impact of substances on adolescents, one can see how risky experimentation can be for 15-year-old.

Counselors who choose to work with substance abuse often seek additional training and experience to best serve this complicated population. Often in my practice, substance abuse reveals itself only after a strong therapeutic alliance has developed. At that point, it is an ethical dilemma to weigh the impact of our therapeutic relationships versus the level of my competence with substance abuse or any other area of specialty. Counselors are wise to carefully screen for substance abuse in intake while also knowing adolescents may likely hide or minimize substance abuse.

Eating Disorders

Counselors who work with eating disorders, similarly to those who work with substance abuse, require a degree of specialization and additional training, yet as many counselors who work with adolescents know, these issues creep up in session with established clients frequently. It is important for counselors who work with adolescents to be well-versed in eating disorders and have a clear understanding of their level of competence surrounding eating disorders.

According to one national survey (Merikangas et al., 2009), 2.9% of adolescents 15 to 18 have experienced an eating disorder. Contributing factors for eating disorders include low self-esteem, lack of coping skills, early childhood abuse, early sexual maturation, and perfectionism (Stice et al., 2011). Along with the significant health concerns that accompany eating disorders, such as heart attack and blood pressure irregularities, suicide is one of the leading causes of death for those diagnosed with an eating disorder (Arcelus et al., 2011). The elevated risk of suicide, long-term health consequences, and the addictive quality of eating disorders complicate working with this population.

An additional important factor for counselors working with eating disorders is awareness of the decreased cognitive function when one is in a state of semi-starvation. From what we know about 15-year-old brain development, this concern is especially worrisome because their brains are under construction. As stated, there are many nuances in working with eating disorders, and counselors would benefit from extended training and supervision.

Depression

Depression at 15 can be disguised by mood swings, increasing autonomy from parents, and masking of depression by the adolescent, intentional or not. Approximately 18% of 14 and 15-year-olds in the United States of America reported a depressive episode in 2020 (Substance Abuse and Mental Health Services Administration [SAMHSA], 2022). According to this national survey, only 41.6% of adolescents who experienced a depressive episode in 2020 received treatment. These numbers seem high, yet the reality is, given the often-secretive nature of adolescent depression and the added stressors post the COVID-19 pandemic, current statistics are likely higher. Adolescents who struggle with depression are at higher risk for substance misuse, self-harm, and suicide (Shaffer & Greenberg, 2002).

Non-Suicidal Self-Injury

Many of my 15-year-old clients engage in non-suicidal self-injury (NSSI). NSSI includes cutting, burning, pinching, head banging, or excessive tattoos/piercings. The most common presentation of NSSI is cutting and burning. Adolescents who self-harm often elicit stereotypes and negative reactions from adults, including counselors. Adolescents who present with self-harm may be seen as "gamey," manipulative, or borderline (Peterson et al., 2008). NSSI is misunderstood, especially regarding adolescents, and is more common than counselors may think. In a survey of 3,060 adolescents, 39.6% reported self-harm within the past year (Zetterqvist et al., 2013). Over 224,000 youth and young adults presented to emergency departments for NSSI in 2020, with females being twice as likely as males (CDC, 2021).

Adolescents self-harm for a variety of reasons. One reason for self-harm is affect regulation. These teens struggle to manage their emotions, including depression, anxiety, frustration, or anger. These clients often feel overwhelmed by feelings and report that NSSI helps them feel regulated and calm. Other clients self-harm as a way to induce more affect; they report feeling numb, empty, or dissociative, and self-harm helps them connect to feelings or reality. Some adolescents report self-harm developed into a form of punishment, often following a perceived failure. Other adolescents report NSSI serves as a way to combat suicidal ideation, and they self-harm as a way to divert taking action on suicidal ideation. Lastly, self-harm can be an adolescent's way to communicate a need or elicit support. Often adults refer to adolescent self-harm as attention-seeking, and I like to help them reframe the behavior as communicating a need and visually expressing their pain. Often an adolescent is unable to express the depth of their feelings or does not feel heard, and reporting self-harm is seen as a way to get the help they need.

Parents are often frustrated and confused by NSSI and need support to understand the complexity of their adolescent's self-harming behavior. I find parents often react out of fear to an adolescent's self-harm, and unfortunately, that fear can be expressed as anger toward the adolescent. Parents also should be encouraged to avoid bribing or punishing adolescents for self-harm. Parents and clinicians need to remember that while NSSI is scary, it often serves as a coping skill for the adolescent. We all want the teen to discontinue self-harm but must be mindful that threatening the teen's coping skill may leave them overwhelmed with the feelings they have been trying to manage.

Suicidal Ideation

Although non-suicidal self-injury often serves a different purpose than suicide, NSSI may accompany suicidal ideation and suicide attempts (Zetterqvist et al., 2013). Adolescents, in general, are a high-suicide-risk population, especially LGBTQ youth. Suicide is the third leading cause of death for adolescents behind automobile accidents and homicide (CDC, 2023). Annually, 19.9% of adolescents consider suicide, 15.3% create a plan, and 9% attempt suicide (CDC, 2023).

Counselors must be prepared to assess for suicide when working with adolescent clients. As with all clients, it is important for a counselor to continually reassess for suicide, not only at intake. As with depression, 15-year-old suicidal ideation can be confusing due to mood swings, impulsivity, and secrecy from parents. An important consideration when managing suicide risk in 15-year-old clients is collaboration with parents or guardians. As scary as adolescent suicidal ideation (SI) is for counselors, parents are even more fearful and may need some assistance managing their fear, developing a safety plan, and gaining psychoeducation around adolescent suicide risk factors.

Problematic Internet Use

Problematic internet use (PIU) is identified as an overuse of the internet alongside cognitive distortions and lack of behavioral control toward internet usage (Davis, 2001). Most professionals who work with adolescents are likely not surprised to know adolescents present with an increased risk of PIU. The internet provides anonymity, escape from reality, interaction, and excitement – all things adolescents crave. Additionally, the internet allows adolescents to try out different ways of being, as a way to explore the developing parts of their personality. Similarly, social media – once limited to Myspace and Facebook – has exploded in the past decade, particularly for adolescents. While social media may have positive outcomes, such as increased socialization, especially in circumstances when face-to-face contact is limited, it also possesses many potential problems for our adolescents. Likes, shares, and comments create mini hits of dopamine, sending a sense of pleasure and success to the user. Adolescents are not the only group susceptible to this type of reinforcement, but their brains are optimally primed to respond to this type of reward.

Additionally, adolescents who used the internet to seek relationships and avoid reality are more likely to develop PIU than those who use the internet for information-seeking (Kormas et al., 2011). Significant time spent gaming, chatting, and viewing pornography has increased the occurrence of PIU. During the COVID-19 pandemic, adolescents relied on the internet for most of their social needs, undoubtedly increasing their risk for PIU.

One of my 15-year-old clients, while recounting some interactions with adults, recently told me, "Treat us like people, but you don't have to pretend to know what it is like for us, because you don't." She is right, we certainly cannot truly understand what it is like to be 15 at this time, but I do believe it is worthwhile for us to be "in touch" with pop culture and media influences that impact our adolescents' lives. The latest learning curve in my practice has been TikTok. I began to hear strikingly similar phrases and terms from multiple clients. I started to connect the dots and confirmed with several clients that indeed many 15-year-olds are exposed to mental health concepts through TikTok. On the one hand, this phenomenon seemed to provide adolescents with a sense of belonging and normalized their experiences with client reporting, "I'm not the only one who feels this way" or "I don't feel so alone." I believe that is true for many of our adolescents although, for others, there seems to be "co-ruminating" through TikTok and other social media platforms. Co-ruminating, a shared experience of excessive focus on problems and negative feelings, is an important consideration of 15-year-olds beyond internet use (Rose, 2021).

Homayoun (2018) presents five additional subtle but impactful negative consequences of social media for adolescents: altered expectations, mixed messages, information overload, an "on all the time" mentality, and "all about the likes" personal values development. She argues that adolescents frequently feel disappointed in their accomplishments based on a constant comparison with whomever they follow online, and they evaluate their own likability or success based on feedback they receive online. These components lead to altered expectations of themselves and the world that are unrealistic. Adolescents (and many adults) struggle to consider that they are comparing their real lives to others' aspirational lives that are projected onto social media. At a time when peer influence surpasses familial influence, the magnitude of input can be hard to combat. Adolescents also receive mixed messages due to hearing adults in their lives espouse the negative consequences of social media use while watching those same adults be "glued" to their phones. Adolescents also receive mixed messages around screens from school, especially during COVID-19. They have been prodded for years to get off their screens and then were abruptly told screens were to be their only connection to peers and school. It is no surprise that adolescents experience information overload from social media.

It not only is overwhelming to process but also creates unrealistic pressure for adolescents to keep up with it all: their friends' lives, politics, and the latest trends, all of which are changing at a rapid pace. Adolescents who engage in social media feel they are "on all the time." We can imagine how external validation through "likes" boosts adolescents' self-esteem yet also has the potential to crush it.

Best Practices for Counseling and Therapy

This section outlines best practices for counseling and therapy for 15-year-old clients. The therapeutic relationship and considerations for adolescent development are paramount. An awareness of one's subjective experiences as an adolescent and biases toward adolescents is essential given the frequently tumultuous nature of this age. There are ethical and legal considerations that are specifically important when working with 15-year-old clients, such as informed consent and confidentiality. Parental involvement is ideal, and parents during this transitional time often need support and psychoeducation. Lastly, I will cover specific interventions and considerations for 15-year-old clients.

Counseling Relationship

As with all clients, the relationship is the essential piece for change. I joke with my supervisees and students that adolescents are great "BS detectors" and can read adults better than we can imagine. I suggest counselors take authenticity, genuineness, and transparency to heart when working with 15-year-olds. Too often, my clients tell me about well-meaning adults in their lives who are "fake" or "pretend to care." Many adolescent clients have been hurt, abused, or at least disappointed by adults in their lives and may come in assessing us for potential danger. I explicitly and implicitly communicate the importance of earning the adolescent's trust to both the client and parent.

Similarly, self-disclosure with adolescents may serve to bridge the relationship. Adult clients more easily understand the professional counseling relationship, and most counselors who work with adults avoid self-disclosure. Child clients are used to adult relationships being primarily one-sided. Fifteen-year-olds are often curious about the adult sitting across from them and may struggle to connect or trust without some relational information. It should be noted that appropriate self-disclosures do not include talking about the counselors' past or current problems unless those problems are minor and resolved (Geldard et al., 2020). I will not discuss my own teenage woes or current problems although I may disclose my thoughts about minor issues or tidbits about me as a human. For example, I may empathetically agree the traffic around the office is bothersome or offer that I also like the band on my client's t-shirt. Adolescents often ask why I became a counselor, and I generally feel comfortable disclosing I had a meaningful relationship with my counselor as an adolescent. It is the truth, and it feels authentic to share if asked by an earnest client.

Developmental Considerations

Existentialism may not be on the forefront of your mind when you consider 15-year-old clients, and it was not on mine either when I began my work with teenagers. Not only are 15-year-olds in the midst of identity development, as discussed in previous sections, but they are also searching for meaning. A sense of meaning can be hard to find in a freshman algebra class, yet 15-year-olds are expected to pay attention and try their best for the promise of a "better future." As we know, adolescents are less future-oriented than adults (Siegel, 2014) and often struggle to consider future planning or future consequences, especially with a lack of internal motivation. Many of my 15-year-old clients report school feels meaningless and they struggle to connect the daily experience of school with their future. A need for meaning extends beyond school, but this example highlights a need for meaning and purpose that many adults may not recognize. Counselors can help 15-year-olds develop a sense of meaning through self-reflection and identity development. Expressive arts can be a beneficial tool in assisting 15-year-old clients to connect to their meaning and future goals.

Keeping in mind Erikson's identity stage of development (Erikson, 1994), counselors remain aware that 15-year-olds are likely to try out different ways of being and different identities. Counselors and parents alike are wise to avoid overemphasizing an element of 15-year-olds' changing identities. I remind parents that 15-year-olds are likely to double down on ideas when challenged, and unless the teen's behavior is harmful, it is helpful to be tolerant and patient with their adolescent's exploration. A 15-year-old client who is exploring identity through hair color, dress, or friend group is developmentally typical and safe. I have noticed when clients are unable to explore identity through safe means, they are at a greater risk of engaging in risk-taking behaviors, such as drug use or unprotected sex. This feels the truest at 15, with that intersection of sensation-seeking and impulse control as well as decreased deference to parental feedback.

Patience for storytelling and then gently bringing the client back to the "issue" is often needed. I often hear new counselors' concerns about 15-year-olds' tendency to story tell and talk at length about their peers, pop culture, or social media activity. All that adolescents share with us is painting a picture of their life and may illustrate their comfort level with deep topics. Geldard et al. (2020) encourage counselors to intentionally use digression when working with adolescents. They recommended counselors notice when clients become distracted or seem emotionally overwhelmed and then assist the client in digressing to a safe topic to gain energy or relax before jumping back into important issues. Additionally, 15-year-old clients are in the process of revising constructs as they process through with a counselor; therefore, counselors may watch adolescent clients contradict themselves and shift from one topic to the next.

Counselor Self-Reflection

I have had the immense pleasure of teaching adolescent counseling courses and supervising counselors in training who are beginning to work with adolescents. I spend a significant amount of time exploring and discussing the counselors' individual experiences in adolescence. Did they get along with their parents? Did they feel included or excluded from their peers? Did they engage in risk-taking behavior, and if so, were there significant consequences? Did they struggle with mental health, and what help, if any, did they receive? I believe this exploration is vital to tease apart what preconceived notions students have about adolescents and what personal experiences may impact their work with adolescents. Given that adolescence is a time full of development, change, and often struggle, it is no surprise many new counselors have intense feelings about this population. Some students are drawn to work with adolescents due to their own positive experiences with a counselor in adolescence (myself included), some admit a desire to save or protect a teenage version of themselves, while others are afraid of being "uncool" or judged by adolescent clients based on their own teen experience. Awareness of one's personal associations and biases toward adolescents is essential prior to working with this population.

Parent Consultation and Psychoeducation

One of the most helpful elements of working with parents of adolescents can be psychoeducation. Often parents benefit from an increased understanding of adolescent development and changes. Many parents report not knowing or understanding their 15-year-old due to what they perceive as dramatic changes in their behavior. One common example is the beginning of the individuation process for 15-year-olds. It is developmentally typical for an adolescent to rely more on their peers and value peer insight over parents, yet many parents feel a sense of rejection from the teen when this begins to happen. More disruptive behaviors, such as talking back, risk-taking, or rebellion, may also be normalized but not condoned. I often say to parents, "This behavior is typical but also an opportunity for you to set some limits." Another important goal for working with the 15-year-old's parent/guardian is to empathize and connect.

Legal and Ethical Considerations for Counselors

Informed Consent

Fifteen-year-old clients enter my office with a variety of expectations and differing levels of external pressure, or coercion, to be in counseling. One of the first questions I ask adolescent clients is, "How do you feel about being here?" Answers from 15-year-old clients seem to range from nervous, sad, or angry to relieved or hopeful. Ideally, I have received some information from the client's parent or caregiver about their level of investment in counseling. Sometimes a parent begrudgingly calls to make the appointment at the request of the adolescent or by a recommendation from the school. Unfortunately, sometimes adolescents show up in my office having just learned they were going to counseling in the parking lot. The goal of an initial meeting with a 15-year-old is to communicate that they are the priority and that they will know and have a say in all that goes on. I attempt to be crystal clear about informed consent with both the adolescent and the parent. An important piece of informed consent with 15-year-olds is explicitly discussing confidentiality and its limits.

Confidentiality

Confidentiality may be one of the most complex aspects of working with 15-year-old clients. As noted, 15 is a pivotal age for brain and cognitive development that further complicates counselors' decisions about disclosing information the adolescent requests to keep private. There are many factors for counselors to consider, including codes of ethics, legal mandates, and clinical assessment of risk.

The ACA *Code of Ethics* (ACA, 2014) mandates counselors explicitly inform clients of the limits of confidentiality. When clients are minors, counselors inform parents of the confidential nature of the counseling relationship consistent with current state laws. Additionally, counselors are to inform all parties about confidentiality, collaborate with parents, and protect the privacy of adolescent clients when possible (ACA, 2014).

From a legal perspective, most states mandate counselors breach confidentially in cases of imminent harm and suspected child abuse. One of the questions for counselors surrounding confidentiality is, "What constitutes imminent harm?" Counselors agree suicidal ideation constitutes imminent harm and may mandate a breach of confidentiality (Michero, 2016).

Master therapists (those counselors identified as experts by their peers) rely heavily on clinical intuition around the parent–adolescent–counselor relationship when making decisions about adolescent confidentiality (Michero, 2016). In research, they described a felt or intuitive sense about adolescents' level of risk and when to inform parents. The parent–adolescent–counselor dynamic includes three relationship dyads: the parent–adolescent, adolescent–counselor, and counselor–parent. The first dyad is the relationship between parent and adolescent. Master therapists considered how helpful the parent may be in working through the issue at hand as well as the parent's potential level of reactivity. They considered the strength of the therapeutic relationship between the adolescent and counselor when making decisions as well as the potential benefit of counseling on the issue. For example, a strong therapeutic alliance and probable improvement of an issue through the counseling process may decrease master therapists' disclosure of information. And finally, they consider the counselor–parent relationship and the amount of trust the parent has in the counselor and the therapeutic process. Master therapists report the best way to decrease ethical dilemmas surrounding confidentially is to collaborate with parents and cover confidentiality thoroughly in informed consent. These considerations do not provide concrete guidance but do provide a framework for decisions around 15-year-old clients and confidentially.

Conclusion

Counseling 15-year-old adolescents can be very meaningful due to the potentially unparalleled impact of the counseling relationship. Fifteen-year-old clients are in the throes of physical, cognitive, social, and emotional development that can leave them feeling overwhelmed. It is an honor to provide a safe space for this special age. Counselors armed with an understanding of their unique development have the power to make a lasting impact on their development and lives.

References

American Counseling Association. (2014). *ACA code of ethics*. Author.

Arcelus, J., Mitchell, A. J., Wales, J., & Nielsen, S. (2011). Mortality rates in patients with anorexia nervosa and other eating disorders: A meta-analysis of 36 studies. *Archives of General Psychiatry*, *68*(7), 724–731. https://doi.org/10.1001/archgenpsychiatry.2011.74

Belter, R., & Grisso, T. (1984). Children's recognition of rights violations in counseling. *Professional Psychology Research and Practice*, *15*, 899–910.

Berk, L. (2017). *Development through the lifespan* (7th ed.). Pearson.

Bowlby, J. (1969). *Attachment and loss: Attachment* (Vol. 1). Basic Books.

Centers for Disease Control and Prevention, National Center for Health Statistics. National Vital Statistics System. (2021). Mortality 2018–2021 on CDC WONDER Online Database, released in (2023). *Data are from the Multiple Cause of Death Files, 2018–2021, as compiled from data provided by the 57 vital statistics jurisdictions through the Vital Statistics Cooperative Program.* http://wonder.cdc.gov/mcd-icd10-expanded.html.

Centers for Disease Control and Prevention, National Center for Injury Prevention and Control. (2023). *Title of the webpage or document*. Disparities in Suicide | Suicide Prevention | CDC.

Davis, R. A. (2001). A cognitive–behavioral model of pathological internet use. *Computers in Human Behavior*, *17*(2), 187–195. https://doi.org/10.1016/S0747-5632(00)00041-8

Erikson, E. H. (1994). *Identity and the life cycle*. W.W. Norton.

Farré, J. M., Montejo, A. L., Agulló, M., Granero, R., Chiclana Actis, C., Villena, A., Maideu, E., Sánchez, M., Fernández-Aranda, F., Jiménez-Murcia, S., & Mestre-Bach, G. (2020). Pornography use in adolescents and its clinical implications. *Journal of Clinical Medicine*, *9*(11), 3625. https://doi.org/10.3390/jcm9113625

Flook, L., Repetti, R. L., & Ullman, J. B. (2005). Classroom social experiences as predictors of academic performance. *Developmental Psychology*, *41*, 319–327. https://doi.org/10.1037/0012-1649.41.2.319

Fowler, J. W., & Dell, M. L. (2006). Stages of faith from infancy through adolescence: Reflections on three decades of faith development theory. In E. C. Roehlkepartain, P. E. King, L. Wagener, & P. L. Benson (Eds.), *The handbook of spiritual development in childhood and adolescence* (pp. 34–45). SAGE. https://doi.org/10.4135/9781412976657.n3

Geldard, K., Geldard, D., & Foo, R. (2020). *Counselling adolescents: The proactive approach for young people* (5th ed.). SAGE.

Grisso, T., & Vierling, L. (1978). Minors' consent to treatment: A developmental perspective. *Professional Psychology, 9*(3), 412–427. https://doi.org/10.1037/0735-7028.9.3.412

Harden, K. P., & Tucker-Drob, E. M. (2011). Individual differences in the development of sensation seeking and impulsivity during adolescence: Further evidence for a dual systems model. *Developmental Psychology*, *47*(3), 739–746. https://doi.org/10.1037/a0023279

Homayoun, A. (2018). *Social media wellness: Helping tweens and teens thrive in an unbalanced digital world.* Corwin, a Sage Company.

Icenogle, G., & Cauffman, E. (2021). Adolescent decision making: A decade in review. *Journal of Research on Adolescence*, *31*(4), 1006–1022. https://doi.org/10.1111/jora.12608

Icenogle, G., Steinberg, L., Duell, N., Chein, J., Chang, L., Chaudhary, N., Di Giunta, L., Dodge, K. A., Fanti, K. A., Lansford, J. E., Oburu, P., Pastorelli, C., Skinner, A. T., Sorbring, E., Tapanya, S., Uribe Tirado, L. M., Alampay, L. P., Al-Hassan, S. M., Takash, H. M. S., Bacchini, D. (2019). Adolescents' cognitive capacity reaches adult levels prior to their psychosocial maturity: Evidence for a "maturity gap" in a multinational, cross-sectional sample. *Law and Human Behavior*, *43*(1), 69–85. https://doi.org/10.1037/lhb0000315. PMID: 30762417; PMCID: PMC6551607.

Kormas, G., Critselis, E., Janikian, M., Kafetzis, D., & Tsitsika, A. (2011). Risk factors and psychosocial characteristics of potential problematic and problematic internet use among adolescents: A cross-sectional study. *BMC Public Health*, *11*, 595. https://doi.org/10.1186/1471-2458-11-595

Merikangas, K. R., Avenevoli, S., Costello, E. J., Koretz, D., & Kessler, R. C. (2009). National comorbidity survey replication adolescent supplement (NCS-A): I. Background and measures. *Journal of the American Academy of Child and Adolescent Psychiatry*, *48*(4), 367–379. https://doi.org/10.1097/CHI.0b013e31819996f1

Michero, E. (2016). *Master therapists' decision-making process concerning adolescent confidentiality: A grounded theory approach* (Publication No. 67531) (Doctoral dissertation, University of North Texas). University of North Texas Digital Libraries.

Moyer, M., & Sullivan, J. (2008). Student risk-taking behaviors: When do school counselors break confidentiality? *Professional School Counseling*, *11*(4), 236–245. http://www.jstor.org/stable/42732829

Moyer, M. S., & Yu, K. (2012). Factors influencing school counselors' perceived effectiveness. *Journal of School Counseling*, *10*(6), 23.

National Academies Press. (2019). *The promise of adolescence: Realizing opportunity for all youth*. NASEM.

Neblett, E. W., Jr., Rivas-Drake, D., & Umaña-Taylor, A. J. (2012). The promise of racial and ethnic protective factors in promoting ethnic minority youth development. *Child Development Perspectives*, 6, 295–303. https://doi.org/10.1111/j.1750-8606.2012.00239.x

Peterson, J., Freedenthal, S., Sheldon, C., & Andersen, R. (2008). Nonsuicidal self injury in adolescents. *Psychiatry*, *5*(11), 20–26. https://pubmed.ncbi.nlm.nih.gov/19724714/

Rose, A. J. (2021). The costs and benefits of co-rumination. *Child Development Perspectives*, *15*(3), 176–181. https://doi.org/10.1111/cdep.12419

Sellers, R. M., & Shelton, J. N. (2003). The role of racial identity in perceived racial discrimination. *Journal of Personality and Social Psychology*, *84*(5), 1079–1092. https://doi.org/10.1037/0022-3514.84.5.1079

Shaffer, D. A., & Greenberg, T. (2002). Suicide and suicidal behavior in children and adolescents. In D. Shaffer & B. D. Waslick (Eds.), *The many faces of depression in children and adolescents*. American Psychiatric Publishing.

Siegel, D. J. (2014). *Brainstorm: The power and purpose of the teenage brain*. Tarcher/Putnam.

Solomon, A. (2012). *Far from the tree: Parents, children and the search for identity*. Scribner.

Steinberg, L. (2014). *Age of opportunity: Lessons from the new science of adolescence*. Houghton Mifflin Harcourt.

Stice, E., Marti, C. N., & Durant, S. (2011). Risk factors for onset of eating disorders: Evidence of multiple risk pathways from an 8-year prospective study. *Behaviour Research and Therapy*, *49*(10), 622–627. https://doi.org/10.1016/j.brat.2011.06.009

Substance Abuse and Mental Health Services Administration. (2022). *Key substance use and mental health indicators in the United States: Results from the 2021 National Survey on Drug Use and Health* (HHS Publication No. PEP22-07-01-005, NSDUH Series H-57). Center for

Behavioral Health Statistics and Quality, Substance Abuse and Mental Health Services Administration. www.samhsa.gov/data/report/2021-nsduh-annual-national-report

Umaña-Taylor, A. J., Quintana, S. M., Lee, R. M., Cross, W. E., Jr., Rivas-Drake, D., Schwartz, S. J., Syed, M., Yip, T., Seaton, E., & The Ethnic and Racial Identity in the 21st Century Study Group. (2014). Ethnic and racial identity during adolescence and into young adulthood: An integrated conceptualization. *Child Development*, *85*(1), 21–39. https://doi.org/10.1111/cdev.12196

Zetterqvist, M., Lundh, L. G., Dahlström, O., & Svedin, C. G. (2013). Prevalence and function of non-suicidal self-injury (NSSI) in a community sample of adolescents, using suggested DSM-5 criteria for a potential NSSI disorder. *Journal of Abnormal Child Psychology*, *41*(5), 759–773. https://doi.org/10.1007/s10802-013-9712-5.

Zimmerman, M. A., Stoddard, S. A., Eisman, A. B., Caldwell, C. H., Aiyer, S. M., & Miller, A. (2013). Adolescent resilience: Promotive factors that inform prevention. *Child Development Perspectives*, 7(4), https://doi.org/10.1111/cdep.12042

Chapter 6

The 16-Year-Old

Molly Moran

Z is a 16-year-old high school student who identifies as queer and gender nonconforming. Although Z has disclosed their gender and sexual identity to a few close friends, they are not out to their family. Z, born Lindsey, was assigned a female gender identity at birth but never felt like a cisgender female. As a child, Z was often referred to as a "tomboy." This did not bother Z as they felt more comfortable around their male-identified friends; however, this changed as Z began to experience physical maturation. Z grew increasingly uncomfortable with their changing body. Recently, they quit the swim team due to the discomfort associated with wearing the required team swimsuit. This level of discomfort and confusion led to feelings of isolation, loneliness, fear, and anxiety. Last month, Z and several other friends were expelled from school for two days because of an alcohol policy violation at a school event. Z felt this consequence was incredibly unfair but did agree to meet with the school counselor to discuss the event and resulting consequences. During this meeting, Z disclosed that they were struggling to understand their identity and felt very alone in that journey. Z described thinking it would be easier to die than to continue living in a body that felt so foreign or to endure the torture that would surely conspire if they were to come out as gender nonconforming. During this meeting, Z learned about the school's gender sexuality alliance (GSA) club and went to a meeting that week. Z met students who identified across the gender and sexual orientation spectrum and felt an incredible sense of affirmation. Z developed close friends and allies through the GSA and even ran for a leadership role. Z grew more curious and open to their experiences and began to explore when and how they might affirm their identity in safe spaces. Z developed a plan to come out to a few supportive teachers at school and began to think about how and when to disclose their gender identity to their mother. Although Z regularly experiences identity-based bullying from several classmates, overall, they feel as though their school is a relatively safe space. Z attributes this sense of safety to teachers who openly support LGBTQIA+ students, a strong GSA, queer students who are in visible leadership roles within the school, and a supportive friend group.

As with Z, 16-year-olds are in a peak developmental period marked by significant biological, cognitive, and psychosocial changes. Sixteen-year-olds experience hormonal changes during puberty that result in physical growth and maturation. Brain development is considerable during this period with changes in structure, function, and circuitry. As connectivity between brain regions strengthens, individuals develop new cognitive capacities and

DOI: 10.4324/9781003196297-9

regulatory abilities. Peer relationships begin to shift as 16-year-olds seek independence from parents and guardians. Adolescence includes several developmental milestones that facilitate the transition to adulthood. It is important to note that the timing and pace of development vary considerably (Hollenstein & Lougheed, 2013). The developmental process is gradual, influenced by many factors, and unique to everyone.

Physical Development

The physical developmental period that occurs at the age of 16 is known as puberty. The process of moving through the stages of puberty varies by sex and chronological age (Laycock & Meeran, 2013). In the United States, individuals assigned female at birth (AFAB) typically begin puberty around the age of 12, complete pubertal development by age 16 (Brix et al., 2019) and have reached peak values in muscle tissue, weight, height, and skeletal mass (Lee & Styne, 2013). For individuals assigned male at birth (AMAB), age 16 is characterized by increases in height, weight, muscle tissue development, skeletal mass, the emergence of body hair, deepening of the voice, and genital maturation (Marshall & Tanner, 1970). AMAB individuals typically complete pubertal development by the age of 18 (Gazzaniga, 2018).

The onset of puberty can vary significantly due to several genetic and environmental factors such as nutrition and exposure to toxins, trauma, and stress (Lee & Styne, 2013). For example, an individual AFAB raised in an environment with social and economic resources, stability, and safety will likely have reached menarche by age 16, whereas a 16-year-old AFAB raised in an environment with limited economic resources and exposure to adverse childhood experiences may not reach menarche for several years. The timing and tempo of puberty and the associated physical changes have several social and psychological implications for 16-year-olds. For example, cisgender males who experience early-onset puberty experience greater acceptance by their peers (Mendle et al., 2010) and, at the same time, are at elevated risk for increased behavioral problems such as bullying and early substance use (Kaltia-Heino et al., 2011) compared to peers who experience typical onset. Conversely, cisgender males who experience later-onset puberty experience elevated rates of anxiety (Graber et al., 2004). Cisgender females who experience early-onset puberty report body dissatisfaction and depression (Reynolds & Juvonen, 2012). Later-maturing cisgender females may experience some distress during adolescence, but the implications are not well-documented. The distress associated with early and late developers does not appear to persist after the period of noticeable differences in maturation (Copeland et al., 2011). For gender nonconforming and transgender individuals such as Z, the onset of puberty and the physical maturation of their bodies can cause significant distress (Murad et al., 2010).

Due to the significant physical changes during this period of development, sleep is an essential restorative process that includes many benefits. Neural connections are strengthened during sleep, and the hormones released during sleep repair damaged brain tissue and clean out toxic metabolic debris (Xie et al., 2013). The Centers for Disease Control and Prevention (CDCP) recommends that adolescents receive between eight and ten hours of sleep per night, yet approximately 72% of high school students report not meeting this recommendation (CDCP, 2019a). Insufficient sleep among adolescents may be a result of later bedtimes, changes in the sleep-wake cycle, early school start times, numerous athletic and/or social obligations, and academic responsibilities (Louzada & Menna-Barreto, 2003). Insufficient sleep is associated with deleterious health and academic consequences such as behavior problems, poor academic performance (Paruthi et al., 2016), and mental health challenges (Lowry et al., 2012).

Brain Development

Brain development during adolescence is significant and includes changes in brain structure, function, and circuitry. The most notable changes that occur in the 16-year-old brain include shifts in the volume of white and gray matter, strengthened connectivity between brain regions, and the gradual maturation of the prefrontal cortex (Gazzaniga, 2018).

During adolescence, many of the synapses formed during childhood are no longer needed or used and are, therefore, pruned, leading to a decline in gray matter. Synaptic pruning leads to stronger, more efficient neural communication. For example, a 16-year-old who is learning a new language is strengthening the neuronal connections needed for language processing and acquisition and is simultaneously pruning neural networks that are no longer needed, such as those related to basic arithmetic.

While gray matter continues to decrease throughout adolescence, white matter increases due to a process called myelination (Giedd, 2015). Adolescence is a period of significant myelination resulting in white matter growth and stronger connections between brain regions (Lenroot & Giedd, 2006; Spear, 2013). Synaptic pruning and myelination essentially rewire the brain to allow for a higher level of information processing. This is often observed when a 16-year-old is able to retrieve prior knowledge and skills to solve an abstract and complex social problem from varying perspectives.

The prefrontal cortex and subcortical regions in the brain undergo extensive development during childhood and adolescence (Juraska & Willing, 2016). Research suggests an increase in connectivity between brain regions, including a rise in dopamine pathways (Wahlstrom et al., 2010), and reconfiguration in the prefrontal cortex during adolescence (Crone & Steinbeis, 2017).

Although basic executive functioning skills start to develop in late childhood and early adolescence, research suggests that brain structures involved in more complex executive functioning such as planning and cognitive flexibility are continuing to stabilize and mature at age 16 (Casey & Caudle, 2013). For example, the dorsal-lateral prefrontal cortex and the anterior cingulate cortex, regions important for integrating feedback to adapt and produce purposeful behaviors, are still being developed at age 16 (Crone & Steinbeis, 2017). As you might expect, a 16-year-old may still have difficulty applying feedback in the moment to modify behaviors. For example, when a counselor is providing feedback to a client about the connection between thoughts, feelings, and behaviors, the client might not be able to integrate the feedback to make changes to behaviors in similar but new situations without multiple examples, observation, and practice. However, with increased connections between brain regions and relevant experiences across contexts, they can start to integrate prior learning to inform future behaviors.

The subcortical region of the brain is responsible for responding to stimuli, constructing new memories, and evaluating emotions, among other regulatory processes. The subcortical region of the brain develops at a much more rapid pace than the prefrontal cortex and, consequently, often dictates decision-making. The delayed maturation of the brain's control center in combination with an active amygdala and strengthened dopamine pathways may lead teens to engage in impulsive, emotionally driven behaviors (Casey & Caudle, 2013). Impulsivity is associated with risk-taking behaviors and is linked with poor decision-making and negative outcomes. However, research suggests that risk-taking is not only developmentally appropriate but also adaptive in that it supports exploration, learning, and skill acquisition (McCormick & Telzer, 2017).

Cognitive Development

Brain development in adolescence coincides with advances in cognitive abilities. Whereas children need concrete examples and physical evidence to understand complex concepts, adolescents can engage in hypothetical or abstract thinking. According to Jean Piaget's (1936) theory of cognitive development, adolescents typically advance to the formal operations stage of development. Adolescents can ponder philosophical questions or moral issues and debate political perspectives. They are also able to reflect on their own thinking and engage in dialogue about their thought process.

At the age of 16, adolescents still tend to gravitate toward what they have observed or what is consistent with their beliefs (Klaczynski & Gordon, 1996). One example of this is the tendency to gravitate toward media that aligns with one's beliefs and/or consistent with familial beliefs. However, they can also contemplate various possibilities, even possibilities that may contradict their own reality (Sigelman & Rider, 2015). In mid to late adolescence, individuals develop the ability to integrate new knowledge through reasoning rather than relying solely on previous knowledge or beliefs. For example, if a 16-year-old was presented with a research question, they may quickly identify a possible answer based upon prior knowledge of the subject, but they may also consider alternatives. Some can even generate several hypotheses and develop a systematic approach to test each hypothesis. While most 16-year-olds can certainly recognize a solid systematic approach to solving problems, not all teenagers are able to engage in the process of scientific reasoning (Schneider & Bullock, 2009), suggesting that not all 16-year-old adolescents have mastered logical reasoning skills. For example, if a 16-year-old is unsuccessful at resolving a conflict with a peer instead of examining the situation from multiple perspectives, identifying, and attempting various solutions, they may experience frustration and give up any attempts to repair the relationship or work through the conflict.

Emotional Development

Many consider adolescence as a period fraught with emotional turbulence. While not all adolescents experience turmoil during this developmental period, many of them do experience heightened emotionality (Dahl & Gunnar, 2009), which may be due to several biological factors. Increases in hormone production and heightened subcortical activity in the brain may result in stronger emotional responses and difficulty managing arousal. By age 16, most adolescents have developed the ability to recognize and evaluate emotions in themselves and others. However, some may struggle to regulate and express emotions productively as the connectivity between the regulatory and emotional response systems in the brain is still being refined. Insufficient sleep may also contribute to irritability and/or increased difficulty managing emotions. In addition to the influence of biological changes in the brain, immense physical changes occur during puberty that can result in feelings of shame, insecurity, or distress, particularly for those who identify as female (Reynolds & Juvonen, 2012). For example, a 16-year-old female identified person who develops breasts at an early age may experience ridicule, teasing, and/or unwanted attention directed at her physical appearance that may lead to insecurity or internalized body shaming.

Navigating new social roles and changes in relationships requires vulnerability and risk-taking, which may evoke strong emotions. As teens engage more with their peers in groups, particularly in task-oriented activities like school projects or sports, they learn how to recognize and work with the emotional dynamics in the group (Larson & Brown, 2007). To be a productive or even an accepted member of the group, one must learn to manage the multitude of feelings associated with task-oriented, group activities and membership. While these experiences might produce a bit of anxiety at first, through collaboration, students begin to develop and practice communication, perspective-taking, and conflict resolution. With these skills, adolescents can engage in emotional exchange with others and better understand emotional processes.

Social and Relationship Development

It is no surprise that peer relationships and social engagement are central in the lives of adolescents. To gain independence and autonomy from parents or guardians, adolescents spend more time with peers and often rely on friends rather than parents/guardians for emotional support. Adolescent relationships differ from childhood friendships in several ways (Sigelman & Rider, 2015). Teen relationships become more intimate and involve a deeper level of commitment and self-disclosure (Rubin et al., 2010). At 16, adolescents begin to shift their focus from individual relationships to the formation of peer groups. Adolescents tend to form peer groups with individuals who have similar interests, beliefs, and values and exhibit similar behaviors. Healthy peer relationships and a sense of belonging to a peer group are associated with several positive psychological outcomes (Sieving et al., 2017). Moreover, it is generally believed that belonging to a peer group is advantageous for identity development. However, adolescents are more susceptible to peer pressure than at any other developmental period (Sumter et al., 2009). When adolescents experience peer pressure to conform to rigid group norms and expectations, identity development can be stifled in some circumstances.

Cultural and Identity Development

Adolescence is marked by immense biological development, a changing social landscape, and ultimately a gradual transition into adulthood. It is understandable that these changes evoke questions about identity, purpose, and role in society. Identity development in adolescence is multidimensional and includes the process of questioning and examining the meaning of group membership, exploring various roles, and gradually crystalizing membership within groups (Phinney & Ong, 2007). Several theories and models exist that elucidate the complicated, developmental process of identity exploration and construction. Identity development is impacted by several factors such as familial influence, sociopolitical climate, and neighborhood or school demographics. Significant variability in the timing and process of identity development exists among 16-year-olds (Huang & Stormshak, 2011). This section is not an exhaustive review of identity development models but rather a brief overview of the general processes of identity formation for 16-year-olds with special attention to gender, sexual orientation, and racial/ethnic identities as these are particularly salient at age 16.

As discussed in Chapter 1, two predominant adolescent identity development theories include Erik Erikson's theory of psychosocial development (1980) and James Marcia's theory of identity development (1993). Erikson suggested that adolescents at age 16 have arrived at the identity vs. role confusion stage of psychosocial development. At this stage, adolescents are faced with the psychological task of determining who they are and who they want to become. Teens may be considering future interests, testing relationships, playing various roles in peer groups, exploring sexual interests, and experimenting with different ways of expressing themselves. There may be significant variation in identity exploration at this stage as the age range is quite large, spanning from 12 to 18 years of age.

Marcia's (1993) theory includes four developmental statuses that adolescents experience as they move toward identity formation: diffusion, foreclosure, moratorium, and achievement. Each status is marked by varying levels of commitment to or interest in identity exploration (see Chapter 1). Research suggests that 16-year-olds ebb and flow through the four statuses; however, a considerable number of 16-year-olds are somewhere between the diffusion and foreclosure status (Marcia, 1993). This suggests that they have not begun the process of identity exploration, feel somewhat ambivalent, or have adopted an identity based upon familial practices.

Racial and Ethnic Identity

Racial and/or ethnic identity is the extent to which race and/or ethnicity has meaning and significance in defining oneself (Nakkula & Toshalis, 2008). Racial, ethnic, and cultural identity models suggest that individuals follow a course of development moving from a place of apathy or negative attitudes of self toward a more positive, integrated sense of self (Cross, 1995; Helms, 1995). While there is considerable variability in the trajectory of racial and/or ethnic identity development, it is believed that exploration and integration of race and ethnicity increase during adolescence (French et al., 2006), particularly for individuals who do not belong to the dominant racial or ethnic group (Else-Quest & Morse, 2015). The timing and tempo of racial and/or ethnic identity development are highly dependent on racial socialization within the family (Quintana, 2007) and the cultural context within school (Graham, 2018). In schools and families that foster a climate of cultural appreciation, celebration, and exploration, individuals have the opportunity to cultivate a deeper understanding of their racial and ethnic identity and, thus, a positive sense of self as a racial being.

Gender Identity

New ways of describing gender continue to emerge, and our understanding of how individuals experience gender continues to expand. The process of gender identity development is influenced by biological and cognitive processes but even more so by socialization (Leaper, 2014). Through social interaction, media, and familial norms, young children begin to develop a gender schema that influences their beliefs about gender and associated roles. As children move into teen years, the desire to be liked and accepted by peers elevates (Steinberg & Monahan, 2007), and as a result, peer interaction and feedback have a significant impact on behaviors and adherence to acceptable roles and activities. Adolescents at age 16 often feel pressure from peers to ascribe to socially appropriate gender norms, which may influence the trajectory of their gender identity development (Cook et al., 2019). For example, a 16-year-old adhering to traditional gender roles or socially acceptable gendered behavior experience reinforcements in the form of social capital such as popularity, while those who do not conform are often excluded or bullied (Toomey et al., 2014). However, as adolescents are exposed to nontraditional gendered behaviors, they begin to think more flexibly about gender (Liben & Bigler, 2002). As the pressure to "fit in" or adhere to group norms becomes less intense, adolescents begin experimenting with gender expression as a means of identity exploration.

Sexual Identity

Sexual identity is an umbrella term that can refer to several aspects of sexuality, such as sexual needs and desires, sexual attraction and expression, values and beliefs about sex, romantic attachment, and sexual orientation. Sexual identity begins to materialize during adolescence. It is a time of sexual exploration and experimentation that can evoke feelings of excitement, fear, and uncertainty. Healthy sexual identity development is dependent on access to sexual health education, affirming and supportive peers, and family. Like other dimensions of identity, sexual identity is unique to everyone, and not all adolescents experience or describe sexuality in a uniform way. For example, in a recent study conducted with a large sample of adolescents (White et al., 2018), a significant percentage of the sample identified as something other than heterosexual, suggesting significant variance in how adolescents understand and experience sexuality. Parenthetically, there has been a dramatic shift in social attitudes about sexual orientation. Consequently, adolescents are expressing same-sex attractions at earlier ages and at higher rates than previous generations. According to the CDCP (2019b), approximately 15.7% of adolescents do not identify as heterosexual – a much larger percentage than in previous years.

Resources and Protective Factors

While 16-year-olds are extremely susceptible to a myriad of risk factors, they are also incredibly resilient. Adolescents have a natural inclination to adapt to environments, foster relationships, and develop skills that can serve as protective factors. As adolescents gain cognitive capacities, they are learning and practicing prosocial communication skills, reasoning skills, and perspective-taking, which aid in the development of healthy relationships, a crucial protective factor for adolescents (Sieving et al., 2017). According to a seminal longitudinal study on protective factors, the following are important for enhancing resilience: utilizing coping strategies, structure and boundaries at home, authoritative parenting, reliable caregiver support, engagement in school and/or community activities, developing hobbies, and positive mentorship at school (Werner, 1992). As you read in the chapter vignette, participating in the GSA and connecting to a caring adult proved to be significant resiliency factors for Z.

For students who hold one or more historically minoritized identities developing prosocial, in-group affiliation and a positive view of their cultural group serves as a protective factor that can promote resilience (Quintana, 2007). A strong sense of belonging to one's cultural group results in positive developmental outcomes across several domains such as increases in self-esteem (Bracey et al., 2004), positive future self-concept, the development of adaptive coping strategies (Moses et al., 2020), and academic achievement (Rivas-Drake et al., 2014). Moreover, several studies suggest that strong cultural identity can mediate the effects of racism and discrimination (Jones et al., 2014; Moses et al., 2020). For LGBTQIA+ adolescents, the presence of a GSA or similar student group that foster community and connection among sexual minority youth serves as a crucial protective factor (Poteat et al., 2016).

Challenges and Risk Factors

Low socioeconomic status, early exposure to trauma, instability in the family/household, abuse, environmental toxins, and limited access to medical care are just a few of the risk factors that may impact human development across the lifespan (American Psychological Association, 2010). The following section will review several risk factors that are particularly salient in the development of the 16-year-old adolescent.

Risky Behaviors

Adolescents are navigating shifts in social networks, new environments, and unfamiliar experiences, which require exploration and some risk-taking. Risk-taking is a normative part of adolescent development and allows teens to learn and develop essential skills for progressing into adulthood. However, with protracted development in the prefrontal cortex coupled with a preoccupation with peer acceptance, adolescents are likely to engage in harmful, risky behaviors with deleterious consequences such as substance use, driving while intoxicated, and unprotected sex. According to the Youth Risk Behavioral Survey (CDCP, 2019b) rates of unprotected sex among adolescents are increasing, leading to unplanned pregnancies and sexually transmitted diseases. Additionally, prevalence rates of substance use within the previous 30 days among high school students are staggering, with approximately 29.2% reporting alcohol use, 21.7% reporting marijuana use, and 15% reporting illicit drug use or misuse of prescription drugs (CDCP, 2019b).

Bullying and School Violence

Most 16-year-olds spend a considerable amount of their day attending school, which can serve as both a protective factor and/or an environment that contributes to negative outcomes. Approximately 20% of high school students reported being a target of bullying, and nearly 7% reported being threatened or injured with a weapon in the previous 12-month period (CDCP, 2019b). Students who hold one or more historically minoritized identities are particularly vulnerable to school-based violence and bullying. For example, 40% of LGBTQIA+ students reported being a target of bullying compared to only 22% of their heterosexual, cisgender peers. Approximately 30% of students who identify as female reported being a victim of bullying compared to only 19% of their male classmates. Bullying and school violence have been associated with elevated rates of anxiety (Copeland et al., 2013), depression, suicidality (Takizawa et al., 2014), and academic difficulties (Rueger, 2014).

Racism and Discrimination

Students of color experience social conditions in schools that lead to disparate health and academic outcomes. It is well-documented that students of color experience disproportionate rates of discipline, chronic absenteeism, and lower graduation rates as compared to their White classmates (U.S. Department of Education: National Center for Educational Statistics, 2018). Several studies have found that school curriculum, policies, and practices are predominantly representative of White, middle-class identities and exclude non-White groups (Paris, 2012). In addition to the structural racism that permeates schools, several studies have documented that students of color regularly experience overt racism and prejudice from peers, staff, and teachers (Irizarry, 2013; Kohli & Solorzano, 2012). Racism and perceived discrimination in adolescence have been associated with increases in psychological distress, depressive symptoms that extend into adulthood, a decline in academic efficacy (Lambert et al., 2009), and elevated rates of substance use (Guthrie et al., 2002).

Adolescents who identify as LGBTQIA+ are the most vulnerable group among teens, particularly if they hold intersecting identities. Adolescents who identify as LGBTQIA+ experience higher rates of bullying, physical violence, and sexual violence than their heterosexual, cisgender peers (CDCP, 2019b). According to The National Survey on LGBTQ Youth Mental Health (Trevor Project, 2021), 75% of LGBTQIA+ adolescents reported experiencing bias-based discrimination, 42% have seriously considered suicide, and 70% reported "poor" mental health during the previous year. This population is at increased risk for substance use, suicidal ideation, poor academic performance, and depression (CDCP, 2019b).

Best Practices for Counseling and Therapy

Working with 16-year-olds in a therapeutic setting can be rewarding, surprising, and downright challenging. Adolescents are often experienced as resistant to counseling and unmotivated in sessions (Gardner, 2015). Fortunately, there is considerable research that provides support for a variety of treatment modalities when working with adolescents who experience an array of presenting concerns. While randomized control trials allow practitioners to identify potential treatment approaches, it is important to note that treatment modality accounts for little, if any, of the variance in client outcomes (Bell et al., 2013; Wampold & Imel, 2015.) Rather, the relationship between the counselor and client is a better predictor of positive outcomes (Labouliere et al., 2017).

Building a strong therapeutic alliance with 16-year-old clients can be difficult, especially for teens who are mandated or uninterested in the counseling process. Early in relationship building, it is beneficial to be honest and transparent about the process of counseling particularly as it relates to confidentiality. Allow clients to ask questions about the process and your experiences as a counselor. In building trust with adolescents, it is appropriate to use some self-disclosure if the counselor can shift focus quickly back to the client. Building trust involves allowing clients to make decisions about their involvement in the counseling process. It may be advantageous to explore previous experiences with or knowledge about therapy with the adolescent, as this gives them an opportunity to be the expert in their own experiences. It may be helpful for the counselor to broach identity differences and openly acknowledge the limits to understanding based on worldview and identity. For example, a counselor can explicitly name the power differential that is often associated with age and invite a conversation with the client about how that could impact the counseling process and relationship.

Exploring identity development may be particularly important as 16-year-olds are beginning to formulate ideas about their sense of self in relation to family, various social and cultural groups, and as autonomous individuals. Counselors can introduce activities that allow clients to explore and articulate values and to develop goals aligned with these values. Counselors can help clients to identify and explore aspects of identity that are salient in the counseling processes and the counseling relationship and/or that may intersect with presenting concerns. For example, if a male-identified counselor was working with a female-identified 16-year-old client experiencing low self-worth, it may be beneficial for the counselor to invite the client to share their experiences with socialized gender roles and expectations, sexism, and social group gender dynamics and to process the experience of discussing these issues with a male counselor. The counselor might also provide information or referrals to support or empowerment groups for female-identifying teens. A counselor is well-positioned to help clients develop a positive cultural identity, which is correlated with many positive mental health and academic outcomes (Jones et al., 2014; Moses et al., 2020).

Many of the challenges and risk factors that adolescents experience are structural in nature, such as discrimination, bullying, and lack of control or choice. A counselor can help adolescents process difficult experiences, develop coping skills, and foster self-awareness, but this may not be enough to buffer against the damage of systemic inequality that many adolescents experience. It is imperative that counselors engage in social justice and advocacy work with and on behalf of clients. "The Multicultural and Social Justice Counseling Competencies" (Ratts et al., 2016) provides a framework for counselors to advocate for clients at the interpersonal, intrapersonal, and institutional levels. To combat the deleterious effects of structural oppression, a counselor not only needs to examine and help clients understand the ways in which power and privilege influence their lived experiences, but they also need to collaborate with institutions to address systemic inequities that may be negatively impacting clients and advocate for equitable policies and laws (Ratts et al.,

2016). A counselor should be aware of local organizations, resources, and community groups that might offer services and supports to clients.

While 16-year-olds can engage in reflective and abstract thinking, they do not always have the capacity to verbalize their emotional experiences, which can result in frustration and stagnation in sessions. Incorporating creative modalities or techniques such as play, art, or drama allows opportunities to process or express emotions in ways that may feel more accessible to teens. Incorporating creative activities may also help to create a more relaxed environment in which the client feels a sense of control and, therefore, decreases resistance (Gardner, 2015). Sixteen-year-old clients may also enjoy interventions related to task-oriented types of activities such as sports, instruments, or dance. Introducing task-oriented activities in session may provide some sense of direction as compared to the ambiguous nature of traditional talk therapies. For example, asking clients to use sports metaphors or using a narrative approach like songwriting could help the client make sense of their presenting concerns.

Utilizing games, recreation, and adventured-based counseling activities in a group setting can serve as a catalyst for processing behavioral patterns or emotional responses. Applying the theoretical framework of experiential education, adventure-based counseling activities allow clients to be active participants in the therapeutic process by providing opportunities for hands-on adventure activities, self and group motivation, and exposure to real and natural consequences and by promoting reflection and integration of knowledge and skills (Gass et al., 2012).

Gass et al. (2012) suggest five areas in which adventure-based activities and experiences are used to enhance the therapeutic process: insight, motivation, skill development, strengthening concept of self, and frame and metaphor. Placing groups of adolescents in an unfamiliar environment and presenting them with unfamiliar challenges can contribute to improvements in communication, problem-solving, leadership, and motor skill development. When faced with challenges and resulting consequences, participants typically gain insight into thoughts and behaviors and, at the same time, gain motivation and confidence when overcoming challenges (Gass et al., 2012). These experiences also provide opportunities for immediate feedback, which allows clients to understand the causes and effects of their behaviors and emotions on other people and the environment. Regardless of the experience or activity, they serve as a metaphor for real-life situations that create meaning for the participant and guide the learning experience.

Conclusion

Adolescence is a unique transitional period that involves significant biological, psychological, and social development. At age 16, teens are particularly vulnerable to risk factors that can impede their development across several dimensions. However, they are also incredibly resilient and have the capacity to build skills that can serve as protective factors throughout their life. It is imperative that counselors working with this population understand the dynamic, complex developmental process that adolescents experience. Counselors have a unique opportunity to create an environment ripe for exploration and growth: a context where adolescents can truly thrive.

References

American Psychological Association. (2010). Children, youth, and families. https://www.apa.org/pi/ses/resources/publications/children-families

Bell, E. C., Marcus, D. K., & Goodlad, J. K. (2013). Are the parts as good as the whole? A meta-analysis of component treatment studies. *Journal of Consulting and Clinical Psychology*, *81*, 722–736. https://doi-org.ezproxy.proxy.library.oregonstate.edu/10.1037/a0033004

Bracey, J. R., Bámaca, M. Y., & Umaña-Taylor, A. J. (2004). Examining ethnic identity and self-esteem among biracial and monoracial adolescents. *Journal of Youth and Adolescence*, *33*(2), 123–132. https://doi.org/10.1023/B:JOYO.0000013424.93635.68

Brix, N., Ernst, A., Lauridsen, L. L. B., Parner, E., Støvring, H., Olsen, J., Henriksen, T. B., & Ramlau-Hansen, C. H. (2019). Timing of puberty in boys and girls: A population-based study. *Paediatric and Perinatal Epidemiology*, *33*(1), 70–78. https://doi.org/10.1111/ppe.12507

Casey, B. J., & Caudle, K. (2013). The teenage brain: Self-control. *Current Directions in Psychological Science: A Journal of the American Psychological Society*, *22*(2), 82–87. https://doi.org/10.1177/0963721413480170

Centers for Disease Control and Prevention. (2019a, May 29). *Sleep and health*. www.cdc.gov/healthyschools/sleep.htm

Centers for Disease Control and Prevention. (2019b). *Youth risk behavior survey*. www.cdc.gov/YRBSS

Cook, R. E., Nielson, M. G., Martin, C. L., & DeLay, D. (2019). Early adolescent gender development: The differential effects of felt pressure from parents, peers, and the self. *Journal of Youth and Adolescence*, *48*(10), 1912–1923. https://doi.org/10.1007/s10964-019-01122-y

Copeland, W. E., Shanahan, L., Costello, E. J., & Angold, A. (2011). Cumulative prevalence of psychiatric disorders by young adulthood: A prospective cohort analysis from the Great Smoky Mountains study. *Journal of the American Academy of Child and Adolescent Psychiatry*, *50*(3), 252–261. https://doi.org/10.1016/j.jaac.2010.12.014

Copeland, W. E., Wolke, D., Angold, A., & Costello, E. J. (2013). Adult psychiatric and suicide outcomes of bullying and being bullied by peers in childhood and adolescence. *Journal of the American Medical Association Psychiatry*, *70*, 419–426. https://doi.org/10.1001/jamapsychiatry.2013.504

Crone, E. A., & Steinbeis, N. (2017). Neural perspectives on cognitive control development during childhood and adolescence. *Trends in Cognitive Sciences*, *21*(3), 205–215. https://doi.org/10.1016/j.tics.2017.01.003

Cross, W. E., Jr. (1995). The psychology of nigrescence: Revising the Cross model. In J. G. Ponterotto, J. M. Casas, L. A. Suzuki, & C. M. Alexander (Eds.), *Handbook of multicultural counseling* (pp. 93–122). SAGE.

Dahl, R. E., & Gunnar, M. R. (2009). Heightened stress responsiveness and emotional reactivity during pubertal maturation: Implications for psychopathology. *Development and Psychopathology*, *21*(1), 1–6. https://doi.org/10.1017/S0954579409000017

Else-Quest, N. M., & Morse, E. (2015). Ethnic variations in parental ethnic socialization and adolescent ethnic identity: A longitudinal study. *Cultural Diversity & Ethnic Minority Psychology*, *21*(1), 54–64. https://doi.org/10.1037/a0037820

Erikson, E. F. (1980). *Identity and the life cycle*. Norton.

French, S. E., Seidman, E., Allen, L., & Aber, J. L. (2006). The development of ethnic identity during adolescence. *Developmental Psychology*, *42*(1), 1–10. https://doi.org/10.1037/0012-1649.42.1.1

Gardner, B. J. (2015). Play therapy with adolescents. In D. A. Crenshaw & A. L. Stewart (Eds.), *Play therapy: A comprehensive guide to theory and practice* (pp. 439–451). Guilford Press.

Gass, M. A., Gillis, H. L., & Russell, K. C. (2012). *Adventure therapy: Theory, research, and practice*. Taylor & Francis Group.

Gazzaniga, M. S. (2018). *Psychological science* (6th ed.). W.W. Norton.

Giedd, J. N. (2015). The amazing teen brain. *Scientific American*, *312*(6), 32–37. https://doi.org/10.1038/scientificamerican0615-32

Graber, J. A., Seeley, J. R., Brooks-Gunn, J., & Lewinson, P. M. (2004). Is pubertal timing associated with psychopathology in young adulthood? *Journal of the American Academy of Child and Adolescent Psychiatry*, *43*(6), 718–726. https://doi.org/10.1097/01.chi.0000120022.14101.11

Graham, S. (2018). Race/ethnicity and social adjustment of adolescents: How (not if) school diversity matters. *Educational Psychologist*, *53*(2), 64–77. https://doi.org/10.1080/00461520.2018.1428805

Guthrie, B. J., Young, A. M., Boyd, C. J., & Kintner, E. K. (2002). Ebb and flow when navigating adolescence: Predictors of daily hassles among African-American adolescent girls. *Journal for Specialists in Pediatric Nursing*, *7*(4), 143–152. https://doi.org/10.1111/j.1744-6155.2002.tb00170.x

Helms, J. E. (1995). An update of Helm's White and people of color racial identity models. In J. G. Ponterotto, J. M. Casas, L. A. Suzuki, & C. M. Alexander (Eds.), *Handbook of multicultural counseling* (pp. 181–198). SAGE.

Hollenstein, T., & Lougheed, J. P. (2013). Beyond storm and stress: Typicality, transactions, timing, and temperament to account for adolescent change. *American Psychologist*, *68*(6), 444–454. https://doi.org/10.1037/a0033586

Huang, C. Y., & Stormshak, E. A. (2011). A longitudinal examination of early adolescence ethnic identity trajectories. *Cultural Diversity & Ethnic Minority Psychology*, *17*(3), 261–270. https://doi.org/10.1037/a0023882

Irizarry, J. G., & Antrop-González, R. (2013). RicanStruction sites: Race, space, and place in the education of DiaspoRican youth. *Taboo: Journal of Culture and Education*, *13*(1), 77–96. https://doi.org/10.31390/taboo.13.1.07

Jones, S. C., Lee, D. B., Gaskin, A. L., & Neblett, E. W. (2014). Emotional response profiles to racial discrimination: Does racial identity predict affective patterns? *Journal of Black Psychology*, *40*(4), 334–358. https://doi.org/10.1177/0095798413488628

Juraska, J. M, & Willing, J. (2016). Pubertal onset as a critical transition for neural development and cognition. *Brain Research*, *1654*(Pt. B), 87–94. https://doi.org/10.1016/j.brainres.2016.04.012

Kaltiala-Heino, R., Koivisto, A.-M., Marttunen, M., & Fröjd, S. (2011). Pubertal timing and substance use in middle adolescence: A 2-year follow-up study: Pubertal timing effects: A new generation of studies. *Journal of Youth and Adolescence, 40*(10), 1288–1301.

Klaczynski, P. A., & Gordon, D. H. (1996). Self-serving influences on adolescents' evaluations of belief-relevant evidence. *Journal of Experimental Child Psychology*, *62*(3), 317–339. https://doi.org/10.1006/jecp.1996.0033

Kohli, R., & Solorzano, D. G. (2012). Teachers, please learn our names! Racial microagressions and the K-12 classroom. *Race, Ethnicity and Education, 15,* 441–462. https://doi.org/10.1080/13613324.2012.674026

Labouliere, C. D., Reyes, J. P., Shirk, S., & Karver, M. (2017). Therapeutic alliance with depressed adolescents: Predictor or outcome? Disentangling temporal confounds to understand early improvement. *Journal of Clinical Child & Adolescent Psychology*, *46*(4), 600–610. https://doi.org/10.1080/15374416.2015.1041594

Lambert, S. F., Herman, K. C., Bynum, M. S., & Ialongo, N. S. (2009). Perceptions of racism and depressive symptoms in African American adolescents: The role of perceived academic and social control. *Journal of Youth and Adolescence*, *38*(4), 519–531. https://doi.org/10.1007/s10964-009-9393-0

Larson, R. W., & Brown, J. R. (2007). Emotional development in adolescence: What can be learned from a high school theater program? *Child Development*, *78*(4), 1083–1099. https://doi.org/10.1111/j.1467-8624.2007.01054.x

Laycock, J., & Meeran, K. (2013). *Integrated endocrinology*. Wiley-Blackwell.

Leaper, C., & Brown, C. S. (2014). Sexism in schools. *Advances in Child Development and Behavior*, *47*, 189–223.

Lee, Y., & Styne, D. (2013). Influences on the onset and tempo of puberty in human beings and implications for adolescent psychological development. *Hormones and Behavior*, *64*(2), 250–261. https://doi.org/10.1016/j.yhbeh.2013.03.014

Lenroot, R. K., & Giedd, J. N. (2006). Brain development in children and adolescents: Insights from anatomical magnetic resonance imaging. *Neuroscience and Biobehavioral Reviews*, *30*(6), 718–729. https://doi.org/10.1016/j.neubiorev.2006.06.001

Liben, L. S., & Bigler, R. S. (2002). The developmental course of gender differentiation. *Monographs of the Society for Research in Child Development*, *67*, 1–146. https://www.jstor.org/stable/3181530

Louzada, F., & Menna-Barreto, L. (2003). Sleep-wake cycle expression in adolescence: Influences of social context. *Biological Rhythm Research*, *34*(2), 129–136. https://doi.org/10.1076/brhm.34.2.129.14490

Lowry, R., Eaton, D. K., Foti, K., McKnight-Eily, L., Perry, G., & Galuska, D. A. (2012). Association of sleep duration with obesity among U.S. high school students. *Journal of Obesity*, *2012*, 476914–476919. https://doi.org/10.1155/2012/476914

Marcia, J. E. (1993). The ego identity status approach to ego identity. In *Ego identity: A handbook for psychosocial research* (pp. 3–21). Springer. https://doi.org/10.1007/978-1-4613-8330-7_1

Marshall, W. A., & Tanner, J. M. (1970). Variations in the pattern of pubertal changes in boys. *Archives of Disease in Childhood*, *45*(239), 13–23. https://doi.org/10.1136/adc.45.239.13

McCormick, E. M., & Telzer, E. H. (2017). Adaptive adolescent flexibility: Neurodevelopment of decision-making and learning in a risky context. *Journal of Cognitive Neuroscience*, *29*(3), 413–423. https://doi.org/10.1162/jocn_a_01061

Mendle, J., Harden, K. P., Brooks-Gunn, J., & Graber, J. A. (2010). Development's tortoise and hare. *Developmental Psychology*, *46*(5), 1341–1353. https://doi.org/10.1037/a0020205

Moses, J. O., Villodas, M. T., & Villodas, F. (2020). Black and proud: The role of ethnic-racial identity in the development of future expectations among at-risk adolescents. *Cultural Diversity and Ethnic Minority Psychology*, *26*(1), 112–123. https://doi.org/10.1037/cdp0000273

Murad, M. H., Elamin, M. B., Garcia, M. Z., Mullan, R. J., Murad, A., Erwin, P. J., & Montori, V. M. (2010). Hormonal therapy and sex reassignment: A systematic review and meta-analysis of quality of life and psychosocial outcomes. *Clinical Endocrinology*, *72*(2), 214–231. https://doi.org/10.1111/j.13652265.2009.03625.x

Nakkula, M., & Toshalis, E. (2008). *Understanding youth: Adolescent development for educators*. Harvard Education Press.

Paris, D. (2012). Culturally sustaining pedagogy: A needed change in stance, terminology, and practice. *Educational Researcher*, *41*(3), 93–97. https://doi.org/10.3102/0013189X12441244

Paruthi, S., Brooks, L. J., D'Ambrosio, C., Hall, W. A., Kotagal, S., Lloyd, R. M., Malow, B. A., Maski, K., Nichols, C., Quan, S. F., Rosen, C. L., Troester, M. M., & Wise, M. S. (2016). Recommended amount of sleep for pediatric populations: A consensus statement of the American

Academy of Sleep Medicine. *Journal of Clinical Sleep Medicine*, *12*(6), 785–786. https://doi.org/10.5664/jcsm.5866

Phinney, J. S., & Ong, A. D. (2007). Conceptualization and measurement of ethnic identity. *Journal of Counseling Psychology*, *54*(3), 271–281. https://doi.org/10.1037/0022-0167.54.3.271

Piaget, J. (1936). *Origins of intelligence in the child*. Routledge & Kegan Paul.

Poteat, V. P., Calzo, J. P., & Yoshikawa, H. (2016). Promoting youth agency through dimensions of gay–straight alliance involvement and conditions that maximize associations. *Journal of Youth and Adolescence*, *45*(7), 1438–1451. https://doi.org/10.1007/s10964-016-0421-6

Quintana, S. M. (2007). Racial and ethnic identity. *Journal of Counseling Psychology*, *54*(3), 259–270. https://doi.org/10.1037/0022-0167.54.3.259

Ratts, M. J., Singh, A. A., Nassar-McMillan, S., Butler, K. S., & McCullough, J. R. (2016). Multicultural and social justice counseling competencies: Guidelines for the counseling profession. *Journal of Multicultural Counseling and Development*, *44*(1), 28–48. https://doi.org/10.1002/jmcd.12035

Reynolds, B. M., & Juvonen, J. (2012). Pubertal timing fluctuations across middle school: Implications for girls' psychological health. *Journal of Youth and Adolescence*, *41*(6), 677–690. https://doi.org/10.1007/s10964-011-9687-x

Rivas-Drake, D., Markstrom, C., Syed, M., Lee, R. M., Umana-Taylor, A. J., Yip, T., Seaton, E. K., Quintana, S., Schwartz, S. J., & French, S. (2014). Ethnic and racial identity in adolescence: Implications for psychosocial, academic, and health outcomes: Ethnic and racial identity in child development. *Child Development*, *85*(1), 40–57. https://doi.org/10.1111/cdev.12200

Rubin, K. H., Coplan, R. J., Bowker, J. C., & Menzer, M. (2010). Social withdrawal and shyness. In P. K. Smith & C. H. Hart (Eds.), *The Wiley Blackwell handbook of childhood social development* (pp. 434–452). Wiley-Blackwell. https://doi.org/10.1002/9781444390933.ch23

Rueger, S. Y., & Jenkins, L. N. (2014). Effects of peer victimization on psychological and academic adjustment in early adolescence. *School Psychology Quarterly*, *29*, 77–88. https://doi.org/10.1037/spq0000036

Schneider, W., & Bullock, M. (2009). *Human development from early childhood to early adulthood: Findings from a 20-year longitudinal study*. Psychology Press.

Sieving, R. E., McRee, A., McMorris, B. J., Shlafer, R. J., Gower, A. L., Kappa, H. M., Beckman, K. J., Doty, J. L., Plowman, S. L., & Resnick, M. D. (2017). Youth-adult connectedness: A key protective factor for adolescent health. *American Journal of Preventive Medicine*, *52*, S275–S278. https://doi.org/10.1016/j.amepre.2016.07.037

Sigelman, C. K., & Rider, E. A. (2015). *Life-span human development* (8th ed.). Cengage Learning.

Spear, L. P. (2013). Adolescent neurodevelopment. *Journal of Adolescent Health*, *52*(2), S7–S13. https://doi.org/10.1016/j.jadohealth.2012.05.006

Steinberg, L., & Monahan, K. C. (2007). Age differences in resistance to peer influence. *Developmental Psychology*, *43*(6), 1531–1543. https://doi.org/10.1037/0012-1649.43.6.1531

Sumter, S. R., Bokhorst, C. L., Steinberg, L., & Westenberg, P. M. (2009). The developmental pattern of resistance to peer influence in adolescence: Will the teenager ever be able to resist? *Journal of Adolescence*, *32*(4), 1009–1021. https://doi.org/ 10.1016/j.adolescence.2008.08.010

Takizawa, R., Maughan, B., & Arseneault, L. (2014). Adult health outcomes of childhood bullying victimization: Evidence from a 5-decade longitudinal British cohort. *American Journal of Psychiatry*, *171*, 777–784. https://doi.org/10.1176/appi.ajp.2014.13101401

The Trevor Project. (2021). *The national survey on LGBTQ youth mental health*. www.thetrevorproject.org/survey-2021

Toomey, R. B., Card, N. A., & Casper, D. M. (2014). Peers' perceptions of gender nonconformity. *The Journal of Early Adolescence*, *34*(4), 463–485. https://doi.org/10.1177/0272431613495446

U.S. Department of Education: National Center for Educational Statistics. (2018). *Student reports of bullying and cyber-bullying: Results from the 2017 school crime supplement to the national crime victimization survey (NCES 2015–056)*. US Dept of Education. https://nces.ed.gov/pubs2019/2019054.pd

Wahlstrom, D., Collins, P., White, T., & Luciana, M. (2010). Developmental changes in dopamine neurotransmission in adolescence: Behavioral implications and issues in assessment. *Brain and Cognition*, *72*(1), 146–159. https://doi.org/10.1016/j.bandc.2009.10.013

Wampold, B. E., & Imel, Z. (2015). *The great psychotherapy debate: The evidence for what makes psychotherapy work* (2nd ed.). Lawrence Erlbaum.

Werner, E. E. (1992). The children of Kauai: Resiliency and recovery in adolescence and adulthood. *Journal of Adolescent Health*, *13*(4), 262–268. https://doi.org/10.1016/1054-139X(92)90157-7

White, A. E., Moeller, J., Ivcevic, Z., & Brackett, M. A. (2018). Gender identity and sexual identity labels used by U.S. high school students: A co-occurrence network analysis. *Psychology of Sexual Orientation and Gender Diversity*, *5*(2), 243–252. https://doi.org/10.1037/sgd 0000266

Xie, L., Kang, H., Takahiro, T., Rashid, D., Maiken, N., Xu, Q., Chen, M. J., Liao, Y., Thiyagarajan, M., O'Donnell, J., Christensen, D. J., Nicholson, C., & Iliff, J. J. (2013). Sleep drives metabolite clearance from the adult brain. *Science (American Association for the Advancement of Science)*, *342*(6156), 373–377. https://doi.org/10.1126/science.1241224

Chapter 7

The 17-Year-Old

Ryan D. Foster and Chris Wilder

Todd was a 17-year-old White heterosexual cisgender male whose mother had called the community counseling center a week prior to set up an intake appointment. When I (RDF) spoke to her to set up the intake, she stated that her son expressed a desire for counseling to deal with some lingering issues at home. The assistant director, Bobbie, completed the intake with Todd. Toward the end of the intake, Bobbie met with me to discuss Todd's preferences for a counselor so that we could place him on the schedule. Bobbie had a wry smile on her face, something that I knew meant she had a quirky idea in her head. She stated that Todd had voiced his preference for a male counselor with a beard, "like Freud," and one who would help him interpret his dreams. I asked Bobbie, "Did he Google me?" She chuckled because I was a practicing Jungian counselor – close enough to Freud, we decided – who often practiced dreamwork, and, yes, I had a full beard. I went with Bobbie back to the counseling room, introduced myself to Todd, and put him on the schedule for the following week.

Todd was like a lot of the clients I (RDF) have counseled who are 17 years old. He was ambitious and confused about the future, excited to turn 18 and *finally* be free, carried quite a bit of unfinished business from past trauma, and engaged willingly and deeply in the process of psychotherapy. During some moments with him, I felt a sense of childlike qualities that pulled us both back to appropriately unrefined parts of his personality. At other times, Todd would share a perception that seemed totally adultlike and depth-oriented. More than anything, my work with Todd was filled with some of the most enjoyable and heartbreaking clinical interactions I have had in my 15 years as a psychotherapist.

In this chapter, using Todd and others as examples, we will discuss the tumultuous age of 17 from a developmental perspective and relate these concepts to their counseling needs. We will review challenges and risk factors that adolescents at this age may experience. Finally, we will introduce you to best practices in counseling and psychotherapy for your 17-year-old clients.

Physical Development

At the age of 17, a few physical changes are complete, and some are notably continuing from earlier ages. Before examining these changes, it is important to note that not all

DOI: 10.4324/9781003196297-10

17-year-olds may follow the typical path of development we describe. For example, children with chromosomal or genetic abnormalities may have differences in physical development. In addition, adolescents who identify as trans may seek medical intervention that impacts typical physical development associated with their biological sex.

Most adolescents have now made it through puberty (Berk, 2018), and it is typical for teens to have reached their full height. Their voices may continue to change with some squeaks and squawks here and there. In addition, their body hair keeps growing, both in places they have been used to seeing it grow and in new spots, too, but thankfully for them, it is in less surprising spots than what they noticed during the last few years.

They continue to modify their behaviors related to physiology, as well. The autonomy that they tend to have allows them to decide how to meet their physical needs, and this liberty can sometimes lead to outcomes contributing to a decline in health and well-being. It is typical for 17-year-olds to spend less time engaging in physical recreation than at any other time in their lives thus far, a decline that began when they were 9 years old (Wall et al., 2011). They are probably not getting enough sleep even though they need around 9 hours per day (Berk, 2018), and having access to devices that emit blue light like cell phones, tablets, and laptops contributes significantly to sleeplessness (Bruni et al., 2015). Finally, many older adolescents are not meeting their nutritional needs (Piernas & Popkin, 2011; Ritchie et al., 2007), a side effect of having greater access to convenience stores packed full of energy drinks, trips to Starbucks, deliciously tempting fast food, and a reduction in frequency with which they sit down with their families to eat meals together.

Brain Development

Behind the mature appearance and mostly completed physical growth is a brain that will not complete the maturing process for another 5 to 7 years. In typically developing teens, the brain achieves its largest physical size in early adolescence: for individuals assigned female at birth (AFAB) about age 11, and those assigned male at birth (AMAB) around age 14 (U.S. Department of Health and Human Services, 2020). Little is known about specific brain maturation for the 17-year-old. We do know that during adolescence, the brain reaches its peak physical size yet continues to mature, growing and pruning some synaptic connections and refining others (National Institute of Mental Health, n.d.). The lack of brain maturity may leave many adults failing to understand why teenagers often behave in irrational, impulsive, and unsafe manners, ignoring consequences of their choices. In this section, we will review maturation processes of the adolescent brain, explore physiological processes affecting brain maturation, discuss external influences on maturation including substance use and nutrition, and review typical adolescent behavioral expressions that occur as a result of a maturing brain.

Please Pardon the Construction

The transition from childhood to adulthood can be difficult and rewarding for the teenager experiencing the growth and for the caregiving adults. Notable changes happen hormonally, intellectually, physically, and socially. Heredity, environment, hormones, nutrition, sleep, stress, and drug use, including alcohol, nicotine, and caffeine, play a critical role in maturing adolescent brains (Arain et al., 2013; Silveri et al., 2008).

Significant structural changes occur as the brain matures. Most brain networks are locally organized during childhood. During adolescence, the maturing brain expands distribution networks and distant regions strengthen their connections. Thus, communication between regions improves as the brain loses gray matter through pruning of unused neurons and synapses (Arain et al., 2013; Karcher & Barch, 2020). While gray matter is decreasing, white matter is increasing, signifying improved efficiency in how various regions of the brain communicate with each other. Gray matter is found primarily on the cortical or surface of the brain, whereas white matter is found in the subcortical or deeper tissues of the brain. An increase in white matter volume suggests strengthened, improved communication between brain regions through a process known as myelination. Myelin comprises proteins and a fatty substance that acts as a covering or sheath that forms around nerves and optimizes transmission of electrical impulses (Arain et al., 2013; Karcher & Barch, 2020; Konrad et al., 2013; Silveri et al., 2008).

Multiple studies demonstrated that the myelination process is a developmental progression that begins before birth and continues through adolescence into early adulthood. The process begins in the back of the brain and works its way to the front (Arain et al., 2013; Giedd, 2004; Johnson et al., 2009). The prefrontal cortex is the seat of executive functioning and is vital but not limited to problem-solving, impulse control, managing intense emotions, and considering consequences of behavioral choices. These processes are the last to mature and explain why impulsive risk-taking and novel behaviors are more predominant in teenagers than adults. Adolescent prefrontal cortex circuitry is still under construction; thus, adolescents may understand an activity is dangerous yet still engage in risky behavior. It also explains why teenagers come home from school without their textbook and realize at 9:30 p.m. they have a test the next day!

On more than one occasion in my time as a high school counselor, I (CW) received late night and weekend phone calls from students and/or parents asking me to let them into the school building to retrieve a textbook or other essential study item because they forgot about a test the next day. This was a valuable learning experience for students, one that hopefully helped them better plan for their next exam, and for parents, who were surprised to learn that as a school counselor, I did not have keys to the building.

Internal and External Influences

It is widely accepted that a surge in the sex hormones estrogen, progesterone, and testosterone contributes to changes in secondary sex characteristics. Sex hormones also contribute to brain maturation and myelinization and affect behavior, learning, and memory. Interrupting the normal maturational processes through poor nutrition and substance use can have significant consequences for a maturing brain (Arain et al., 2013; Silveri et al., 2008). Neurons and connective networks may be damaged, and teens who rely on substances to manage stress are at risk for anxiety and depression and fail to learn from experiences gained by responsible decision-making (Berk, 2018).

Cognitive Development

Cognitive development refers to the maturation of thinking processes, perception, reasoning, and meaning-making. Brains of 17-year-olds are growing new cells, white matter is increasing, gray matter is decreasing, and the interface and communication among brain regions are strengthening, resulting in more efficient brains (Arain et al., 2013; Karcher & Barch, 2021; Konrad et al., 2013; Silveri et al., 2008). An ability to hold in less self-centered ideas and engage in more complex thinking processes marks late adolescence and allows 17-year-olds to explore wide-ranging global concepts like ethics, justice, policy, morality, and political issues that require abstract reasoning and thinking. Their views may be idealistic with little tolerance for opposing opinions, yet 17-year-olds are framing their identities and charting courses of who they shall become (Berk, 2018; Ciccia et al., 2009; Ragelienė, 2016).

Cognitively, 17-year-olds are in a stage of development known as the formal operations stage (Inhelder & Piaget, 1955/1958). Piaget speculated that children/teenagers were not only adding to their existing knowledge base but also were undergoing a qualitative shift in how they think. The ability to think abstractly, hypothetically, and critically denotes the formal operations stage. For example, my (RDF) client Todd would often opine out loud about his dad's physical abuse and its relationship to an unjust world for innocent children.

Reliance on crystallized intelligence (CI) is a common cognitive-developmental feature in late childhood and early adolescence. CI relies on previously gained information and is reflected through memory, vocabulary, and general knowledge (Brown, 2016). Examples of CI include memorizing facts, solving equations, reading, and riding a bike. CI depends on an ability to assimilate experiences and build upon acquired knowledge and skills (Berk, 2018; Ciccia et al., 2009; Kuhn, 2006; Office of Population Affairs, Department of Health and Human Services, n.d.). For 17-year-olds, this can create internal. Their CI is operational; however, it is built upon earlier experiences. As they are exposed to an increasing number and depth of adult experiences and decisions, they sometimes lack a solid foundation that guides how they should move through these new adventures and choices. For example, applying to college for first-generation teens from impoverished backgrounds can be immensely overwhelming. They know where they want to be and can imagine it fully, but the path to get there is complex, and they have little experiential knowledge to navigate the process.

Fluid intelligence is an emerging attribute in late adolescence and includes an ability to reason and distinguish patterns. Younger children and early adolescents can grasp some abstract concepts. However, the maturing brains of late adolescents are better equipped to engage in more malleable abstract thinking or an ability to problem-solve that is not dependent on specific knowledge or experience (Cochrane et al., 2019). Abstract thinking is considered a higher-order reasoning skill and includes creating, analyzing, reasoning, problem-solving, and speaking figuratively. Abstract thinking extends beyond tangible certainties. Closely related to abstract thinking is metacognition, or thinking about thinking, and it refers to an ability to understand, evaluate, and critically analyze oneself as a learner and thinker. For example, a successful strategy in preparing for SAT testing, a common experience at 17 years old, is planning *how* to study for the exam given its novel testing style.

Emotional Development

One of the more observable features of maturing 17-year-olds is emotional development. With a growing sense of independence and an increased interest in romantic partnerships and sex (Berk, 2018; Office of Population Affairs, Department of Health and Human Services, n.d.; Salerno et al., 2015), they may have a clearer understanding of their sexual orientation and develop a deeper capacity for caring and empathy toward others. They may be prone to sadness or depression, affecting academic performance and perhaps leading to alcohol or drug use. Learning to identify and manage intense emotions is an important task of healthy emotional development as 17-year-olds enter young adulthood. This period is vital to skill-building, during which these teens are working to improve life skills, integrate novel experiences like romantic relationships, and explore educational and career decisions while gaining insight into self and others. Reality does not impede optimism about the future as can be seen in the following example.

It was late March of his senior year in high school when Chris finally realized that high school would be over soon and he needed to do something with his life. All his friends were going to college, and he decided he should, too. Only one of his family members had finished high school, let alone attend college. He discussed his college options with his parents, a music scholarship to a private school over 3 hours away. He decided this would be a good fit. Chris's parents objected. They had not saved money for his education, and besides, there was a community college in town, and they insisted he attend there if he was to go to college. Rejecting their wishes to stay home, Chris told his family that he was going away to college regardless of their opinion and lack of financial support. That was my (CW) story. I did not know what to expect and had no experience to guide my decision-making. Planning to attend college was foreign to me. How would I pay for it? What did I need to do to prepare? I should have asked myself multiple important questions, but I did not have an experiential base from which to ask. As I look back at that time in my life, I ask myself, "What were you thinking?"

Maturation of the frontal lobe makes it likely that 17-year-olds understand consequences of their actions but still make risky choices. They remain susceptible to peer influence and emotional reactivity, which complicates their ability to organize thoughts and make good decisions. Decision-making presents unique challenges and opportunities for late adolescent teens. Because synaptic pruning and strengthening is an ongoing process into early adulthood, teens, more so than adults, are likely to make emotional decisions. When allowed to think and reflect on a decision, late adolescent teenagers are likely to make informed and responsible decisions. The need for quick, in-the-heat-of-the-moment decisions tends to have more emotions tied to the process with little regard to outcomes (Berk, 2018; Ciccia et al., 2009; Office of Population Affairs, Department of Health and Human Services, n.d.).

Alex was a biracial, cisgender male. His father was African American and his mother of Hispanic heritage. Alex had two younger brothers and came from an intact family who regularly practiced Christianity. I (CW) saw Alex and his parents in my office after an incident left his parents confused about what happened and concerned about his future. Shortly before his 17th birthday, Alex sneaked out of the family home and took his mother's car without permission. He drove to another city to "rescue" his girlfriend. She was upset with her parents over restrictions placed on her due to academic problems. Alex drove over two hours from his home to pick her up, and on his way back home, law enforcement pulled them over. Neither one had a driver's license, and police held them in custody until their parents could pick them up.

During our family session, Alex's parents could not understand what possessed their first-born, football-playing, honor-roll, church-attending teenager to act so impulsively. In therapy, Alex tried his best to explain but struggled to articulate his motives in a way that satisfied his parents' need for answers. Alex stated he wanted to get his girlfriend out of a hostile environment where her stepfather had imposed restrictions that they thought were excessive. Alex succumbed to the emotionality of his girlfriend, allowed his own emotions to take precedence over rational thought, and acted impulsively. He knew it was wrong to drive without a license but felt compelled to get his girlfriend out of her house. He had not considered how he would explain to his parents how his girlfriend ended up at the family home. Biology, environment, and protective factors like parenting and caregiver guidance affect multifaceted emotional states of teenagers (Arain et al., 2013; Berk, 2018). Youth emotional states may vacillate rapidly, and unpredictable moods can lead to increased conflict with adults and siblings.

Furthermore, teens become more self-conscious about their physical appearance and may struggle as they compare their bodies to peers and young adults (Berk, 2018; Bos et al., 2020; Salerno et al., 2015). Emily was a 17-year-old cisgender Asian American female who came to counseling with me (CW) reporting symptoms of depression and anxiety. During intake, Emily reported she had been experiencing a wide range of emotions, including anger and frustration, accompanied by bouts of unexplained crying. Emily came from a supportive home. She had close friendships, was involved in several extracurricular activities, and made good grades. Over several weeks of therapy, Emily realized she would get angry with herself after scrolling through her social media accounts and comparing her appearance to that of friends and social influencers. The snapshots of thin, attractive people "living their best life" often led to negative self-talk about her body and life.

Social and Relationship Development

Seventeen-year-olds explore their identities in the context of social groups (Erikson, 1993). As 17-year-olds work toward greater autonomy, they find that peer groups have a major influence on development of independence (Tanti et al., 2011). Many 17-year-olds have been driving for a year or so and may be working or looking for jobs, and these social contexts can open up their role and ego identity processes even more as they are no longer bound to the confines of a home or school environment. Cliques and subgroups end at this age and are somewhat a thing of the past, allowing these teens to ensure goodness of fit between their own ego identity and "the sameness and continuity of one's meaning for others" (Erikson, 1993, p. 94).

Technology is a contemporary medium through which identity development takes place. Modern adolescents are considered digital natives, having never known a world in which technology was not handheld, immediately responsive, and available to anybody who could afford it. Although 17-year-olds have a capacity to experience deeper relational intimacy as they grow, leading them to seek far more time with friends than with parents and family, the ways in which they tend to seek it is through digital connection. Adolescents have easy access to devices that connect digitally and allow them to interact on social media, via text messaging, and through other digital communication platforms. In 2018, around 95% of teens reportedly owned a smartphone, and most of them have built a suite of social media apps, with rates of use among adolescents in a Pew survey as follows: YouTube (85%), Instagram (72%), Snapchat (69%), Facebook (51%), and Twitter (32%) (Anderson & Jiang, 2018). We speculate that using these and newer social media platforms to connect with their peers has skyrocketed since the 2018 Pew survey.

In our clinical experiences, we have no conclusion as to whether the influence of social media and digital nativism on identity is overall beneficial or consequential. With any social endeavor, there are risks and challenges, opportunities and meaning. It seems to us that digital socialization makes all these potentials more immediate and potent for 17-year-olds. We might sound cliché in stating that technology moves so rapidly and social media apps change so quickly in their frequency of use – one example is adolescent use of Facebook, which dropped around 20% within a three-year timespan of Pew surveys (Anderson & Jian, 2018; Lenhart, 2015) – that it is hard for a clinician to have a grounded sense of how changes in social connection impact older adolescents broadly.

Culture and Identity Development

Increasingly, therapists are called to view clients through a lens of intersectionality, that is, viewing them holistically and in the complexity of their interacting identities and experiences. Therefore, it is essential to consider how aspects of a 17-year-old's culture and identity influence each other and, beyond that, to what degree a client adopts each intersecting aspect of who they believe they are and what their family expects of them, and to what degree they are even considering their identities and values. Modern adolescents tend to lean toward self-identification, and in that respect, therapists might find that their clients are experimenting with their contextual views of themselves. Therefore, one main concept for therapists to consider in terms of culture is how a client experiences their intersections of culture, in what ways they wish to experiment with expressing them, and how they believe they are perceived by others. For example, an African American adolescent cisgender male who is walking home from school in an impoverished urban neighborhood is thinking about safety and survival in ways that impact how he thinks about who he is and how he fits into the greater community and the world, and he views his future quite differently than others from a non-minoritized culture. Similarly, a 17-year-old diagnosed with Down syndrome perceives their job and career identities and opportunities in a more limited fashion due to internalized societal messages than a person who has a more privileged ability status.

A central struggle at this age in terms of various influences on an intersectional identity such as racial and ethnic identity, sexual and gender identity, ability differences, socioeconomic status, and religious and spiritual identity is couched in identity vs. role confusion (Erikson, 1993). Because 17-year-olds are often on the tail end of this phase, they may be experiencing consequences of an unresolved identity. They may appear to have no idea what they want to do with the rest of their lives. They may seem rather surface in their thoughts about themselves and their future. On the other hand, they may seem deeply committed to who they are, how they describe themselves, and what they want out of life. However, despite Erikson's use of the word "crisis" in his *labeling* of this period of life, his *description* of what happens is more attuned to words like "exploration" and "commitment" (Kroger, 2012). A typical example of this process is exploration of career decisions as part of seeking their place in adult society.

Four identity statuses have emerged from research regarding Erikson's (1993; see Chapter 1 in this text) exploration and commitment concepts. These identity statuses are directly influenced by elements of an adolescent's intersectional identities. Around age 17, people may have stayed in one of the four statuses since early adolescence, or they may have experimented and transitioned between more than one status (Kroger, 2012). Certainly, the cultural environment of a teen's family and the ways in which that teen adopts those values – and the degree to which that teen thinks that they even have a choice in the matter – has a significant influence on their identity status.

Resources and Protective Factors

Although 17-year-olds seek increased autonomy and depth of relationships with friends and intimate partners, they still benefit from parental involvement and guidance. Authoritative parenting can be an essential resource for older adolescents (Berk, 2018). Practically speaking, these teens need caregivers who support their efforts at autonomy but also will be an empathic and compassionate presence when they screw up. Authoritative parenting tends to result in a teen with a solid self-concept (McKinney et al., 2008), acting as a protective factor for novel challenges. In addition, adolescents who have good relationships with their parents – that is, teens who perceive more positive affect than negative – tend to choose friends who are comparatively as healthy. As an illustration, in a relationship counseling session, I facilitated a dialogue between a mother and her 17-year-old daughter. Mom had previously clearly communicated a curfew to her daughter who violated this rule recently, coming home from a party late. The daughter was upset about the consequences she faced, yet mom provided emotional support for her. This parent-child structure often results in a teen who has a good relationship with her parent.

Friends and peers continue to have a major influence on a 17-year-old's decision-making and value set. Positive relationships with peers can act as protective factors and contribute to academic achievement and social engagement (Berk, 2018). Peers can influence self-concept, as older adolescents rely heavily on matching their view of self with how they believe others view them. In addition, teens who are involved in extracurricular activities at school or through community organizations report less depression and anxiety and greater life satisfaction and optimism (Oberle et al., 2020).

Challenges and Risk Factors

Because a typical 17-year-old is undergoing massive brain changes, including subcortical areas that are maturing whereas prefrontal areas do not match the same level of maturation (Konrad et al., 2013), coupled with a decrease in dopamine production (Giedd, 2004), they are neurobiologically vulnerable to thrill-seeking and risky behaviors – the same old childhood activities just do not do it for them anymore (Powell, 2006). Within this neurobiological context, it is no surprise that the United Nations Office on Drugs and Crime (2018) identified ages 15 to 17 as a "critical risk period for the initiation of substance use" (p. 15). Unfortunately, 70% of deaths around this age are a result of automobile accidents, homicide, suicide, or other physical injuries (Eaton et al., 2012).

Teenagers who experience chronic stress are at greater risk for atypical brain functioning and development that can leave them vulnerable to depression and anxiety (Doane et al., 2013; Sheth et al., 2017) as well as eating disorders, substance abuse, and academic issues (Thapar et al., 2012). Chronic stress during adolescence can emerge from neglect and abuse (Manly et al., 1994), chronic illness of self or family members (Kliewer, 1997; Worsham et al., 1997), perceived discrimination (Trent et al., 2019), and poverty (McLoyd, 1998). Chronic stress appears to be causally related to anhedonia during adolescence (Sheth et al., 2017), a key symptom of depression. Relatedly, adolescents who experience depression are at greater risk for suicidal behavior (Windfuhr et al., 2008). Adverse childhood experiences (ACEs) begin to demonstrate some of their effects and, if unaddressed, can lead to development of severe mental health concerns.

My (RDF) client Todd had several ACEs, including parental divorce at a young age and a physically and emotionally abusive biological father. During counseling, Todd revealed that his mother drank alcohol to the point of inebriation every evening. One particularly shocking moment he discussed was walking in on his mother performing oral sex on a man she was dating after she and her date had consumed alcohol and become drunk. He reported feelings of anhedonia within his relationship with his mother and symptoms of depression in general, which concerned me a great deal. To mitigate this chronic stress in Todd's life, I invited his mother to a parent consultation during which I inquired about her alcohol use. She readily admitted to abusing alcohol and reluctantly accepted my referral to her own individual therapist at our counseling center.

Many of the risks that older adolescents face arise due to their increased autonomy and social engagement with peers and exploring new ways of connecting in dating relationships. One such risk is intimate partner violence. Approximately 9% of high school students reported experiencing dating violence (Eaton et al., 2012). These experiences can lead to increased risk of dating violence, stalking, or rape in adulthood. Relatedly, adolescent use of social media and the internet can expose them to other forms of sexual violation such as sexting (Chassiakos et al., 2016).

One last major area of risk worth discussing is the onset of chronic mental disorders during late adolescence. Symptoms for serious mental health disorders such as bipolar disorder, schizophrenia and other psychotic disorders (U.S. Department of Health and Human Services, 2020), and personality disorders begin to appear in late adolescence (Preston et al., 2021a, 2021b). Clinically, symptoms of mental health disorders can appear differently than they do during adulthood, putting adolescents who suffer from these diagnoses at risk of delayed identification and treatment.

Best Practices for Counseling and Therapy

Therapy at any age is influenced primarily by the therapeutic relationship as an agent of change on which the therapist has the greatest influence (Wampold & Imel, 2015). The nature of that relationship for a 17-year-old depends on several variables, including the setting in which the client is being counseled, their cultural context, and the therapist's theoretical approach. A school counselor will typically have a limited direct care role in the high school setting when compared to an outpatient, residential, or intensive outpatient therapist. It is important to note that there is no one-size-fits-all therapeutic approach to working with a 17-year-old. However, older adolescents have mastered the art of detecting bullshit, so there seems to be one particularly significant factor in a successful therapeutic relationship with them – authenticity (Holliman & Foster, 2016).

Holliman and Foster (2016) identified some distinct ways that therapists could communicate authenticity that can help the believability of the therapist for an adolescent client. One way to model authenticity is through *personal confidence*, meaning that a therapist has worked on a deep level of self-acceptance and feeling of being enough (Rogers, 1961). Another component of authenticity involves *modifying language and speech*, which boils down to therapists saying "what they actually *want* to say to clients" instead of "what they believe they *should* say" (Holliman & Foster, 2016, p. 64).

A third component of authenticity with 17-year-old clients is *dissipating tension*. Holliman and Foster (2016) defined this as "an authentic way of responding to the underlying and often unspoken issues that exist in the [therapeutic] relationship" (p. 64). In dissipating tension, therapists engage in ways that are not additive to a naturally risky relationship. Therapists must genuinely care about the adolescent's world and not what their parents might want the therapist to believe. In addition, a physical environment that is welcome and comfortable for older adolescents is essential. A hearty sense of humor helps with dissipating tension, too. I remember engaging in dissipating tension the moment I met Todd in person after Bobbie had completed the intake. I popped my head into the session room when Bobbie and Todd were finishing up, after it was decided that I would be a good match for his therapist preferences, and said in a deep exuberant voice, "You rang?" somewhat like Lurch from *The Addams Family*.

Going off script is another way of communicating authenticity (Holliman & Foster, 2016). This involves the therapist dropping their basic skills textbook, attending to the ways in which the teen client has created an expected script for the therapist to follow, and then abandoning that script. One script that an adolescent client could assign me (RDF) might be "middle aged counselor who makes too many stupid dad jokes." In going off script, I would intentionally play an opposite role, allowing more room for creativity and far more attention to here-and-now discovery in the therapeutic process.

A final tactic is *sharing the unexpected* (Holliman & Foster, 2016). Many times, counselors try to find something different to *do* during session, and the point here is to find some way to *be* different from other adults in the client's life. Often, adult authority figures are in defense mode with teens. The therapist's intention here should be to engage in an egalitarian relationship in which they demonstrate deep vulnerability and presence, owning up to their mistakes in the therapeutic relationship.

Expressive Arts

When we train counselors to work with older adolescents, often they want to know what techniques and strategies to use. Our go-to strategy with a 17-year-old is to integrate expressive arts approaches with some talk therapy, which seems to be more engaging for this age group (Sori & Heckler, 2003). There are several advantages to using expressive arts with older teenagers. First, therapists can find a vast number of expressive arts activities doing an internet search and quite a few books that provide detailed prompts. Furthermore, many expressive arts activities used with pre-adolescents or younger adolescents can be adapted for use with older adolescents. Second, expressive arts are an indirect route to a teenager's psyche, often gently sneaking past a client's defenses. These activities do not require the adolescent to talk at length about things that may trigger emotions such as shame or parts of their lives about which they feel embarrassed. Third, expressive arts can act as metaphor and symbol and can help teens observe their internal worlds in ways that allow for just enough distance to move through healing processes. Engaging in expressive arts can sometimes feel much safer and more trusting than traditional talk therapy alone. Finally, expressive arts materials, prompts, and processes can be adapted to the client's individual abilities, culture, status, background, preferences, boundaries, and sensory systems.

Humanistic Sandtray Therapy

We have found one particular expressive arts medium to be our go-to strategy with 17-year-old clients: sandtray. Typically, sandtray involves a large rectangular tray filled with sand and a collection of symbolic miniature figures (Armstrong, 2008). Clients are given a prompt to create a scene in the sand that is representative of an aspect of their life. It is common for sandtray therapists to process clients' scenes in the sandtray with them.

Sandtray emerged from Margaret Lowenfeld's world technique, and there are several underlying philosophies to the approach (Homeyer & Sweeney, 2022). The approach that we use is humanistic sandtray therapy (HST; Armstrong, 2008; Armstrong et al., 2017; Foster, in press). HST is based on a blend of person-centered and Gestalt theories and is a non-directive form of sandtray processing. In HST, therapists assume that the therapeutic relationship is the agent of change that provides a safe, authentic environment in which clients benefit by gaining immediate awareness of self.

Several factors make this approach useful for a client in late adolescence. HST can involve all five senses and engages many neurobiological systems (Armstrong et al., 2017; Foster, 2022). In its most basic form, it is a visual and tactile approach. Even for clients with vision limitations, the kinesthetic quality of HST makes it ideal to engage sensory experiences that can activate memories of painful experiences (Badenoch, 2008), which can be meaningfully processed. For adolescent clients and particularly those who have experienced trauma, having an alternate method of self-expression can feel safer than talk therapy. It can also help adolescents developmentally, as they are still exploring ways to capture their experiences abstractly and the symbolic nature of HST is responsive to these needs.

HST creates an opportunity for catharsis that bypasses the many sets of rules 17-year-olds tend to develop about how to express emotions, what emotions are acceptable to express, and when they should express them (Armstrong et al., 2017). HST provides a new pathway for clients to experience emotion without fear of losing control because their emotions can be captured and bound by the tray. Ultimately, HST can be an effective approach to adolescent therapy because it is couched in a safe therapeutic relationship, activates neurobiological integration, involves holistic sensory experiencing, and requires little content to be shared with the therapist due to its focus on awareness and here-and-now experiencing. All these variables are important in any therapeutic approach with a 17-year-old client.

Conclusion

Seventeen-year-olds might well be one of our favorite ages of clients with whom to work. They bring such developmental polarities to the counseling room: an adultlike physical appearance embodying childhood hopes and dreams that are beginning to feel closer for them, increasing complexity in intimate relationships, greater emotional and cognitive self-understanding limited by the lack of a fully developed frontal lobe, and rewards and challenges that are linked to their ever-increasing autonomy. We find that it is easy to be pulled into these various polarities when working with our 17-year-old clients, creating assumptions that they are either less or more advanced than they are in areas of development. Like almost all adolescents, 17-year-olds can be a complicated and energizing age with which to engage in the therapeutic process – and well worth all the moments of head scratching, heartbreak, attunement, confusion, discovery, and depth.

References

Anderson, A., & Jiang, J. (2018, May 31). Teens, social media & technology 2018. *Pew Research Center*. www.pewresearch.org/internet/wp-content/uploads/sites/9/2018/05/PI_2018.05.31_TeensTech_FINAL.pdf

Arain, M., Haque, M., Johal, L., Mathur, P., Nel, W., Rais, A., Sandhu, R., & Sharma, S. (2013). Maturation of the adolescent brain. *Neuropsychiatric Disease and Treatment*, *2013*(default), 449–461. https://doaj.org/article/071f91c12be241dcb6f989e700e7ad55

Armstrong, S. A. (2008). *Humanistic sandtray therapy*. Ludic Press.

Armstrong, S. A., Foster, R. D., Brown, T., & Davis, J. (2017). Humanistic sandtray therapy with children and adults. In E. S. Leggett & J. N. Boswell (Eds.), *Directive play therapy: Theories and techniques* (pp. 217–253). Springer.

Badenoch, B. (2008). *Being a brain-wise therapist: A practical guide to interpersonal neurobiology*. W. W. Norton & Company.

Berk, L. E. (2018). *Development through the lifespan* (7th ed.). Pearson.

Bos, D. J., Dreyfuss, M., Tottenham, N., Hare, T. A., Galvan, A., Casey, B. J., & Jones, R. M. (2020). Distinct and similar patterns of emotional development in adolescents and young adults. *Developmental Psychobiology*, *62*(5), 591–599. https://doi.org/10.1002/dev.21942

Brown, R. E. (2016). Hebb and Cattell: The genesis of the theory of fluid and crystallized intelligence. *Frontiers in Human Neuroscience, 10*. https://doi.org./10.3389/fnhum.2016.00606

Bruni, O., Sette, S., Fontanesi, L., Baiocco, R., Laghi, F., & Baumgartner, E. (2015). Technology use and sleep quality in preadolescence and adolescence. *Journal of Clinical Sleep Medicine, 11*(12), 1433–1441. https://doi.org/10.5664/jcsm.5282

Chassiakos, Y. R., Radesky, J., Christakis, D., Moreno, M. A., Cross, C., & Council on Communications and Media. (2016). Children and adolescents and digital media. *Pediatrics, 138*(5). https://doi.org/10.1542/peds.2016-2593

Ciccia, A. H., Meulenbroek, P., & Turkstra, L. S. (2009). Adolescent brain and cognitive developments: Implications for clinical assessment in traumatic brain injury. *Topics in Language Disorders, 29*(3), 249. https://doi.org/10.1097/TLD.0b013e3181b53211

Cochrane, A., Simmering, V., & Green, C. S. (2019). Fluid intelligence is related to capacity in memory as well as attention: Evidence from middle childhood and adulthood. *PLoS ONE, 14*(8), 1–24. https://doi.org/10.1371/journal.pone.0221353

Doane, L. D., Mineka, S., Zinbarg, R. E., Craske, M., Griffith, J. W., & Adam, E. K. (2013). Are flatter diurnal cortisol rhythms associated with major depression and anxiety disorders in late adolescence? The role of life stress and daily negative emotion. *Development and Psychopathology, 25*(3), 629-642. https://doi.org/10.1017/S0954579413000060

Eaton, D. K., Kann, L., Kinchen, S., Shanklin, S., Flint, K. H., Hawkins, J., Harris, W. A., Lowry, R., McManus, T., Chyen, D., Whittle, L., Lim, C., & Wechsler, H. (2012). Youth risk behavior surveillance-United States, 2011. *Morbidity and Mortality Weekly Report. Surveillance Summaries, 61*(4), 1–162.

Erikson, E. H. (1993). *Childhood and society*. Norton.

Foster, R. D. (2022). *Humanistic sandtray therapy treatment manual*. Humanistic Sandtray Therapy Institute.

Foster, R. D. (in press). *Humanistic sandtray therapy: The definitive guide to philosophy, therapeutic conditions, and the real relationship*. Routledge

Giedd, J. N. (2004). Structural magnetic resonance imaging of the adolescent brain. *Annals of the New York Academy of Sciences, 1021*(1), 77–85. https://doi-org./10.1196/annals.1308.009

Holliman, R. P., & Foster, R. D. (2016). Embodying and communicating authenticity in adolescent counseling. *Journal of Child and Adolescent Counseling*, 2(1), 61–76. https://doi.org/10.1080/23727810.2016.1160353

Homeyer, L. E., & Sweeney, D. S. (2022). *Sandtray: A practical manual* (4th ed.). Routledge.

Inhelder, B., & Piaget, J. (1958). *The growth of logical thinking from childhood to adolescence: An essay on the construction of formal operational structures*. Basic Books. (Original work published 1955)

Johnson, S. B., Blum, R. W., & Giedd, J. N. (2009). Adolescent maturity and the brain: The promise and pitfalls of neuroscience research in adolescent health policy. *Journal of Adolescent Health, 45*(3), 216–221. https://doi.org/10.1016/j.jadohealth.2009.05.016

Karcher, N. R., & Barch, D. M. (2021). The ABCD study: Understanding the development of risk for mental and physical health outcomes. *Neuropsychopharmacology: At the Intersection of Brain, Behavior, and Therapeutics*, 46(1), 131–142. https://doi.org/10.1038/s41386-020-0736-6

Kliewer, W. (1997). Children's coping with chronic illness. In S. A. Wolchik & I. N. Sandler (Eds.), *Handbook of children's coping: Linking theory and intervention* (pp. 275–300). Springer.

Konrad, K., Firk, C., & Uhlhaas, P. J. (2013). Brain development during adolescence. *Deutsches Aerzteblatt International, 110*(25), 425–431. https://doi.org/10.3238/arztebl.2013.0425

Kroger, J. (2012). The status of identity: Developments in identity status research. In P. K. Kerig, M. S. Schulz, & S. T. Hauser (Eds.), *Adolescence and beyond: Family processes and development* (pp. 64–83). Oxford University Press.

Kuhn, D. (2006). Do cognitive changes accompany developments in the adolescent brain? *Perspectives on Psychological Science*, *1*(1), 59–67. https://doi.org/10.1111/j.17456924.2006.t01-2-.x

Lenhart, A. (2015). Teens, social media and technology overview. https://www.pewresearch.org/wp-content/uploads/sites/9/2015/04/PI_TeensandTech_Update2015_0409151.pdf

Manly, J. T., Cicchetti, D., & Barnett, D. (1994). The impact of subtype, frequency, chronicity, and severity of child maltreatment on social competence and behavior problems. *Developmental Psychopathology*, *6*(1), 121–143. https://doi.org/10.1017/S0954579400005915

McKinney, C., Donnelly, R., & Renk, K. (2008). Perceived parenting, positive and negative perceptions of parents, and late adolescent emotional adjustment. *Child and Adolescent Mental Health*, *13*, 66–73. https://doi.org/10.1111/j.1475-3588.2007.00452.x

McLoyd, V. C. (1998). Socioeconomic disadvantage and child development. *American Psychologist*, *53*(2), 185–204. https://doi.org/10.1037//0003-066x.53.2.185

Oberle, E., Ji, X. R., Kerai, S., Guhn, M., Schonert-Reichl, K. A., & Gadermann, A. M. (2020). Screen time and extracurricular activities as risk and protective factors for mental health in adolescence: A population-level study. *Preventive Medicine*, *141*. https://doi.org/10.1016/j.ypmed.2020.106291

Office of Population Affairs Department of Health and Human Services. (n.d.). *Adolescent development explained*. https://opa.hhs.gov/adolescent-health/adolescent-development-explained/cognitive-development

Piernas, C., & Popkin, B. M. (2011). Increased portion sizes from energy-dense foods affect total energy intake at eating occasions in U.S. children and adolescents: Patterns and trends by age group and sociodemographic characteristics, 1977–2006. *American Journal of Clinical Nutrition*, *94*, 1324–1332. https://doi.org/10.3945/ajcn.110.008466

Powell, K. (2006). Neurodevelopment: How does the teenage age brain work? *Nature*, *442*, 865–867. https://doi.org/10.1038/442865a

Preston, J. D., O'Neal, J. H., Talaga, M. C., & Moore, B. A. (2021a). *Child and adolescent psychopharmacology made simple* (4th ed.). New Harbinger.

Preston, J. D., O'Neal, J. H., Talaga, M. C., & Moore, B. A. (2021b). *Handbook of clinical psychopharmacology for therapists* (9th ed.). New Harbinger.

Ragelienė, T. (2016). Links of adolescents identity development and relationship with peers: A systematic literature review. *Journal of the Canadian Academy of Child & Adolescent Psychiatry*, *25*(2), 97–105.

Ritchie, L. D., Spector, P., Stevens, M. J., Schmidt, M. M., Schreiber, G. B., Striegel-Moore, R. H., Wang, M., & Crawford, P. B. (2007). Dietary patterns in adolescence are related to adiposity in young adulthood in Black and White females. *Journal of Nutrition*, *137*, 399–406. https://doi.org/10.1093/jn/137.2.399

Rogers, C. R. (1961). *On becoming a person*. Houghton Mifflin.

Salerno, A., Tosto, M., & Antony, S. D. (2015). Adolescent sexual and emotional development: The role of romantic relationships. *Procedia—Social and Behavioral Sciences*, *174*, 932–938. https://doi.org/10.1016/j.sbspro.2015.01.714

Sheth, C., McGlade, E., & Yurgelun-Todd, D. (2017). Chronic stress in adolescents and its neurobiological and psychopathological consequences: An RDoC perspective. *Chronic Stress*, *1*, 1–22. https://doi.org/10.1177/2470547017715645

Silveri, M. M., Tzilos, G. K., & Yurgelun-Todd, D. A. (2008). Relationship between white matter volume and cognitive performance during adolescence: Effects of age, sex and risk for drug use. *Addiction*, *103*(9), 1509–1520. https://doi.org/10.1111/j.1360-0443.2008.02272.x

Sori, C., & Heckler, L. (2003). *The therapist's notebook for children and adolescents: Homework, handouts, and activities for use in psychotherapy*. The Hayworth Clinical Practice Press.

Tanti, C., Stukas, A. A., Halloran, M. J., & Foddy, M. (2011). Social identity change: Shifts in social identity during adolescence. *Journal of Adolescence*, *34*(3), 555–567. https://doi.org/10.1016/j.adolescence.2010.05.012

Thapar, A., Colishaw, S., Pine, D. S., & Thapar, A. K. (2012). Depression in adolescence. *The Lancet*, *379*, 1056–1067. https://doi.org/10.1016/S0140-6736(11)60871-4

Trent, M., Dooley, D. G., & Dougé, J. (2019). The impact of racism on child and adolescent health. *Pediatrics*, *144*(2), 1–14. https://doi.org/10.1542/peds.2019-1765

U.S. Department of Health and Human Services. (2020). *The teen brain: 7 things to know*. National Institute of Mental Health. www.nimh.nih.gov/health/publications/the-teen-brain-7-things-to-know

United Nations. (2018). *World drug report 2018*. Office on Drugs and Crime. www.unodc.org/wdr2018

Wall, M. I., Carlson, S. A., Stein, A. D., Lee, S. M, & Fulton, J. E. (2011). Trends by age in youth physical activity: Youth Media Campaign Longitudinal Survey. *Medicine and Science in Sports and Exercise*, *40*, 2140–2147. https://doi.org/10.1249/MSS.0b013e31821f561a

Wampold, B. E., & Imel, Z. E. (2015). *The great psychotherapy debate: The evidence for what makes psychotherapy work* (2nd ed.). Routledge.

Windfuhr, K., While, D., Hunt, I., Turnbull, P., Lowe, R., Burns, J., Swinson, N., Shaw, J., Appleby, L., Kapur, N., & The National Confidential Inquiry into Suicide and Homicide by Young People with Mental Illness. (2008). Suicide in juveniles and adolescents in the United Kingdom. *Journal of Child Psychology and Psychiatry*, *49*(11), 1157–1167. https://doi.org/10.1111/j.1469-7610.2008.01938.x

Worsham, N. L., Compas, B. E., & Ey, S. (1997). Children's coping with parental illness. In S. A. Wolchik & I. N. Sandler (Eds.), *Handbook of children's coping: Linking theory and intervention* (pp. 195–213). Springer.

Part IV

Late Adolescence/Early Adulthood

Chapter 8

The 18- to 19-Year-Old

Amanda Lara and Katherine E. Purswell

The ages of 18 and 19 mark a milestone in U.S. culture as these once-adolescents transition into official adulthood. As an 18-year-old citizen in the United States, the new adult acquires a series of privileges and responsibilities including the right to vote in federal, state, and local elections and the right to enlist in the military. The milestone also marks a change in legal implications; at the age of 18, the young adult can be more commonly charged with a crime to the fullest extent of the law without the possibility of a juvenile sentence or expungement. Accountability shifts to the young adult as parents can no longer access school or medical records without consent. Given the nature of the serious long-term consequences of these new privileges, the prevailing cultural expectations of logical decision-making and problem-solving appear beyond the brain and emotional development of this age group. At the same time, this age may be filled with opportunity as the young adult makes decisions about their future. Therapists can be particularly important in supporting 18- and 19-year-olds in making the transition to adulthood.

Amalia is an outgoing and ambitious 18-year-old African American female entering her first year of university. Amalia is eager to establish new relationships at college and enjoy the freedom associated with living away from her nuclear family. Amalia dreams of the new tattoos, piercings, and cigarettes that she can now legally obtain without parental consent. She is largely hopeful about her future.

While Amalia is excited about her new opportunities, she finds herself feeling sadness and worry about the end of her high school years. Amalia has come to rely on the routine of the school day. She knows that it will be challenging to maintain her friendships as some of her peers will be entering other universities or the full-time workforce while she studies. Amalia is consumed with doubt. She is aware of the pressure to quickly pick a major of study and begin the typical four-year journey to a career. Amalia is discouraged at the prospect of being a racial minority in her new college town. She is unsure of her career path and believes that she must continue her education because her parents have told her that she must either attend college or enter the workforce. Amalia sometimes feels overwhelmed by the demands of adulthood and vehemently expresses that she is not ready for "adulting."

Like most young adults, Amalia is being asked to commit to a vocational path despite not having yet explored enough of herself, others, and the world to understand what would best suit her values and identity. Considering the following changes in Amalia and

DOI: 10.4324/9781003196297-12

other 18- and 19-year-olds can assist parents, teachers, and other helping professionals in providing appropriate support that adheres to the strengths of this population.

Physical Development

By the age of 18, physical and sexual body changes related to puberty have completed. An 18- or 19-year-old individual is typically done growing; this is true across genders. As young adults can expect few changes in their bodies, there is a greater sense of acceptance of their physical appearance in comparison to earlier adolescent years (Eisenberg et al., 2006). However, Bucchianeri et al. (2013) noted that body dissatisfaction overall does not decrease by age 18 and concerns for body image extend well beyond young adulthood. There is still a preoccupation with physical appearance, seemingly driven in part by the use of social media. Researchers found that exposure to social media may negatively affect a young adult's body image and food choices (Rounsefell et al., 2019).

Consider 19-year-old cisgender male Lucas. Lucas was raised by a conservative, working-class family and identifies as gay. He recently began working 50-hour weeks in a body shop and spends his free time playing sports and going to the gym. Lucas can run, jump, and climb with enviable agility. After a few months of his new routine, Lucas begins to feel physically weak at the gym after work and is sleeping no more than five hours every night. He does not attribute the weakness to fatigue from his physically demanding job and rigid schedule, but rather to his own lack of determination. Lucas knows logically that he cannot spend more time at the gym without becoming unreliable at work or losing more hours of sleep. He opts to reduce his sleep time to allow himself more exercise time.

Lucas has noticed that his mood is better when he exercises. This trend is true for many young adults. In college-aged men, an increase in exercise frequency is associated with less daytime dysfunction and decrease in depressed mood; in college-aged women, an increase in exercise frequency is associated with improved sleep quality, increased positive affect, and decreased depressed mood (Glavin et al., 2022).

However, should Lucas continue to deprive his body of sleep, the consequences could be significant, as sleep is a significant factor that predicts quality of life for younger adults. On average, 32% of adults aged 18 to 24 reported getting less than the recommended 7 to 9 hours of sleep per night (Liu et al., 2016). Lack of proper sleep could ultimately lead to a work accident, as sleep deprivation is associated with impaired cognitive performance (Institute of Medicine, 2006). Sleep deprivation also impacts overall mood, emotion reactivity, and anxiety symptoms (Palmer et al., 2023).

Sexual Development

The latent sexuality present in earlier adolescence has already emerged in most young adults ages 18 and 19 (Kumar-Kar et al., 2015). Sexual maturity typically occurs after pubertal onset, which can range from ages 8 to 14. Both early and late onset of puberty can create concerns that can last into young adulthood. Youth who experience early sexual development are more likely to engage in unprotected sex, have more sexual partners, have a higher risk of sexually transmitted infections (STIs), and have more non-consensual sexual experiences (Boislard et al., 2016). Late sexual onset is associated with low body image (Boislard et al., 2016). Understanding a young adult's individual experiences and timelines related to puberty and sexual development is important for supporting them in developing healthy relationship and sexual behaviors and navigating their relationship to their own bodies.

By the late teens and early 20s, most young adults have had a vaginal or oral sexual experience regardless of marital status (Herbenick et al., 2010). Therefore, education about STIs is crucial for teens and young adults. Researchers have noted that STIs might be a more prominent risk for those who engage in early experiences of vaginal sex as they were found to have more sexual partners than individuals who had not engaged in vaginal sex (Santelli et al., 1998). Bisexual females were also more likely than heterosexual females to have sexual intercourse, early sexual activity, more sexual partners, more unprotected sex, and to use alcohol or drugs before engaging in sex (Rasberry et al., 2018). Additionally, LGBTQ+ youth are more at risk for STIs due to higher-risk sexual behavior, resulting in twice as high rates of STIs as in heterosexual cisgender males (Benson & Hergenroeder, 2005). This increased prevalence and risk may be attributed to inadequate sexual education that is inclusive of all sexual orientations, LGBTQ+ youth hiding their sexual activity due to discrimination or parental rejection, and internal pressure for LGBTQ+ to assert their sexual identity or attempt to meet heteronormative expectations by being more sexually active (Ybarra et al., 2016). The risk for STIs is increased by the use of drugs or alcohol for youth of all genders and sexual orientations.

Young adults are more likely to use effective contraception after comprehensive sex education, a finding that shows 18- and 19-year-olds can make healthy decisions about sex with guidance and support (Cheedalla et al., 2020; Jaramillo et al., 2017). Research indicates that gay and bisexual men have more positive attitudes about condoms and increased peer group acceptance of safer sex practices than heterosexual young adults (Johns et al., 2018). Therapists supporting adolescents and young adults are essential in identifying individual risk related to sexual activity and helping parents/caregiver and youth access inclusive resources related to healthy sexual behaviors and use of protection to reduce risk of STIs and unintended pregnancies.

Brain Development

In American culture, a person is considered an adult with significant privileges and responsibilities granted at age 18. However, these societal expectations do not align with the reality that the brains of young adults are not fully developed. The prefrontal cortex (PFC) is responsible for executive functions, such as representational knowledge, operational processing skills, and self-regulation, and is partly responsible for self-awareness and introspection. The PFC does not reach maturity until the age of 25 or beyond, meaning that 18- to 19-year-olds do not have fully developed decision-making and problem-solving skills (Giedd, 2004). Therefore, it can be expected that 18- and 19-year-olds continue to demonstrate some level of impulsivity, risk-taking, and decreased insight into their feelings compared to adults with fully developed PFCs. Young adults may also be prone to ignoring consequences and seeking immediate gratification. For example, an 18-year-old may prioritize hanging out late with friends over working on college applications that are due the following day.

White matter, which is responsible for the connectivity between different areas of the brain, increases from early to late adolescence (Arain et al., 2013), though by 18 and 19 it still has not reached the volume of most other adults (Giedd, 2004). However, 18- and 19-year-olds have developed enough white matter that connectivity in the corpus callosum and cerebellum promotes creativity and intelligence that was not present prior to these ages. This increase in white matter also results in more rapid and efficient communication between the prefrontal cortex, where executive functioning originates, and the limbic system, where emotions are processed (Johnson et al., 2009). Thus, young adults can be expected to exhibit an emotional maturity and regulation that is different from that of early adolescents who may be more prone to reactive decision-making.

For 19-year-old Lucas, reducing feelings of shame toward his body might appear to outweigh the consequences of showing up late to work due to fitting in an early gym session. With time though, Lucas determines that he would rather not lose his job due to tardiness. Lucas ultimately chooses to create a balanced routine. Lucas' example shows the ways in which the developing brain provides opportunities for learning and growth.

Cognitive Development

Given the development of the brain's structure at ages 18 and 19, young adults are exhibiting more abstract and future-oriented thinking. Like 18-year-old Amalia, young adults are concerned with their future: what their peers will be doing, what their careers will look like, and what intimate or social relationships they will develop and maintain. Piaget (1965) identified the final developmental stage of his cognitive theory as the onset of abstract thought. Piaget theorized that most people reach the final stage of formal operations but that the timing is dependent upon multiple factors including personal and educational experiences. For example, growing up in an environment where critical thinking is practiced and valued would promote the development of more advanced abstract thinking skills. In addition to being able to think abstractly, a person develops stronger conceptual abilities and deepening awareness of complex emotions. Thus, young adults ages 18 and 19 demonstrate the ability to consider different points of view and think hypothetically. They can be challenged with philosophical and idealistic problems and have the capability to understand underlying issues.

Consider Amalia's resolution to a dispute with her college roommate. Amalia and her roommate have two distinct routines – Amalia is a morning person, and her roommate is a self-declared night owl. Their routines are determined for the semester given their class schedules and clash in close quarters. Amalia is frustrated that her roommate stays up late with the light on, and her roommate has expressed that she is angry with Amalia for listening to music in the morning. Amalia acknowledges that it would be difficult for her roommate to sleep in with music, and her roommate acknowledges that it would be difficult to fall asleep with all the lights on. After hearing each other's perspectives on the issue, they agree to compromise. Amalia will wear headphones in the morning to listen to music, and her roommate will use a desk lamp to study at night.

The compromise that Amalia and her roommate agree upon was not just the product of critical thinking skills. As this age group strengthens their abstract thinking skills, a shift in morality can be noted as well. An 18- or 19-year-old synthesizes more information than a younger teenager when considering what is just and right. Kohlberg (1984) identified the characteristics of the two final stages in his moral development model as developing an awareness of different points of view and, ultimately, establishing ethical principles for guidance. Because one's capacity for perspective-taking is dependent on one's ability to think abstractly, moral development is strongly connected to cognitive development.

Young adults with postconventional morality want to hear another's conflicting perspective because they can now recognize that people can hold different values and beliefs (Kohlberg, 1984; Lally & Valentine-French, 2019). It is not enough for a young adult to hear "I don't want you to stay out late because that is the rule in this home." They may be more responsive to explanations like, "I feel worried when I don't know where you are late at night, and I need to hear from you." Additionally, individuals ages 18 and 19 might relate more to learning another's perspective because they have developed a deeper understanding of the social context and impact of behavior and have a desire to do not just what is good but what is right for society.

Emotional Development

Eighteen- and nineteen-year-olds can address feelings and emotions in exciting new ways due in part to the shifts in brain development. At this point in development, the brains of young adults ages 18 and 19 are very sensitive to their emotional environment (Johnson et al., 2009). Young adults may interpret situations as threatening and may respond more impulsively than older adults. Young adults also display reduced cognitive performance to negative emotional cues compared to older adults (Cohen et al., 2016). At the same time, 18- and 19-year-olds are also building their capacity for greater emotional regulation and stability. Emotional capacity and regulation may be inconsistent and highly influenced by sleep, stress, timing, and social context.

Consider again Lucas' attempts to balance his schedule. Lucas' mother notices that he appears weary, and she wants to offer advice. She approaches Lucas and says, "You're looking tired lately. Maybe you should cut back on some stuff and focus on your work." Lucas sees the concerned look on his mother's face and immediately feels anger. He believes he is trying his best and is hurt to hear that his mother is not acknowledging his efforts. Lucas walks away from his mother, letting her know that he finds her to be controlling. His mother is left confused and worried for her son. What she fails to see is that her advice was perceived as criticism by Lucas.

Social and Relationship Development

By ages 18 and 19, young adults experience a shift in social and relational needs. They are making their own decisions and developing a community consciousness that results in a stronger valuing of commitment in their social relationships. Young adults crave opportunities to gain independence from their family unit and gravitate toward seeking acceptance from their peers (NASEM, 2019). As 18- and 19-year-olds experience changes in their educational setting and routines related to graduating from high school, moving away from home, or starting new jobs or careers, they may struggle to balance their desire and need for independence and their ongoing need for support from family and parents/caregivers. As they move in and out of the family in new ways, it may be a challenge for them to navigate their changing identity and roles in their families. Parents may also struggle in creating new expectations and boundaries as their 18- or 19-year-old alternates between asserting their independence and seeking emotional, economic, and/or social support.

Variability in romantic relationships is common for young adults. Young adults are often motivated to date or seek romantic partnership and intimacy. While early romantic and sexual relationships are associated with a higher prevalence of STIs in adolescents, these types of relationships are not considered intrinsically risky for young adults. As discussed previously, comprehensive sex education can help to mitigate some of the risk in engaging in sexual behaviors. Participation in romantic relationships can be a protective factor and source of social support and connection for some young adults. One study found that single young adults rate their life satisfaction lower and level of loneliness higher than young adults who occasionally date (Gonzales Aviles et al., 2020). Going to college, moving out of the family home, or starting a job can expand a young adults' social and romantic opportunities and increase exposure to more diverse communities and perspectives. These major life transitions may also disrupt 18- or 19-year old's social relationships as friendships from high school or home become more disconnected or change due to distance and no longer participating in shared social environments. This can be a period of both social expansion and isolation as late adolescents move in and out of new and old social contexts.

Culture and Identity Development

From an Eriksonian perspective of development, 18- and 19-year-olds are typically navigating the crisis of identity vs. role confusion. According to Erikson (1968), the focus of this fifth stage is to develop a clear sense of self, and the existential question to be asked is "Who am I?" Expanding on Erikson's theory, Marcia (1966) elaborated that this stage of identity development is marked by exploration and commitment. Chapter 1 includes details of these theories. Most 18- to 19-year-olds are still exploring many aspects of their identity, while other aspects may be more stable. Specifically, individuals who are positively resolving this stage generally have a cohesive sense of self but may still be exploring some particular identities such as racial/ethnic identity. As seen in the case of Amalia, some peers are entering college, while others might be entering directly into the workforce. Opportunities for socialization and exposure will differ in either circumstance and impact cultural and identity development.

Ethnic and Racial Identity Development

Ethnic and racial identity (ERI) development in young adulthood is facilitated largely by the strides in cognitive development made in middle and late adolescence. In a study examining Latino young adults, Sladek and colleagues (2023) found that ERI exploration and resolution increased over time in the transition from high school to college. Umaña-Taylor et al. (2014) also described ERI development in young adults based on their cognitive capabilities. While a younger teen is focused on the categorization and exploration of different ethnic and racial reference groups, an 18- or 19-year-old can consider the intersections of multiple identities to produce a coherent overall identity (Crenshaw, 1989; Grzanka, 2020). For example, a Chinese American genderqueer 19-year-old with a disability would likely be able to articulate how these various identities come together to be something more than just the "sum" of their various experiences with each unique identity while continuing to integrate their identities into a cohesive sense of self.

Gender and Affectional Identity Development

Because 18- to 19-year-olds are typically entering new environments post-high school (full-time workforce, higher education, "gap year" experiences) and because of the prevalence of gender and affectional identity conversations in the current social and political discourse in the US, young adults are likely to be exposed to new ways of thinking about these distinct but interrelated identities. For example, a 19-year-old college student who attended a high school where diverse gender identities were generally affirmed may meet other students or professors who hold very different views. Conversely, an 18-year-old from a more socially conservative part of the country may encounter an openly gay person for the first time in a new job. Either of these experiences could challenge the person's cognitive schema around gender and sexuality and could lead them to confirm or change their own perspective (Robbins & McGowan, 2016).

More and more high school- and college-aged youth are identifying as queer or trans, with nearly 20% of youth ages 18 to 25 identifying as LGBT (Gallup Poll Social Series, 2022). For 18- to 19-year-olds who have more expansive gender identities or with minoritized affectional identities, leaving home or spending more time outside the home could provide space for deeper exploration and expression of these identities, especially for young people in less affirming environments (Robbins & McGowan, 2016). Some clients may experience feelings of joy or elation at being able to fully express their identity for the first time. Others may feel a sense of confusion or self-doubt, especially if they still see the less affirming values as valid. Therapists can support these young adults in better understanding themselves and developing a cohesive identity that fits for them and reflects their true sense of self.

Resources and Protective Factors

One potential protective factor for 18- and 19-year-olds is related to their brain and cognitive development. As the prefrontal cortex continues to mature and young adults gain more cognitive complexity, they are able to think and problem-solve in more nuanced and creative ways than when they were younger. Young adults are able to make better use of executive functioning skills including planning ahead and exercising more impulse control. These skills are useful as they take on more adult responsibilities and navigate more social situations independently. Supporting young adults in exploring their options, listening to their values and beliefs as they navigate decisions, and providing emotional support as they learn through experience are helpful in strengthening their confidence and capacity for problem-solving and decision-making.

Family relationships and support continue to be a protective factor for 18- and 19-year-olds even as they seek more independence from the adults in their families. When parents and other important adults are able to provide nonjudgmental support for 18- and 19-year-olds' forays into adulthood, young adults can feel less alone and overwhelmed. Family and parental support, stability, and engagement reduce the risk of substance misuse and mental and emotional disorders (Centers for Disease Control and Prevention, 2023). Family members and parents can also play a critical role in supporting identity development in late adolescence and early adulthood. Research has shown that family support of young adults' sexual identity was associated with the young adult associating positive thoughts with queer identity and community (Taylor, 2023). Eighteen- and nineteen-year-olds can seem like they do not value the opinions of parents and other family members, but, in reality, support from parents and family members can help ease their transition into adulthood in ways that impact their continued development.

Challenges and Risk Factors

Various factors influence the maturation of the brain including genetics, sex hormones, environment, substance use, and nutritional status (Arain et al., 2013). Given the numerous factors that can alter healthy brain development, young adults are prone to risk factors such as impulsivity and risk-taking. It can be expected that young adults ages 18 and 19 might experiment with risky sexual activity, alcohol and substance use, or other dangerous behaviors. While experimentation is not indicative of a chronic issue, it can lead to long-term consequences that these young adults may not consider. Young adults with pre-existing risk factors, such as previous difficulties with executive functioning tasks due to biology, previous developmental disruptions, or trauma, have a higher likelihood of sensation-seeking behaviors becoming problematic (NASEM, 2019). For example, if a 19-year-old has unresolved trauma, experimentation with alcohol may lead to self-medication. Additionally, periods between first use and experimentation to regular use or misuse of substances may be brief. Rates of cannabis use disorder peak at the age of 18 (Vasilenko et al., 2017) with 20–30% of youth moving from first use of marijuana to regular use within the first year of experimentation (Wittchen et al., 2008). Beyond cannabis use, 90% of adults who smoke daily first tried smoking by the age of 18 and e-cigarettes continue to rise in popularity with high school students and young adults (Centers for Disease Control and Prevention, 2023a). Counselors working with clients ages 18 and 19 need to understand how youth are engaging with substances and sexual behavior including contextual and individual risk and protective factors.

Another challenge with the 18- and 19-year-old population is related to their awareness of their emotions and behavioral patterns. As their PFCs are not fully developed, some young adults may have less self-awareness than their slightly older peers. Thus, they may not be willing to seek help when they need it because they may attribute a personal problem to something external to them or perceive accepting support as a challenge to their burgeoning independence. For example, a 19-year-old who experiences many unwanted breakups may blame the other people rather than looking inward or examining their own communication or relational patterns. This person may not see the need to attend therapy. This opposition is not to be confused with therapeutic resistance but rather can be a manifestation of limited introspection or a desire to establish and prove independence.

Of course, many 18- and 19-year-olds have much higher levels of self-awareness than they did in early adolescence. This observation reflects another challenge of this age group: the variability in development. As mentioned previously, 18- and 19-year-olds are legally considered adults, but the extent to which their social environment expects them to act like adults can differ considerably based on cultural, familial, socioeconomic, and individual factors. For example, an 18-year-old in a lower income household may have already been working after school and on the weekend for years and is now expected to be financially independent, while a 19-year-old in a more financially wealthy income bracket may not be expected to get even a part-time job until after college. Variability in life experience, culture, responsibilities, and support (tangible, financial, social, informational, or emotional) profoundly impacts an individual's transition into adulthood and relative independence or dependence in late adolescence.

Finally, a significant challenge when working with 18- and 19-year-olds is that they may have recently transitioned out of pediatric care. Young adults may lose access to mental health support through high school counselors or social workers. While consent laws vary across states, in general, age 18 marks the allowable age to consent to treatment. Some young adults might be seeking treatment for the first time of their own volition. Young adults may encounter barriers to accessing treatment on their own depending on their knowledge of the healthcare system or access to services that are integrated in an educational or professional environment. For example, an 18-year-old whose family members would only take them to unlicensed religious "counselors" may be excited to get to choose their own therapist for the first time. However, the potential client may not know where to start or how to find and pay for quality services. They could quickly become overwhelmed with the process. Perceived stigma, poor mental health literacy, and a preference for self-reliance may also keep young adults from seeking mental health services (Gulliver et al., 2010).

Best Practices for Counseling and Therapy

While it is important to be proactive and connect young adults to services as soon as possible, there are instances where what appears to be a concern or symptom of a mental health disorder may, in fact, be a developmental characteristic typical of 18- and 19-year-olds. For example, seeking independence from the family unit can be interpreted as self-isolating behavior when it may reflect a healthy developmental drive. Formal and informal assessment can be useful in understanding the nature, scope, and severity of a concern.

Assessment

When selecting assessments for use with 18- and 19-year-olds, it is vital to consider the norming group used to develop the assessment to ensure that the evaluation accurately represents the individual. Pediatric tools are often no longer appropriate for late teens and young adults. The Columbia Suicide Severity Rating Scale (CSSRS) and the Patient Health Questionnaire (PHQ-9) can be helpful tools for understanding the complexity of symptoms and identifying the most appropriate level of care. Additionally, informal assessment that centers the young adult's culture, identity, and development is essential to identifying how to best support them in navigating challenges, barriers to resources, or challenges within their social systems and environments.

Career and Relationship Counseling

At the age of 18 and 19, individuals are concerned with their futures, so career counseling may be helpful to explore values and career pathways or if a young adult is experiencing feelings of overwhelm or stress related to career exploration. As romantic partnerships and sexual relationships are often a focus during this period of development, 18- and 19-year-olds may engage in counseling to explore relationship concerns and support their identity development in the context of romantic and peer relationships. Even if 18- and 19-year-olds are not experiencing severe mental health symptoms, insight-oriented counseling can give young adults a space to practice their growing introspection skills. As therapists use reflective listening and other facilitative skills, they can scaffold continued cognitive and emotional development and support ongoing identity development.

Therapeutic Process

Once a young adult has found themselves in a chair (or screen) across from you, helping them to feel engaged and take ownership of the counseling process is vital. Although it is helpful to consider the protective and risk factors discussed in this chapter, each 18- or 19-year-old has their own experiences, identities, and environments that shape who they are. It is essential for counselors to remember that the individual sitting across from you is who carries their own experiences and is still exploring who they are in this world as they more deeply engage in the social and cultural aspects of adulthood.

Arain et al. (2013) encourage adults to shift from overprotecting to allowing adolescents to make mistakes in order to develop self-regulation and strengthen executive functioning. For example, if a 19-year-old is talking about quitting a stable part-time job for one that seems more uncertain, a therapist could help the young adult process the pros and cons of the new job but should avoid offering advice to try to protect them from potential future discomfort when the new job does not measure up to their expectations. If the job works out, the therapist can celebrate with the client, and if it does not, then the therapist can provide accepting support as the 19-year-old explores what went wrong and how to avoid the same situation again.

Opportunities to develop self-awareness through journaling and mindfulness practices may be especially beneficial to 18- and -19-year-olds. Because the young adult's PFC is not yet fully developed, clinicians may facilitate introspection using tools designed to have clients reflect on their experiences with attention to positive and negative consequences of behavior and decisions. Skillful reflective listening can also serve to facilitate introspection.

In addition, skills-based workshops with a focus on the development of executive functioning skills, such as time management, memory skills, note taking, and interpersonal effectiveness skills, may also be helpful adjuncts to therapy for 18- to 19-year-olds.

Cognitive Behavioral Therapy (CBT)

One choice for addressing typical challenges experienced by young adults is cognitive behavioral therapy (CBT). Anxiety built by uncertainty and mood fluctuations that manifest as irritability and isolation are often seen in young adults at this important phase of life. Often, there are complaints of fatigue (Tanith Herring et al., 2022). What 18- and 19-year-olds might not recognize is these problems can be impacted by the client's beliefs, thoughts, and behavior. CBT is an evidence-based practice that focuses on the relationship between thoughts, feelings, and behaviors (Beck, 2011). A clinician can assist a young adult in understanding how a negative belief can develop into negative emotions. For example, a young adult with social anxiety whose mind begins to race as soon as they get into bed can use thought-stopping techniques to interrupt automatic, negative thoughts about what everyone must be thinking about them based on their social interactions that day.

Dialectical Behavior Therapy (DBT)

When there is a concern for suicidality, impulsive or disruptive behavior, social conflict, or poor coping skills, dialectical behavior therapy (DBT) may be beneficial for developing necessary skills in young adults (Linehan, 1993). For young adults experiencing challenges in their relationships and difficulties with mood regulation, DBT can be useful as it focuses on a set of skills designed to target these issues while building insight through mindfulness. The development of mindfulness skills has also been associated with an increase in the use of adaptive behaviors, such as exercise, in young adults (Dash et al., 2021). The effectiveness of DBT in young adults appears to be especially true for the college student population, as most can benefit from the skills-based approach (Pistorello et al., 2012). For example, distress tolerance skills, such as running, used to cope in the short term may prevent a young adult from engaging in impulsive and harmful choices, such as self-injury, that may exacerbate the situation. DBT can be delivered in different modalities, including group or individual therapy.

Motivational Interviewing

As young adults treasure their independence, motivational interviewing can be a helpful intervention given that it affirms client choice and autonomy. When a young adult is confronted about their decisions to engage in harmful behavior, the result is often strong resistance. Motivational interviewing is an evidence-based practice; the goal is to work collaboratively with the client to reduce harmful behaviors (SAMHSA, 2021). After establishing rapport and expressing empathy, clinicians can use "change talk" and "sustain talk" to guide and evoke rather than persuade and direct a young adult toward behavioral changes (Naar-King & Suarez, 2010). Motivational interviewing can be beneficial for young adults engaging in substance use, risky sexual behavior, and disordered eating.

Process-Focused Approaches

While many young adults can benefit from the shorter-term, more structured therapy approaches described previously, others may need more emotion-focused or longer-term approaches such as existential, person-centered, or relational-cultural counseling. For example, Samuel, a 19-year-old cisgender male, had been subjected to religious "counseling" through his family's church where he had been told he just needed to pray and trust God more and his depression would go away. When Samuel began full-time work and moved out of his parents' home, he sought out therapy services. Samuel had experienced persistent physical abuse as a child, and it took months of relationship-focused counseling before he trusted the counselor enough to start discussing the emotional pain inflicted on him by the adults in his childhood. As the counseling relationship continued, much of Samuel's work involved exploring and building his identity apart from the role of "problem child" placed on him by his family. Other 18- and 19-year-olds may appreciate more relational and philosophical-based counseling approaches because these approaches lend themselves to clients exploring identities and using their developing cognitive skills.

Conclusion

Ages 18 and 19 are marked by the transition from adolescence into adulthood. These young adults are seeking opportunities to understand who they are in relation to their communities. While they can sometimes appear to be stubborn and exhibit resistance, these behaviors are their efforts to establish independence. Their identity exploration is aided by the cognitive capabilities that have solidified. At this stage in development, support rather than direction is most effective in supporting young adults. The growth at ages 18 and 19 provides the foundation for future development in adulthood.

References

Arain, M., Mathur, P., Rais, A., Nel, W., Sandhu, R., Haque, M., Johal, L., & Sharma, S. (2013). Maturation of the adolescent brain. *Neuropsychiatric Disease and Treatment*, *9*, 449–461. https://doi.org/10.2147/ndt.s39776

Beck, J. S. (2011). *Cognitive behavior therapy: Basics and beyond* (2nd ed.). Guilford Press.

Benson, P., & Hergenroeder, A. (2005). Bacterial sexually transmitted infections in gay, lesbian, and bisexual adolescents: Medical and public health perspectives. *Seminars in Pediatric Infectious Disease)*, *16*(3), 181–191. https://doi.org/10.1053/j.spid.2005.04.007

Boislard, M. A., van de Bongardt, D., & Blais, M. (2016). Sexuality (and lack thereof) in adolescence and early adulthood: A review of the literature. *Behavioral Sciences (Basel, Switzerland)*, *6*(1), 8. https://doi.org/10.3390/bs6010008

Bucchianeri, M. M., Arikian, A. J., Hannan, P. J., Eisenberg, M. E., & Neumark-Sztainer, D. (2013). Body dissatisfaction from adolescence to young adulthood: Findings from a 10-year longitudinal study. *Body Image*, *10*(1), 1–7. https://doi.org/10.1016/j.bodyim.2012.09.001

Centers for Disease Control and Prevention. (2023a). *Mental health: Poor mental health impacts adolescent well-being*. www.cdc.gov/healthyyouth/mental-health/

Centers for Disease Control and Prevention. (2023b). *Youth and tobacco use*. www.cdc.gov/tobacco/data_statistics/fact_sheets/youth_data/tobacco_use/index.htm

Cheedalla, A., Moreau, C., & Burke, A. E. (2020). Sex education and contraceptive use of adolescent and young adult females in the United States: An analysis of the National Survey of Family Growth 2011–2017. *Contraception: X*, *2*, 100048. https://doi.org/10.1016/j.conx.2020.100048

Cohen, A., Breiner, K., Steinberg, L., Bonnie, R., Scott, E., Taylor-Thompson, K., Rudolph, M., Chein, J., Richeson, J., Heller, A., Silverman, M., Dellarco, D., Fair, D., Galván, A., & Casey, B. J. (2016). When is an adolescent an adult? Assessing cognitive control in emotional and nonemotional contexts. *Psychological Science*, *27*(4), 549–562. https://doi.org/10.1177/0956797615627625

Crenshaw, K. (1989). Demarginalizing the intersection of race and sex: A black feminist critique of antidiscrimination doctrine, feminist theory, and antiracist politics. *University of Chicago Legal Forum*, *1989*(1), 139–167.

Dash, S., Bourke, M., Parker, A. G., Trott, E., & Pascoe, M. (2021). Mindfulness is associated with reduced barriers to exercise via decreasing psychological distress in help-seeking young adults: A cross-sectional brief report. *Early Intervention in Psychiatry*, *16*(9), 1049–1054. https://doi.org/10.1111/eip.13249

Eisenberg, M. E., Neumark-Sztainer, D., & Paxton, S. J. (2006). Five-year change in body satisfaction among adolescents. *Journal of Psychosomatic Research*, *61*(4), 521–527. https://doi.org/10.1016/j.jpsychores.2006.05.007

Erikson, E. H. (1968). *Identity: Youth and crisis*. Norton.

Gallup Poll Social Series. (2022). *U.S. LGBT identification steady at 7.2%*. https://news.gallup.com/poll/470708/lgbt-identification-steady.aspx

Giedd, J. N. (2004). Structural magnetic resonance imaging of the adolescent brain. *Annals of the New York Academy of Sciences*, *1021*(1), 77–85. https://doi.org/10.1196/annals.1308.009

Glavin, E. E., Matthew, J., & Spaeth, A. M. (2022). Gender differences in the relationship between exercise, sleep, and mood in young adults. *Health Education & Behavior*, *49*, 128–140. https://doi.org/10.1177/1090198120986782

Gonzales Aviles, T., Finn, C., & Neyer, F. K. (2020). Patterns of romantic relationship experiences and psychosocial adjustment from adolescence to young adulthood. *Journal of Youth and Adolescence*, *50*, 550–562. https://doi.org/10.1007/s10964-020-01350-7

Grzanka, P. (2020). From buzzword to critical psychology: An invitation to take intersectionality seriously. *Women and Therapy*, *43*(3–4), 244–261. https://doi.org/10.1080/02703149.2020.1729473

Gulliver, A., Griffiths, K. M., & Christensen, H. (2010). Perceived barriers and facilitators to mental health help-seeking in young people: A systematic review. *BMC Psychiatry 10*(113). https://doi.org/10.1186/1471-244X-10-113

Herbenick, D., Reece, M., Schick, V., Sanders, S. A., Dodge, B., & Fortenberry, J. D. (2010). Sexual behavior in the United States: Results from a national probability sample of men and women ages 14–94. *The Journal of Sexual Medicine*, *7*(5), 255–265. https://doi.org/10.1111/j.1743-6109.2010.02012.x

Institute of Medicine. (2006). *Sleep disorders and sleep deprivation: An unmet public health problem*. The National Academies Press. https://doi.org/10.17226/11617

Jaramillo, N., Buhi, E. R., Elder, J. P., & Corliss, H. L. (2017). Associations between sex education and contraceptive use among heterosexually active, adolescent males in the United States. *The Journal of Adolescent Health*, *60*(5), 534–540. https://doi.org/10.1016/j.jadohealth.2016.11.025

Johns, M., Liddon, N., Jayne, P., Beltran, O., Steiner, R., & Morris, E. (2018). Systemic mapping of relationship-level protective factors and sexual health outcomes among sexual minority youth: The role of peers, parents, and partners, and providers. *LGBT Health*, *5*(1). https://doi.org/10.1089/lgbt.2017.0053

Johnson, S. B., Blum, R. W., & Giedd, J. N. (2009). Adolescent maturity and the brain: The promise and pitfalls of neuroscience research in adolescent health policy. *The Journal of Adolescent Health*, *45*(3), 216–221. https://doi.org/10.1016/j.jadohealth.2009.05.016

Kohlberg, L. (1984). *The psychology of moral development: The nature and validity of moral stages*. Harper & Row.

Kumar-Kar, S., Choudhury, A., & Singh, A. P. (2015). Understanding normal development of adolescent sexuality: A bumpy ride. *Journal of Human Reproductive Sciences*, *8*(2), 70–74. https://doi.org/10.4103/0974-1208.158594

Lally, M., & Valentine-French, S. (2019). *Lifespan development: A psychological perspective* (2nd ed.). Creative Commons. http://dept.clcillinois.edu/psy/LifespanDevelopment.pdf

Linehan, M. (1993). *Skills training manual for borderline personality disorder*. Guilford Press.

Liu, Y., Wheaton, A. G., Chapman, D. P., Cunningham, T. J., Lu, H., & Croft, J. B. (2016). Prevalence of healthy sleep duration among adults – United States, 2014. *Morbidity and Mortality Weekly Report*, *65*, 137–141. https://doi.org/10.15585/mmwr.mm6506a1

Marcia, J. E. (1966). Development and validation of ego-identity status. *Journal of Personality and Social Psychology*, *3*(5), 551–558. https://doi.org/10.1037/h0023281

Naar-King, S., & Suarez, M. (2010). *Motivational interviewing for adolescents and young adults*. Guilford Press.

National Academies of Sciences, Engineering, and Medicine (NASEM). (2019). *The promise of adolescence: Realizing opportunity for all youth*. The National Academies Press. https://doi.org/10.17226/25388

Palmer, C. A., Bower, J. L., Cho, K. W., Clementi, M. A., Lau, S., Oosterhoff, B., & Alfano, C. A. (2023). Sleep loss and emotion: A systematic review and meta-analysis of over 50 years of experimental research. *Psychological Bulletin*. Advance online publication. https://doi.org/10.1037/bul0000410

Piaget, J. (1965). *The moral judgment of the child*. Free Press (Original work published 1932).

Pistorello, J., Fruzzetti, A. E., Maclane, C., Gallop, R., & Iverson, K. M. (2012). Dialectical Behavior Therapy (DBT) applied to college students: A randomized clinical trial. *Journal of Consulting and Clinical Psychology*, *80*(6), 982–994. https://doi.org/10.1037/a0029096

Rasberry, C. N., Lowry, R., Johns, M., Robin, L., Dunville, R., Pampati, S., Dittus, P. J., & Balaji, A. (2018). Sexual risk behavior differences among sexual minority high school students—United States, 2015 and 2017. *MMWR Morbidity and Mortality Weekly Report*, *67*, 1007–1011. http://dx.doi.org/10.15585/mmwr.mm6736a3

Robbins, C. K., & McGowan, B. L. (2016). Intersectional perspectives on gender and gender identity development. *New Directions for Student Services*, *2016*(154), 71–83. https://doi.org/10.1002/ss.20176

Rounsefell, K., Gibson, S., McLean, S., Blair, M., Molenaar, A., Brennan, L., Truby, H., & McCaffery, T. (2019). Social media, body image, and food choices in young adults: A mixed methods systematic review. *Nutrition & Dietetics*, *2020*(77), 12–40. https://doi.org/10.1111/1747-0080.12581

Santelli, J. S., Brener, N. D., Lowry, R., Bhatt, A., & Zabin, L. S. (1998). Multiple sexual partners among U.S. adolescents and young adults. *Family Planning Perspectives*, *30*(6), 271–275. https://doi.org/10.2307/2991502

Sladek, M. R., Gusman, M. S., & Doane, L. D. (2023). Ethnic-racial identity development trajectories across the transition to college. *Journal of Youth and Adolescence*, *52*, 880–898. https://doi.org/10.1007/s10964-022-01724-z

Substance Abuse and Mental Health Services Administration. (2021). *Using motivational interviewing in substance use disorder treatment. Advisory.* Substance Abuse and Mental Health Services Administration (SAMHSA).

Tanith Herring, G., Loades, M. E., Higson-Sweeney, N., Hards, E., Reynolds, S., & Midgely, N. (2022). The experience of cognitive behavioural therapy in depressed adolescents who are fatigued. *Psychology & Psychotherapy*, *95*(1), 234–255. https://doi.org/10.1111/papt.12365

Taylor, A. B., & Neppl, T. K. (2023). Sexual identity in lesbian, gay, bisexual, transgender, and queer or questioning emerging adults: The role of parental rejection, and sexuality specific family support. *Journal of Family Issues*, *44*(2), 409–428. https://doi.org/10.1177/0192513X211050063

Umaña-Taylor, A. J., Quintana, S. M., Lee, R. M., Cross, W. E., Jr, Rivas-Drake, D., Schwartz, S. J., Syed, M., Yip, T., Seaton, E., & Ethnic and Racial Identity in the 21st Century Study Group. (2014). Ethnic and racial identity during adolescence and into young adulthood: An integrated conceptualization. *Child Development*, *85*(1), 21–39. https://doi.org/10.1111/cdev.12196

Vasilenko, S. A., Evans-Polce, R. J., & Lanza, S. T. (2017). Age trends in rates of substance use disorders across ages 18–90: Differences by gender and race/ethnicity. *Drug and Alcohol Dependence*, *180*, 260–264. https://doi.org/10.1016/j.drugalcdep.2017.08.027

Wittchen, H. U., Behrendt, M., Höfler, M., Perkonigg, A., Lieb, R., Bühringer, G., & Beesdo, K. (2008). What are the high risk periods for incident substance use and transitions to abuse and dependence? Implications for early intervention and prevention. *International Journal of Methods in Psychiatric Research*, *17*(S1), S16–S29. https://doi.org/10.1002/mpr.254

Ybarra, M. L., Rosario, M., Saewyc, E., & Goodenow, C. (2016). Sexual behaviors and partner characteristics by sexual identity among adolescent girls. *The Journal of Adolescent Health: Official Publication of the Society for Adolescent Medicine*, *58*(3), 310–316. https://doi.org/10.1016/j.jadohealth.2015.11.001

Chapter 9

The 20- to 21-Year-Old

Dominique A. Avery and Karen Jubert

Lula is a 20-year-old junior in college. They are Latinx, come from a smaller town, lower SES, and identify with a strongly connected family and collectivistic community. In the last year, they have come out as genderqueer at college, started using they/them pronouns, and began to present their gender as more androgynous. They are in a relationship with a college senior, Bo, at the same school who is a 21-year-old cisgender male. He is from a higher SES, Western-acculturated family, and is biracial white/Asian. Lula is concerned about Bo's upcoming graduation after which he is planning to travel and doesn't have a specific career path. Lula will return to live with their family this summer and feels pressure to move back home after graduation to get a "good job."

Lula occasionally engages in social binge drinking but has no pattern of other problematic substance use. They are experiencing some anxiety that has been present since elementary school but are not currently suicidal. Lula is feeling uncertain about the future and how to navigate family and intimate partner relationships. They have not come out as genderqueer to their family, and although they believe their family will be supportive, there is not a lot of gender diversity in their small hometown. The recent changes have increased their anxiety, and they are seeking counseling at the college counseling center.

The ages of 20 and 21 fall within the period of emerging adulthood. The theory of emerging adulthood was first introduced by Arnett in 2000 to explain the period after age 18 when, although legally an adult, many have not yet reached the three criteria that mark the transition to adulthood: accepting personal responsibility, independent decision-making, and financial independence Arnett (2007). Additionally, emerging adulthood is described by five main characteristics: instability, possibilities, self-focus, in-betweenness, and identity explorations (Arnett, 2015). By age 20 to 21, some features such as sexual and physical development may be near completion, but emotionally and neurologically, the brain does not fully transition from an adolescent brain to an adult brain until the mid-20s. Additionally, issues such as identity formation, social and familial relationships, and career are particularly heightened.

There has been debate over the conceptualization of the ages 18 to 29 as a distinct developmental period due to the contextual nature of individuals as they transition from adolescence to adulthood (Arnett, 2015; Arnett et al., 2011). The theory of emerging adulthood was developed on Western-acculturated populations although it has now been researched and substantiated as a global and cross-cultural phenomenon (Swanson, 2016). However,

DOI: 10.4324/9781003196297-13

Syed and Mitchell (2013) caution that the theory of emerging adulthood may not universally apply to all racial and ethnic groups, especially those that are collectivistic for whom individualization vs. independence takes a different developmental route. Furthermore, class and socioeconomic status impact factors such as college attendance, career choice, and living situations (Arnett, 2015; Landberg et al., 2019). Despite the critiques, emerging adulthood is a widely accepted stage of development (Swanson, 2016).

The theory of emerging adulthood arose to capture the subjective nature of the phase between adolescence and adulthood due to the rising age of life transitions in industrialized nations (Arnett, 2000). For many, the early years of their 20s are a period of in-betweenness, where individuals are no longer fully under the supportive structures of their family of origin and K–12 education but frequently have not yet fully achieved the common milestones of adulthood: marriage, parenthood, career, and independent living. For example, the average age of marriage in the United States has continued to rise since the 1950s and now hovers around age 30 (U.S. Census Bureau, 2022). Similarly, individuals ages 20–21 are less likely to have given birth to their first child compared to past decades (Central Intelligence Agency US, 2023). We have chosen to use the theory of emerging adulthood to discuss many of the typical experiences of ages 20 to 21, without assuming universality, while attending to the various contextual nuances. For example, at age 20 to 21, marriage and childbirth are not uncommon. Additionally, routes such as employment after high school, associate degrees, or certificate education may lead to earlier starts to careers.

Five Features of the Theory of Emerging Adulthood

Arnett (2015) characterized emerging adulthood by five main features: identity explorations, self-focus, in-betweenness, instability, and possibilities. These domains are not exclusive to this age range but are most prevalent during ages 18 to 25 (Arnett & Mitra, 2020). Identity exploration is one of the defining aspects of early adulthood (Arnett, 2000, 2015), and the early 20s are often occupied by the questions "Who am I?," "What do I want to do with my life?," and, "Who do I want to build relationships with (friendships and sexual/romantic)?" All these identity exploration questions are self-focused as emerging adults learn to care for themselves in newly independent ways.

When emerging adults are asked if they feel they have reached adulthood, the answer is: in some ways, yes, and, in other ways, no, which demonstrates the feeling of in-betweenness (Arnett, 2015). The in-betweenness of exploration and delay in settling into adulthood milestones mark an extension of Erikson's (1950) stage of adolescence defined by identity vs. role confusion. Likewise, exploration of identity is often accompanied by increased instability (Arnett, 2015) due to frequent shifts in location and housing because of moves for college attendance, shifts in relationship status, or changes in employment. While many may focus on the negative aspects of this life stage such as increased risk-taking, higher levels of substance use, and struggles with mental health and independence, it is also important to keep in mind this is an age of possibilities as emerging adults explore how they want to live their lives (Arnett, 2000). The five features of emerging adulthood are evident in the clients described in the case study and are further explored in each of the sections of this chapter.

Physical Development

Although most aspects of physical development have finished by the ages of 20 to 21, ongoing brain development (Bethlehem et al., 2022) and weight gain (Zagorsky & Smith, 2011) will continue through this period. Emerging adults tend to be physically healthy; 91% report they are in excellent, very good, or good health (Alawode & Nicholson, 2023). The highest causes of death are external rather than health-related complications. The main health concerns are risky lifestyle choices (e.g., smoking, sedentary behavior, binge drinking) that may determine health outcomes in later adulthood (Daw et al., 2017) and higher rates of drug and alcohol use (Substance Abuse and Mental Health Services Administration [SAMHSA], 2022). Additionally, among those ages 20 to 24, cisgender males die at 3.5 times the rate of cisgender females (CDC, 2020) with unintentional injury as the leading cause of death for both sexes. Homicide is the second leading cause of death for cisgender males and the third cause for cisgender females. For cisgender females, suicide is the second leading cause of death and the third cause for cisgender males. Emerging adults also pay less attention to their physical health and have the lowest rates of health literacy and use of preventative health services, compared to other adults, even if they have access to healthcare or current health insurance (Alawode & Nicholson, 2023).

The independence associated with emerging adulthood may look different for those needing long-term dependence on caregivers. For those with chronic health conditions, the transition from pediatric to adult care systems presents challenges. The quality of the transition into adult care is dependent on adequate preparation and intentional timing (Coyne et al., 2019). The transition may also have emotional challenges such as acclimatizing to a different healthcare culture, loss of security in relationships, and fears over taking greater responsibility for their medical care. Additionally, the feeling of being between care, lack of belonging, and culture shock (Coyne et al., 2019) mirrors the general in-betweenness of this phase of development. Good communication about the process (Coyne et al., 2019) and supporting self-determination (McDougall et al., 2010) are important factors for positive outcomes. Self-determination is important to all emerging adults at this stage of life but is especially important to those with chronic conditions and/or disabilities (McDougall et al., 2010).

The Second Puberty of Transgender Transitions

Sexual maturation is complete in cisgender adolescents by age 20 to 21. However, medical interventions such as hormone blockers delay or halt the onset of puberty for transgender and genderqueer youth (Coleman et al., 2022). The ages of 18 to 24 are the most common time when trans adolescents first begin to transition or fully express their gender identity (Herman et al., 2022). They may seek hormone replacement therapy or gender-affirming medical treatments that constitute second puberty (Coleman et al., 2022). Medical interventions such as hormone blockers have become more widely researched (Ehrensaft et al., 2018) and available in some areas, while anti-transgender legislation limiting the availability of gender-affirming health care is on the rise (Trans Legislation Tracker, n.d.), making the future of access to gender-affirming medical care uncertain. College has been a space where Lula has explored their gender identity and gender expression. Within counseling, they need support navigating how they will present when returning to their hometown. Additionally, counseling is often a necessary step in the gate-keeping model of transgender healthcare and could be useful to Lula if they decide to pursue medical transition.

Brain Development

In the last few decades, neuroscience research has substantiated the continuation of brain development through the mid-20s. Chapter 1 includes a full discussion of brain development. During the ages of 20–21, the brain is transitioning from an adolescent brain to an adult brain, which mirrors the developmental characteristic of in-betweenness. Emerging adulthood marks a time of strengthening and stabilizing existing structural and functional neural connections (Andrews et al., 2020; Luna et al., 2020). By the mid-20s, the most dramatic structural changes of synaptic pruning and myelination are mostly complete.

Structurally, most of the brain development during emerging adulthood occurs in the prefrontal cortex including the areas involved in executive function, attention, reward systems, and social processes (Tamnes et al., 2017). Longitudinal brain scans show development moving from the top, in the primary somatosensory areas of the dorsal parietal lobe, then progressing forward and down with the cortex and the PFC maturing last (Bethlehem et al., 2022; Tamnes et al., 2017). Within the sensory and motor regions, connections between the frontoparietal and limbic networks involved in memory, mentalizing (ability to interpret mental states, feelings, and the actions of others), and social cognition continue to strengthen (Andrews et al., 2020). Additionally, there are structural-developmental differences from earlier adolescence. Emerging adults have more mature development of the areas of the brain associated with the control of implicit and explicit emotional regulation (Pozzi et al., 2021).

Changes in brain development mirror psychosocial changes. Advances in developmental neuroscience in the last few decades have helped debunk many of the myths about the adolescent brain and behavior such as adolescents as irrational, less risk-averse, and unable to perceive risks (Steinberg, 2008). During emerging adulthood, risk-taking decreases, especially in the context of social pressure, which corresponds with a decrease in sensation-seeking, greater executive functioning, emotional regulation, and decision-making capacities (Romer et al., 2017). Steinberg (2008) proposes gradual structural and functional changes in the prefrontal cortex correspond with the cognitive control system's capacity for self-regulation. As a result, although behaviors such as unprotected sex, drug and alcohol use, and unsafe driving typically peak during the ages of 18–25, they, too, gradually decline.

Cognitive Development

Elements of cognitive development for emerging adults include making decisions, solving problems, accepting responsibility, navigating change, and gaining self-understanding in response to the demands of life during this transition to adulthood (Arnett, 2000; Arnett & Mitra, 2020). For example, Lula is at a crossroads of deciding about whether or not to come out to their parents, figuring out if they will give in to the pressure of moving back home post-graduation, and making decisions about the future of their romantic relationship. Lula's major life decisions are representative for many emerging adults and the process of ambiguous and complex decision-making aids cognitive development (Arnett & Mitra, 2020). As emerging adults navigate life situations, cognitive maturity parallels identity development and understanding of self and others (Arnett, 2007a). Life situations may include activities such as choosing a career, changing jobs, acting on their beliefs or values, managing relationship roles, using their time, making conscientious determinations on unclear matters, or allowing themselves to pivot as needed when new information is presented (Arnett & Mitra, 2020). Thus, cognitive development during emerging adulthood is a time of possibilities as they develop an increased capacity for reasoning and understanding the world around them.

Developmental cognitive expectations should be contextual because early childhood trauma and adverse childhood experiences contribute to stalled maturation of the brain and are the most consistent predictive factor in later cognitive dysfunction (Su et al., 2019). Cognitive immaturity from adverse experiences affect an emerging adult's capacity for growth in their relationships, learning, motivation, memory, social behavior, and some executive functioning (Immordino-Yang et al., 2019). For example, early trauma often impacts the quality of social and romantic relationships. Trauma-focused counseling can improve relationship quality and PTSD symptoms, which cause impairment of memory and ability to process new information.

Aspects of emotional well-being such as chronic sleep deprivation, effects of poor nutrition and gut health, feelings of isolation, and suicidal ideation affect cognitive functioning (Immordino-Yang et al., 2019). Additionally, disparities of racial stress, experiences of discrimination, and racial disproportionality of social determinants of health impact cognitive development among emerging adults (Chen et al., 2022; Immordino-Yang et al., 2019). However, many activities are related to positive cognitive development and resilience. Educational and social relationships increase brain efficiency and engagement in higher-level cognitive functions (Immordino-Yang et al., 2019). Developmental tasks such as decisions about lifestyle, careers, and committed relationships enhance disciplined thinking and symbolic thinking (Immordino-Yang et al., 2019). Lula has many protective factors for their cognitive function including absence of childhood trauma and supportive relationships. The decisions they are struggling with are typical of the cognitive life-stage tasks described before. Strong social support could be helpful in successfully navigating decision-making and, therefore, strengthening cognitive processes.

Emotional Development

Ages 20 to 21 can be an exciting time filled with possibilities but is also a time of increased emotional instability making it difficult to distinguish between normative identity development processes and difficulties that will persist as mental health concerns (Arnett et al., 2014). Frequent transitions contribute to instability in emerging adulthood and can cause psychological distress due to role confusion (Lane, 2015). For Lula, the move home has triggered anxiety and stress as they try to reconcile how to navigate their identity and relationships in these two different environments. Secure attachments are related to psychological well-being (Schwartz, 2016), and Lula's belief in the support they will receive from their parents is a protective factor. Additionally, positive peer relationships support emerging adults' ability to navigate developmental challenges and contribute to emotional well-being. Therefore, familial and social context is interconnected to emotional development as emerging adults navigate identity development questions of "Who am I?" and "How do I fit in?"

Emerging adults have increased emotional regulation capacity compared to adolescents (Pozzi et al., 2021) but have the highest risk for substance use and other mental health disorders (SAMHSA, 2022). The first onset of half of all mental health disorders occurs by the age of 24 (Jones, 2013). Similarly, ages 18 to 27 years old are at the highest risk of developing substance use disorders (Jones, 2013; SAMHSA, 2022), whereas anxiety disorders tend to have an earlier onset (median age 11) and mood disorders tend to develop later with a median onset of 30 (Jones, 2013). Childhood psychological maltreatment is strongly associated with a weaker sense of self and is a predictor of PTSD symptoms among emerging adults (Watts et al., 2023). However, a significant protective factor is the belief in future possibilities and a sense of optimism, which can help buffer against stress, anxiety, and depression (Arnett, 2015).

Social and Relationship Development

For emerging adults, the social and relationship dynamics of friendships, family relations, and romantic and sexual encounters are pivotal developmental concerns (Arnett, 2006). Erikson's (1950) psychosocial theory includes the successful navigation of intimate relationships, both friendship and sexual/affectional partnerships but does not adequately account for the unique nature of the period, which includes aspects of both adolescent and early adulthood psychosocial stages. Relationships and supportive social connections play a critical role in mental and emotional well-being during this period of transition (Lane, 2015). For ages 20 to 21, this is a period of exploration and instability (Arnett, 2015), and of opportunities and possibilities (Lane, 2015), thus the potential exists for transformative and rewarding social and relationship experiences. Within college settings, this evolves through peer connections from joining major-specific, interest-oriented, or identity-based student organizations; attending campus networking events; getting involved in team sports; and/or taking on leadership roles. Within the larger community setting, social and relationship experiences develop through participating in community service activities, hobbies, or interest groups; joining various organizations; or being involved with religious or spiritual entities.

Social Identity Development

During emerging adulthood, social roles expand beyond the influence of caregivers toward more autonomous relationships and greater integrated social identity as a romantic partner, friend, or adult family member (Arnett, 2006). They face the pressure of a social-clock for achieving the markers of adulthood: finishing college, starting a new career/job, getting married, or buying a home (Arnett, 2007). Emerging adults may experience distress and feelings of inadequacy or discontentment by not meeting their own or others' timing of major social milestones. Emerging adults may also struggle socially if they are among vulnerable populations such as those who age out of foster care (Courtney et al., 2021; Rosenberg & Abbott, 2019), have histories with the criminal justice system (Arnett, 2007; Park, 2022), belong to a marginalized community, or live with mental health or chronic illness (Milder et al., 2023). In contrast, some emerging adults may have more freedom from social-clock expectations because family members can supply support to them through these transitional years (Fingerman et al., 2012). Thus, they may take longer to figure out their next life steps or may experiment more with potential life directions. The socioeconomic differences between Bo and Lula are evident in how each is managing their social-clock. Bo's family can supply the financial support to experience an extended period of travel before settling into adulthood markers. In contrast, Lula and their family have interconnected financial dependence whereas moving back home and getting a "good job" may alleviate financial stress on both Lula and their family, leading to a different social developmental path.

Relationships

As emerging adults become less dependent on their family of origin, friends begin to grow as central sources of intimacy and social support (Arnett, 2006). Friendships among emerging adults are likely to be based on connection due to similar culture, beliefs, ethnicity, hobbies, and behaviors (McPherson et al., 2001). Friendships may be affected by the instability that marks this period due to transitions in starting college, moving away from home, beginning a career, changes in romantic partnerships, or becoming a parent. Major life events shape identity development and influence the roles of friendships. Counseling can be a space for Lula to deepen their understand of familial, social, and romantic relationships. Helpful interventions could include exploring their social network and who is within their circles of support by identifying people within their inner circle of intimate relationships, then expanding out to friendships, acquaintances, and transactional relationships.

In emerging adulthood, adult responsibilities are delayed, thus many 20- to 21-year-olds benefit from stronger connections with their caregivers for financial, emotional support, and decision-making guidance (Arnett, 2015; Fingerman et al., 2012). Family relationship dynamics such as intensive parenting styles (emotional, financial, practical, advice-giving, or social support provided from parents) contribute to better psychological outcomes (Fingerman et al., 2012). Race and ethnicity may shape family-of-origin perspectives of independence vs. interdependence (Syed & Mitchell, 2013), as seen in the differences between Lula's collectivistic family and Bo's Western-acculturated family expectations.

Intimacy and emotional support can come from friendships, romantic partners, and sexual relationships (Arnett, 2000). Relationship patterns are increasingly diverse among emerging adults. For example, some delay marriage until their late 20s; wait until after marriage to have children; have children before marriage with a cohabitating partner; choose not to have children; remain single; or maintain long-term monogamous, multiple partner, or polyamorous relationships. Additionally, emerging adults use more flexible ways of connecting including spontaneous gatherings (Arnett, 2000) and social media

(Arnett, 2015). Noncommitted, emotionally inconsequential sexual interactions through hook-ups, friends with benefits, one-night stands, or stay-over relationships are more common among this age group (Arnett, 2006; Burdette et al., 2009; Jamison & Ganong, 2011). Navigating the emotional uncertainty of relationship conflicts, first relationship break-ups, boundaries, and healthy vs. abusive relationships is common during this developmental period (Arnett, 2006).

Culture and Identity Development

Emerging adulthood is characterized by identity formation (Arnett, 2000) within a cultural context. As emerging adults negotiate identity development, there are three main areas of exploration: love, worldview, and work (Arnett, 2000). Love and romance become more committed and intimate as emerging adults explore physical and emotional connections through sexual activity and cohabitation (Arnett, 2000). Arnett poses a common identity-focused question that captures the developmental needs of this period: "Given the kind of person I am, what kind of person do I wish to have as a partner through life?" (p. 473). Thus, identity development and intimate relationships are closely intertwined.

Worldview is the lens through which a person processes information and forms the values and beliefs through which they make sense of the world (Arnett, 2000, 2015). Worldview is shaped by one's early childhood experiences, family of origin, culture, religious values, and present identity exploration. Dominant social norms form a master narrative that influences how individuals view their cultural identity and engage in culturally bound behaviors such as gender roles. Exploration of new environments and experiences may lead emerging adults to question the worldview they developed earlier in life (Arnett, 2000). Erikson (1950) conceptualized development during emerging adulthood as a renegotiation of identity as an individual moves from childhood to incorporating wider societal contexts of adulthood. More recent discursive identity development models expand beyond the individual focus to include master narratives (McLean et al., 2016). McLean et al. (2016) highlights the interconnectedness of personal and structural processes in gender identity development for emerging adulthood. Frequent relocation and exposure to new social contexts may allow for the reauthoring of childhood master narratives as we see in the case of Lula.

Identity factors, such as the urge to establish oneself, arise through the exploration of educational and work options in preparation for more focused roles as adults (Arnett, 2000). The path to establishing oneself can take many different forms including direct engagement in work after high school, going to college or trade school, exploration and travel, establishing a family, or prolonged time at home. Socioeconomic status (SES) affects the options available, and lower SES emerging adults feel more pressure to establish themselves sooner (Landberg et al., 2019). The exploration of work experiences brings about identity-focused questions: "Who am I?" (personality); "What do I love to do?" (interests); "What are my skills and abilities?" (strengths); "What matters to me and my family?" (values); "What motivates me?" (inspiration and motivation); "How ready am I for change?" (readiness); and "What do I want or need" (beliefs, desires, and aspirations). However, satisfaction and fulfillment are not always the result of emerging adults exploring love, work, and worldview, and some may experience disappointment, rejection, isolation, or exclusion (Arnett, 2000). Nevertheless, emerging adulthood is a time of possibility and opportunity as they find their place in relationships and occupations.

The age of emerging adulthood is a period of exploration for individuals to figure out who they are and how they fit in society, find a sense of belonging, align values, and build solidarity (Arnett, 2000; Syed & Mitchell, 2013). They may seek a reflection of themselves in those around them as a form of validation and acceptance (Arnett, 2000). However, Syed and Mitchell (2013) debate if the Western concepts of emerging adulthood apply to minoritized racial and ethnic groups because they may have shortened or lengthened identity formation due to increased family responsibilities or added identity development issues of acculturation. For emerging adults seeking to find places of belonging and a secure sense of self, racial and ethnic identity formation is one of the more variable areas of development. Societal barriers such as privilege, stigma, discrimination, stereotypes, White supremacy, racism, and other oppressive systems can affect identity development (Syed & Mitchell, 2013). Most models have focused on the *process* of ethnic identity development, while Syed and Azmitia (2008) developed an ethnic identity development model with a large, ethnically diverse college population to fill a gap in understanding the *content* of ethnic identity for emerging adults. Syed and Azmitia's study yielded four categories of narratives: experiences of prejudice, feelings of connection or belonging to their racial/ethnic group, awareness of being different within their own ethnic group or from others, and awareness of underrepresentation or being in the minority. The relevance each of the four themes will have in the life of an emerging adult will depend on many factors such as their privileged vs. minoritized racial/ethnic status, social/peer context, and stage of racial/ethnic identity development.

Lula's and Bo's experiences are characteristic of the race/ethnicity and class factors that shape emerging adulthood. Lula is experiencing conflict between their family of origin's collectivistic values and the individual, self-exploration path their partner plans to take after college. Lula's ethnic/racial and gender identity development has heightened during their time at college through exposure to new social contexts and course content. The pressure Lula feels to return and establish themselves within their home community compared to Bo, who is acculturated in Western expectations of freedom to explore and shape his identity individually before setting down, are common racial/ethnic differences (Syed & Mitchell, 2013). One of the goals of counseling, therefore, would not be to help Lula conform to one standard of identity development over the other but rather to discover their values and desired path in moving toward adulthood. Lula's lower SES background also likely adds to the pressure to establish themselves post-graduation rather than continued exploration (Landberg et al., 2019). For Lula, these are big identity questions about relationships and the values they are developing as an emerging adult.

Resources and Protective Factors

The further development of a sense of self and finding a place in the world present an exciting time for emerging adults. Those ages 20 to 21 are entering a period of greater emotional and cognitive stability and decreases in risky behaviors (Pozzi et al., 2021;

Romer et al., 2017; Steinberg, 2008). An important protective factor for emerging adults is the presence of family and social support systems (Coyne et al., 2019; Jankowski et al., 2021; Lane, 2015; Schwartz, 2016). Those with good support systems tend to have better mental health and overall well-being.

Extended Services as Protective Factors

For adolescents in foster care, extended services have been shown to have widespread, positive benefits (Courtney et al., 2021), especially in reducing racial disparities (Rosenberg & Abbott, 2019). Emerging adults receiving extended services are 3 times more likely to be enrolled in school, 1.3 times more likely to be employed, and experience increased housing stability. Extending care to age 21 leads to 2.7 times reduction in homelessness compared to those who exited at age 18 (Courtney et al., 2021). Social and emotional benefits include being two times less likely to become young parents than those exiting at 18 (Rosenberg & Abbott, 2019), having a reduced risk of entering the justice system (Park, 2022), and having stronger emotional and social support systems (Courtney et al., 2021). The Family First Prevention Services Act (2017) allows states to extend foster care services until the age of 23. Most states extend services, varying from ages 19 to 23 (Child Welfare Information Gateway, 2022). In summary, extended care shows the importance of ongoing structural and relational support through ages 20 to 21.

Challenges and Risk Factors

The most prevailing risk factors for ages 20 to 21 are suicide, mental illness, and substance use. Suicide is the second-highest cause of death for cisgender females and third-highest for cisgender males (CDC, 2020). Transgender adolescents have higher rates of suicide (James et al., 2016), but supportive social and family environments are a significant mediating factor (Olson et al., 2016). Ages 18 to 25 are more likely than any other adult age category to have a mental illness (SAMHSA, 2022). They are more likely to have a major depressive episode and significantly more likely than older adults to have had serious suicidal thoughts (13.0% of ages 18–25), made a suicide plan (4.9% of ages 18–25), or attempted suicide (2.7% of ages 18–25). Suicidal thoughts and behaviors among emerging adults occur at similar rates to younger adolescents. They also have the highest rates of needing substance use treatment (25.1% of ages 18–25, compared to 7.6% of ages 12 to 17, and 15.1% of 26 and older). However, they do not receive interventions for substance use disorders at corresponding rates, only 4.1% of ages 18 to 25 received treatment. Similarly, emerging adults are less likely than older adults to receive treatment for other mental health disorders but have higher rates of perceived unmet needs.

Illicit drug use peaks during the ages of 18 to 25, with 38.0% using an illicit drug in the last year (SAMHSA, 2022). Marijuana is the most often used illicit drug (35.4% ages 18 to 25) followed by misuse of prescription pain relievers, tranquilizers or sedatives, hallucinogens, and cocaine. Binge drinking is also a common risk behavior among emerging adults. Although alcohol use is common throughout adolescence and emerging adulthood, age 21 is when alcohol becomes legal to consume in the United States and is a major social milestone for many emerging adults. Among the age group 18 to 25, 29.2% had engaged in binge drinking in the previous 30 days (SAMHSA, 2022). Lula, for example, does not regularly use drugs or alcohol but discloses occasional social binge drinking. Binge drinking is correlated with structural and functional abnormalities in the still developing prefrontal cortex and subcortical structures of the brain (Pérez-García et al., 2022). Functional changes related to binge drinking include compromised executive functions of decision-making and reward-related decision-making, increased difficulty performing inhibitory control (necessary for goal-oriented behavior) tasks, and abnormalities in working memory. Decision-making, goal-oriented behavior, and working memory are all crucial aspects of academic success and maintaining employment, which are key developmental tasks for ages 20 to 21. Due to the high rates of alcohol and drug use and low rate of accessing treatment, counseling for this age group should include screening for substance use.

Best Practices for Counseling and Therapy

Emerging adulthood is a time of taking on greater responsibility for mental health services. Yet, persons ages 20 to 21 may not seek help for mental health services due to beliefs about the need for independence and autonomy (Wilson et al., 2011) or because of racial/ethnic disparities in access and availability of relevant mental health care (NeMoyer et al., 2022). However, the involvement of family and social support is related to help-seeking behaviors. Wilson et al. (2011) found emerging adults are more likely to disclose mental illness or suicidal thoughts to intimate partners, but, for many, family members have the biggest influence on making connections to counselors. Due to the influence of families in the lives of emerging adults, counseling including family members or family systems–focused counseling may be relevant, especially when working to build support systems. Additionally, the heightened influence of peers for emerging adults means group interventions are well-suited to support identity exploration and the development of a sense of self in the social context (Giannone et al., 2020). Smaller, structured groups allow for closer relationship building and support when used with identity formation questions such as LGBTQIA+ topics, cultural identity development, and trauma support.

Relationship counseling may be useful in supporting emerging adults in navigating sexual/affectional relationships. A counseling focus on intimate relationships is useful for developing healthy relationship skills and assessing for intimate partner violence. Counselors should also regularly screen for drug and alcohol use and consider co-occurring treatment due to high rates of substance use and underutilization of treatment (SAMHSA, 2022). Counselors should include routine suicide screenings because of the high rate of suicidal thoughts and behaviors among this age group (SAMHSA, 2022).

Developmentally, emerging adults have reached similar emotional and cognitive capacities as adults; thus, most counseling interventions are likely to be developmentally appropriate. Expressive therapies such as art, music, poetry, writing, dance, or drama can be useful healing outlets for emerging adults to process memories and feelings that may be difficult to put into words. Counselors should consider the specific risk, situational, and identity factors when selecting approaches for working with ages 20 to 21. The impact of trauma (Su et al., 2019) and cumulative exposure to racial stress (Chen et al., 2022) are important contextual factors in counseling emerging adults. Frequent instability means that social support and attachment are particularly important in the counseling relationship (Lane, 2015), and the counselor should attend to intra-counseling relationship building in addition to external social supports. For many emerging adults attending college, continuity of care is an important support when moving between school and home during breaks. This can be addressed using brief and time limited approaches, the use of telehealth, or referrals. Counselors should also provide referrals to supplemental resources such as health services, social supports, career or housing services, etc. to aid the successful transition to the markers of adulthood. Due to the support emerging adults still need, decision-making, career-focused, or brief task-oriented counseling can be helpful to resolve issues such as deciding where to live, attending college/technical training or not, choosing a career path, and making many other "adult" decisions.

Telehealth allows for continuity of services during moves, decreases financial and transportation barriers, and increases access in rural areas. Since the COVID-19 pandemic, telehealth has become a standard modality within mental health. Telehealth offers benefits such as continuity of care with a preferred counselor, increased connection to specialist services, and ease of access. However, counselors should attend to considerations such as remote crisis response, diminished nonverbal communication, disruptions to confidentiality, and laws and rules when working across stateliness, and it may not be appropriate for all clients or conducive to all modalities such as expressive arts.

Case Conceptualization and Interventions

Lula is experiencing a period of instability and a feeling of in-betweenness that is common for emerging adults. While expected for this period of life, these changes and uncertainty about the future have exacerbated underlying anxiety. Although Lula denies current suicidal ideation, they have disclosed social binge drinking. It will be important to build trust and continue to assess for alcohol use or suicidal ideation.

Short-term approaches may help Lula with immediate problem-solving and decrease anxiety as the end of the school year and significant life transitions approach. Solution-focused counseling is effective in alleviating anxiety with college students (Novella et al., 2022). Telehealth has the potential benefit of continuation of services after Lula returns home for the summer. It may be helpful to connect Lula to genderqueer online social support to help with any feeling of isolation in their small hometown. Additionally, due to Bo's graduation and Lula's recent gender identity exploration, it could be useful to connect Lula with counseling groups, cultural centers, or student organizations on campus when they return to school to bolster social support (Giannone et al., 2020).

Lula is grappling with some large identity questions that could be addressed in longer-term, identity integration–focused counseling. Counseling focused on the emotional process of discovering identity, values, and beliefs (Schwartz et al., 2005) would help Lula negotiate conflicting expectations. Narrative therapy and other post-modern approaches are well-suited to integrating the nuances of social, cultural, environmental, and other contextual factors faced by emerging adults navigating identity development. Narrative therapy processes of identifying, deconstructing, and reauthoring the dominant story are well-suited to support Latinx clients such as Lula to integrate the contrasting cultural, familial, and environmental pressures they experience during transition periods (Farrell & Gibbons, 2019).

Conclusion

The ages of 20 to 21 are an exciting time of possibilities for identity development but also a time when risk factors such as substance use and suicide cannot be ignored. Positive support systems from friends, family, and intimate partners are indicative of good outcomes for this developmental period despite instability and uncertainty (Coyne et al., 2019; Jankowski et al., 2021; Lane, 2015; Schwartz, 2016). Counseling is one support system that can help emerging adults navigate the five main features of this period: instability, possibilities, self-focus, in-betweenness, and identity explorations (Arnett, 2015). The characteristics of this period are not age-bound (Arnett & Mitra, 2020), and many contextual factors will influence the nuanced differences in how individuals navigate the journey from adolescence into adulthood.

References

Alawode, O. A., & Nicholson, H. L. (2023). Health literacy and uptake of annual physical check-ups among emerging adults in the United States: Findings from the behavioral risk factor surveillance system. *Sociology Compass*, *17*(4), e13081. https://doi.org/10.1111/soc4.13081

Andrews, J. R., Ahmed, S. P., & Blakemore, S. (2021). Navigating the social environment in adolescence: The role of social brain development. *Biological Psychiatry*, *89*(2), 109–118. https://doi.org/10.1016/j.biopsych.2020.09.012

Arnett, J. J. (2000). Emerging adulthood: A theory of development from the late teens through the twenties. *American Psychologist*, *55*(5), 469–480. https://doi.org/10.1037//0003-066X.55.5.469

Arnett, J. J. (2006). The psychology of emerging adulthood: What is known, and what remains to be known? In J. J. Arnett (Ed.), *Emerging adults in America: Coming of age in the 21st century* (pp. 303–330). American Psychological Association.

Arnett, J. J. (2007). Emerging adulthood: What is it and what is it good for? *Society for Research in Child Development*, *1*(2), 68–73. https://doi.org/10.1111/j.1750-8606.2007.00016.x

Arnett, J. J. (2015). *Emerging adulthood: The winding road from the late teens through the twenties* (2nd ed.). Oxford University Press.

Arnett, J. J., Kloep, M., Hendry, L. B., & Tanner, J. L. (2011). *Debating emerging adulthood: Stage or process?* Oxford University Press.

Arnett, J. J., & Mitra, D. (2020). Are the features of emerging adulthood developmentally distinctive? A comparison of ages 18–60 in the United States. *Emerging Adulthood*, *8*(5), 412–419. https://doi.org/10.1177/2167696818810073

Arnett, J. J., Žukauskienė, R., & Sugimura, K. (2014). The new life stage of emerging adulthood at ages 18–29 years: Implications for mental health. *The Lancet Psychiatry*, *1*(7), 569–576. https://doi.org/10.1016/s2215-0366(14)00080-7

Bethlehem, R. A. I., Seidlitz, J., White, S. N., Vogel, J., Anderson, K. J., Adamson, C., Adler, S. S., Alexopoulos, G. S., Anagnostou, E., Areces-Gonzalez, A., Astle, D. E., Auyeung, B., Ayub, M., Bae, J., Ball, G. C., Baron-Cohen, S., Beare, R., Bedford, S. A., Benegal, V., . . . Lee, S. H. (2022).

Brain charts for the human lifespan. *Nature, 604*(7906), 525–533. https://doi.org/10.1038/s41586-022-04554-y

Burdette, A. M., Ellison, C. G., Hill, T. D., & Glenn, N. D. (2009). "Hooking up" at college: Does religion make a difference? *Journal for the Scientific Study of Religion, 48*(3), 535–551. https://doi.org/10.1111/j.1468-5906.2009.01464.x

Centers for Disease Control and Prevention. (2020). Fatal data visualization. *WISQARS: Web-Based Injury Statistics Query and Reporting System.* https://wisqars.cdc.gov/data/explore-data/home

Central Intelligence Agency US. (2023). Mother's mean age at first childbirth. *World Factbook.* www.cia.gov/the-world-factbook/field/mothers-mean-age-at-first-birth/

Chen, R., Weuve, J., Misra, S., Cuevas, A., Kubzansky, L. D., & Williams, D. R. (2022). Racial disparities in cognitive function among middle-aged and older adults: The roles of cumulative stress exposures across the life course. *The Journals of Gerontology: Series A, 77*(2), 357–364. https://doi.org/10.1093/gerona/glab099

Child Welfare Information Gateway. (2022). *Extension of foster care beyond age 18.* www.childwelfare.gov/topics/systemwide/laws-policies/statutes/extensionfc/

Coleman, E., Radix, A. E., Bouman, W. P., Brown, G. V., De Vries, A. C., Deutsch, M., Ettner, R., Fraser, L., Goodman, M. C., Green, J. C., Hancock, A. B., Johnson, T. E., Karasic, D. H., Knudson, G., Leibowitz, S. F., Meyer-Bahlburg, H. F. L., Monstrey, S., Motmans, J., Nahata, L., . . . Sabir, K. (2022). Standards of care for the health of transgender and gender diverse people: Version 8. *International Journal of Transgender Health, 23*(suppl.1), S1–S259. https://doi.org/10.1080/26895269.2022.2100644

Courtney, M. E., Okpych, N. J., & Park, S. (2021). *Report from CalYOUTH: Findings on the relationships between extended foster care and youths' outcomes at age 21.* Chapin Hall at the University of Chicago.

Coyne, I., Sheehan, A. M., Heery, E., & While, A. (2019). Healthcare transition for adolescents and young adults with long-term conditions: Qualitative study of patients, parents and healthcare professionals' experiences. *Journal of Clinical Nursing, 28*(21–22), 4062–4076. https://doi.org/10.1111/jocn.15006

Daw, J., Margolis, R., & Wright, L. (2017). emerging adulthood, emergent health lifestyles: Sociodemographic determinants of trajectories of smoking, binge drinking, obesity, and sedentary behavior. *Journal of Health and Social Behavior, 58*(2), 181–197. https://doi.org/10.1177/0022146517702421

Ehrensaft, D., Giammattei, S., Storck, K., Tishelman, A. C., & Keo-Meier, C. L. (2018). Prepubertal social gender transitions: What we know; what we can learn-A view from a gender affirmative lens. *International Journal of Transgenderism, 19*(2), 251–268. https://doi.org/10.1080/15532739.2017.1414649

Erikson, E. H. (1950). *Childhood and society.* W. W. Norton & Co.

Family First Prevention Services Act of 2017, H.R. 253 (2017). www.congress.gov/bill/115th-congress/house-bill/253

Farrell, I. C., & Gibbons, M. M. (2019). Using narrative therapy to assist college-age Latino immigrants. *Journal of College Counseling, 22*(1), 83–96. https://doi.org/10.1002/jocc.12116

Fingerman, K. L., Cheng, Y. P., Wesselmann, E. D., Zarit, S., Furstenberg, F., & Birditt, K. S. (2012). Helicopter parents and landing pad kids: Intense parental support of grown children. *Journal of Marriage and Family, 74*(4), 880–896. https://doi.org/10.1111/j.1741-3737.2012.00987.x

Giannone, Z. A., Ben-David, S., Cox, D. W., & Kealy, D. (2022). Emerging adults' experiences of brief group interventions: Two approaches to possible selves. *Counselling Psychology Quarterly, 35*(2), 444–466. https://doi.org/10.1080/09515070.2020.1870438

Herman, J. L., Flores, A. R., & O'Neill, K. K. (2022). How many adults and youth identify as transgender in the United States? *Williams Institute*. https://williamsinstitute.law.ucla.edu/wp-content/uploads/Trans-Pop-Update-Jun-2022.pdf

Immordino-Yang, H. M., Darling-Hammond, L., & Krone, C. R. (2019). Nurturing nature: How brain development is inherently social and emotional, and what this means for education. *Educational Psychologist*, *54*(3), 185–204. https://doi.org/10.1080/00461520.2019.1633924

James, S. E., Herman, J. L., Rankin, S., Keisling, M., Mottet, L., & Anafi, M. (2016). *The report of the 2015 U.S. transgender survey*. National Center for Transgender Equality. https://transequality.org/sites/default/files/docs/usts/USTS-Full-Report-Dec17.pdf

Jamison, T. B., & Ganong, L. (2011). "We're not living together:" Stayover relationships among college-educated emerging adults. *Journal of Social and Personal Relationships*, *28*(4), 536–557. https://doi.org/10.1177/0265407510384897

Jankowski, P. J., Hall, E. R., Crabtree, S. A., Sandage, S. J., Bronstein, M., & Sandage, D. (2021). Risk, symptoms, and well-being: Emerging adult latent profiles during treatment. *Journal of Counseling & Development*, *99*(4), 440–451. https://doi.org/10.1002/jcad.12396

Jones, P. B. (2013). Adult mental health disorders and their age at onset. *British Journal of Psychiatry*, *202*(s54), s5–s10. https://doi.org/10.1192/bjp.bp.112.119164

Landberg, M., Lee, B., & Noack, P. (2019). What alters the experience of emerging adulthood? How the experience of emerging adulthood differs according to socioeconomic status and critical life events. *Emerging Adulthood*, *7*(3), 208–222. https://doi.org/10.1177/2167696819831793

Lane, J. A. (2015). Counseling emerging adults in transition: Practical applications of attachment and social support research. *The Professional Counselor*, *5*(1), 15–27. https://doi.org/10.15241/jal.5.1.15

Luna, B., Tervo-Clemmens, B., & Calabro, F. J. (2021). Considerations when characterizing adolescent neurocognitive development. *Biological Psychiatry*, *89*(2), 96–98. https://doi.org/10.1016/j.biopsych.2020.04.026

McDougall, J., Evans, J., & Baldwin, P. (2010). The importance of self-determination to perceived quality of life for youth and young adults with chronic conditions and disabilities. *Remedial and Special Education*, *31*(4), 252–260. https://doi.org/10.1177/0741932509355989

McLean, K. C., Shucard, H., & Syed, M. (2016). Applying the master narrative framework to gender identity development in emerging adulthood. *Emerging Adulthood*, *5*(2), 93–105. https://doi.org/10.1177/2167696816656254

McPherson, M., Smith-Lovin, L., & Cook, J. M. (2001). Birds of a feather: Homophily in social networks. *Annual Review of Sociology*, *27*(1), 415–444. https://doi.org/10.1146/annurev.soc.27.1.415

Milder, M. K. L., Bazier, A., Ward, S., Rand, K. L., & Hirsh, A. T. (2023). Resilience, social support, and health in emerging adults with and without chronic health conditions. *Emerging Adulthood*, *11*(3), 557–571. https://doi.org/10.1177/21676968221148322

NeMoyer, A., Cruz-Gonzalez, M., Alvarez, K., Kessler, R. C., Sampson, N. A., Green, J. C., & Alegría, M. (2022). Reducing racial/ethnic disparities in mental health service use among emerging adults: Community-level supply factors. *Ethnicity & Health*, *27*(4), 749–769. https://doi.org/10.1080/13557858.2020.1814999

Novella, J. K., Ng, K., & Samuolis, J. (2022). A comparison of online and in-person counseling outcomes using solution-focused brief therapy for college students with anxiety. *Journal of American College Health*, *70*(4), 1161–1168. https://doi.org/10.1080/07448481.2020.1786101

Olson, K. R., Durwood, L., DeMeules, M., & McLaughlin, K. A. (2016). Mental health of transgender children who are supported in their identities. *Pediatrics*, *137*(3), 1–8. https://doi.org/10.1542/peds.2015-3223

Park, K. (2022). Is juvenile justice system involvement context-dependent?: The differential experiences of older foster youth in the context of extended foster care. *Child and Adolescent Social Work Journal*. https://doi.org/10.1007/s10560-022-00840-w

Pérez-García, J., Suárez-Suárez, S., Doallo, S., & Cadaveira, F. (2022). Effects of binge drinking during adolescence and emerging adulthood on the brain: A systematic review of neuroimaging studies. *Neuroscience & Biobehavioral Reviews*, *137*, 1–27. https://doi.org/10.1016/j.neubiorev.2022.104637

Pozzi, E., Vijayakumar, N., Rakesh, D., & Whittle, S. (2021). Neural correlates of emotion regulation in adolescents and emerging adults: A meta-analytic study. *Biological Psychiatry*, *89*(2), 194–204. https://doi.org/10.1016/j.biopsych.2020.08.006

Romer, D., Reyna, V. F., & Satterthwaite, T. D. (2017). Beyond stereotypes of adolescent risk taking: Placing the adolescent brain in developmental context. *Developmental Cognitive Neuroscience*, *27*, 19–34. https://doi.org/10.1016/j.dcn.2017.07.007

Rosenberg, R., & Abbott, S. (2019). Supporting older youth beyond age 18: Examining data and trends in extended foster care. *Child Trends*. www.childtrends.org/publications/supporting-older-youth-beyond-age-18-examining-data-and-trends-in-extended-foster-care

Schwartz, S. J. (2016). Turning point for a turning point: Advancing emerging adulthood theory and research. *Emerging Adulthood*, *4*(5), 307–317. https://doi.org/10.1177/2167696815624640

Schwartz, S. J., Kurtines, W. M., & Montgomery, M. J. (2005). A comparison of two approaches for facilitating identity exploration processes in emerging adults. *Journal of Adolescent Research*, *20*(3), 309–345. https://doi.org/10.1177/0743558404273119

Steinberg, L. (2008). A social neuroscience perspective on adolescent risk-taking. *Developmental Review*, *28*(1), 78–106. https://doi.org/10.1016/j.dr.2007.08.002

Su, Y., D'Arcy, C., Yuan, S., & Meng, X. (2019). How does childhood maltreatment influence ensuing cognitive functioning among people with the exposure of childhood maltreatment? A systematic review of prospective cohort studies. *Journal of Affective Disorders*, *252*, 278–293. https://doi.org/10.1016/j.jad.2019.04.026

Substance Abuse and Mental Health Services Administration. (2022). *Key substance use and mental health indicators in the United States: Results from the 2021 National Survey on Drug Use and Health*. www.samhsa.gov/data/report/2021-nsduh-annual-national-report

Swanson, J. A. (2016). Trends in literature about emerging adulthood. *Emerging Adulthood*, *4*(6), 391–402. https://doi.org/10.1177/2167696816630468

Syed, M., & Azmitia, M. (2008). A narrative approach to ethnic identity in emerging adulthood: Bringing life to the identity status model. *Developmental Psychology*, *44*(4), 1012–1027. https://doi.org/10.1037/0012-1649.44.4.1012.

Syed, M., & Mitchell, L. A. (2013). Race, ethnicity, and emerging adulthood. *Emerging Adulthood*, *1*(2), 83–95. https://doi.org/10.1177/2167696813480503

Tamnes, C. K., Herting, M. M., Goddings, A., Meuwese, R., Blakemore, S., Dahl, R. E., Güroğlu, B., Raznahan, A., Sowell, E. R., Crone, E. A., & Mills, K. L. (2017). Development of the cerebral cortex across adolescence: A multisample study of inter-related longitudinal changes in cortical volume, surface area, and thickness. *The Journal of Neuroscience*, *37*(12), 3402–3412. https://doi.org/10.1523/jneurosci.3302-16.2017

Trans Legislation Tracker. (n.d.). *Tracking the rise of anti-trans bills in the U.S.* https://translegislation.com/learn

U.S. Census Bureau. (2022). Median age at first marriage: 1890 to present. *The Census Bureau*. www.census.gov/content/dam/Census/library/visualizations/time-series/demo/families-and-households/ms-2.pdf

Watts, J. R., Lazzareschi, N. R., Liu, Y., & O'Sullivan, D. (2023). Childhood psychological maltreatment, sense of self, and PTSD symptoms in emerging adulthood. *Journal of Counseling & Development*, *101*(1), 96–105. https://doi.org/10.1002/jcad.12455

Wilson, I. G., Rickwood, D., Bushnell, J., Caputi, P., & Thomas, S. N. (2011). The effects of need for autonomy and preference for seeking help from informal sources on emerging adults' intentions to access mental health services for common mental disorders and suicidal thoughts. *Advances in Mental Health*, *10*(1), 29–38. https://doi.org/10.5172/jamh.2011.10.1.29

Zagorsky, J. L., & Smith, P. (2011). The freshman 15: A critical time for obesity intervention or media myth? *Social Science Quarterly*. https://doi.org/10.1111/j.1540-6237.2011.00823.x

Chapter 10

The 22- to 25-Year-Old

Rachel Jacoby, Kimberly Molnar and Taylor Falardeau

Kaycee, a 23-year-old cisgender female who identifies as Irish American and who recently graduated from college at State University, is beginning her first post-college job as a third-grade teacher at a K–5 school in her hometown. Kaycee is struggling with life post-college. She feels grateful to have a job right away, especially since many of her friends have been unable to find work in their respective fields. Nevertheless, she has struggled with the in-between feeling of growing into an adult with the hopes of marriage, stability, and a family while simultaneously missing the freedom of her college days. Kaycee's partner, Alyx, a 24-year-old cisgender female, has posed the conversation of marriage and home-ownership to Kaycee. However, having this discussion increases Kaycee's anxiety toward what her future holds.

This chapter explores ages 22 to 25. Whether this age range falls into adolescence or adulthood has been an ongoing discussion that has centered around age, brain development, social/emotional development, and life transitions. According to researchers (Arnett, 2006, 2007; Coker et al., 2023), this age range is more appropriately classified as emerging adulthood, the period when people actively explore various possibilities related to relationships, work, and becoming a contributing member of society (Coker et al., 2023; Eriksson et al., 2020). As discussed in prior chapters, emerging adulthood can be a time of uncertainty and exploration (Arnett, 2006).

Five Features of Emerging Adulthood

The concept of emerging adulthood was developed by Arnett (2006), and one of his contributions to developmental psychology was to successfully push the conversation away from generational factors as measures of development. Instead, he described the developmental underpinnings for this age range. According to Arnett (2006), five core features distinguish emerging adulthood from preceding periods of adolescence: the age of identity exploration, the age of instability, the self-focused age, the age of feeling in-between, and the age of possibilities (Arnett, 2006). The age of identity exploration is most typical in industrialized societies and is characterized as a period when people address opportunities and choices that will collectively shape the foundation of their adulthood and overall worldviews (Arnett, 2006). In short, it is asking oneself, "Who am I?" and seeking the answer through self-discovery and clarification of wants and needs (Arnett, 2019). This

DOI: 10.4324/9781003196297-14

task is more simply stated than achieved, and 22- to 25-year-olds may struggle due to the combination of high independence and high instability characteristic in this age range.

The age of instability refers to frequent adjustments and pervasive exposure to new possibilities related to social, occupational, and academic pursuits. These pursuits may also result in instability in habitation (Arnett, 2006, 2019). Whereas identity exploration sets the tone for selected opportunities and future directions, the age of instability reminds emerging adults of the fickleness of our choices. What was once a desired pathway may be uncovered as the "wrong" choice. Although developmentally appropriate, revising plans may result in wistfulness for times when these 22- to 25-year-olds felt they had their lives all figured out, and they may feel a sense of urgency to establish a plan for their future (Arnett, 2019).

Though not as egocentric as their adolescent counterparts, 22- to 25-year-olds are exceptionally self-focused, in that they continually consider where they want to be, what they want out of life, and who will be a part of that journey. This pivotal period emphasizes self-sufficiency, self-agency, and personal meaning-making. Instead of living up to the expectations placed upon them (e.g., maintaining the same boundaries as in adolescence, carrying on generational career traditions), emerging adults focus on what drives them and feels congruent with the person they are becoming as they ease into independence. Although independence has its advantages, making decisions autonomously can also feel overwhelming. To successfully navigate this stage, individuals can consider the guidance of their friends and family but must seek to understand what they want, where they want to be, and who they want to be on their life journey.

When in the phase of self-discovery, a person may simultaneously feel they have surpassed adolescence yet not fit into the characterizations of adulthood as outlined by Arnett (2007): accepting accountability and responsibility for yourself, being autonomous in your decision-making, and finding financial independence. This period is one of trial and error, filled with questions, doubt, and ambiguity. For example, they may be acutely aware of the discomfort that comes when finishing post-secondary school with the rest of their lives ahead of them. These individuals could feel ill-prepared to fulfill roles and responsibilities of being an adult fully on their own (e.g., buying a home, establishing new relationships). The developmental task of the age of feeling in-between is to bear witness to the transition between adolescence and adulthood.

Emerging adulthood has the potential to be viewed solely as uncertain and unstable. However, with the ambiguity of this phase comes the opportunity to look at this period optimistically. For 22- to 25-year-olds, this is a time to explore the many possibilities waiting ahead. Even when overambitious expectations lead to disappointments, young adults have the opportunity to shift direction and make new plans. They might also notice they have the chance to redefine their lives and step away from generational traumas that have impeded wellness within the family, something that is made easier when trusted connections are accessible. Without genuine support, navigating changing directions may be difficult for 22- to 25-year-olds, and possibilities will seem scarce. For emerging adults who are molding their lives in alignment with their vision for the future, undergoing a transformation from who they were to who they are becoming can be a daunting, albeit rewarding, task.

Physical Development

The human body as a whole reaches its capacity for optimal functioning in emerging adulthood when most physiological systems reach full maturity and the functionality of these systems reach their crest. Physiological systems that reach peak functionality during emerging adulthood include the immune, digestive, musculoskeletal, respiratory, nervous, and circulatory systems (Broderick & Blewitt, 2020; Whitbourne & Whitbourne, 2016). On average, these systems progressively develop until the age of 22 when they start to decline. The timing of peak functionality and development of specific systems are influenced by genetic and social factors (Broderick & Blewitt, 2020).

Achieving good health in this stage is not guaranteed, and individual differences must be considered based on experiences, practice, and habits (Broderick & Blewitt, 2020). For example, world-class athletes must train and maintain their physical skills. Poor habits, such as smoking, can hinder peak physical development. Individual variations in peak performance can also be influenced by factors like disability or diverse abilities, with different abilities and experiences shaping what peak performance means (Broderick & Blewitt, 2020). Engaging in risk-taking behaviors is still common during this period, and 22- to 25-year-olds are not exempt from the need to care for their bodies (Whitbourne & Whitbourne, 2016).

Sexual Health and Reproduction

One physiological system that bears further consideration is the reproductive system. Consistent with the physical development of emerging adults, sexual functioning is at its peak between the late teens and early 30s (Hahn et al., 2018). Research has shown variations in sexual activity among emerging adults. Although many emerging adults trend toward developing long-term sexual relationships with partners (Bae & Kogan, 2020), constructs such as "hookup culture" and "friends with benefits" are also applied frequently to this developmental stage (Olmstead et al., 2018). Some young adults are part of polyamorous or non-monogamous relationships. Those with long-term romantic sexual partners tend to have sex more often and may eschew protection more frequently than those engaged in casual sex.

The capacity for reproduction also reaches its peak in early adulthood, making this developmental stage one of the most physically optimal times in life for fertility (Alexander et al., 2014). Further, the prevalence of factors that interfere with reproduction, such as barriers to conception, prenatal complications, and miscarriages, are at their lowest (Alexander et al., 2014). Although it is comparatively easy to reproduce during this stage, individual choices about parenthood may vary. With the advent of modern contraception, birth rates in Western countries are highly controlled, and many individuals enter parenthood in their 30s and 40s.

Brain Development

During emerging adulthood, gray matter, the structures of the brain that contain mainly neurons, continues to thin. Likewise, white matter, consisting of axons, expands, and dendrites, continues to form (Sinnott, 2014). Conversely, the prefrontal cortex, responsible for executive functioning, continues and then ends its period of growth in emerging adulthood (Sinnott, 2014). Thus, 22- to 25-year-olds demonstrate greater complexity of their thoughts, learning, and understanding than they did in late adolescence (Taber-Thomas & Perez-Edgar, 2015).

Although structures of the brain reach maturation during early adulthood, the brain continues to grow and refine, contributing to improvements in cognitive functioning (Broderick & Blewitt, 2020; Sinnott, 2014), and peak brain performance occurs later in adulthood (Sheffler, et al., 2021). For example, a 24-year-old may be able to process novel information and make a decision quickly but may not fully consider the various implications of their decision in the way a 35-year-old could.

Like the contextual complexity of physical development in this stage, the maturation and development of the brain is highly dependent on relative factors (Sinnott, 2014). A person's physical environment and social world may drastically contribute to brain development (Broderick & Blewitt, 2020; Taber-Thomas & Perez-Edgar, 2015). Environmental toxins, chronic stress, socioeconomic status, and social factors (e.g., education level, systemic oppression, and social discrimination) may influence brain chemistry (Assari, 2020; Noble et al., 2020). Furthermore, predisposition to developing mental health disorders is at its highest in emerging adulthood (Taber-Thomas & Perez-Edgar, 2015).

Cognitive Development

The period from ages 22 to 25 marks a significant stage of cognitive development, characterized by the expansion and fine-tuning of higher-order thinking abilities as individuals transition from adolescence to full-fledged adulthood. Notably, executive functions play a pivotal role in this developmental journey and encompass an array of enhanced cognitive abilities, such as problem-solving, decision-making, planning, and impulse control. As emerging adults grapple with new challenges in areas like education, career, and personal experiences, they progressively cultivate and fine-tune these executive functions, enabling them to make more informed and considered choices (Siegel, 2013). For example, if a 23-year-old client is trying to make a decision about whether to stay at their job or to find a new one, they are more able than in the past to engage in complex problem-solving by examining multiple angles of the situation, ignoring irrelevant information, and coming to a decision about the best course of action.

A fundamental component of development during emerging adulthood, cognitive flexibility assumes particular significance. Cognitive flexibility is the capacity to confront novel situations while maintaining adaptability in the face of associated challenges (Kurt & Gunduz, 2020). Cognitive flexibility helps young adults adapt to their changing environment during the age of instability.

In addition to cognitive flexibility, the cognitive development of emerging adults is intrinsically linked to higher education. Studies have consistently demonstrated that college and post-secondary education play a significant role in fostering advancements in critical thinking and postformal thought, and emerging adults, regardless of their educational backgrounds, exhibit a heightened capacity for monitoring their learning and thinking processes (King & Kitchener, 2015). For example, if a client is struggling with self-doubt and finding it challenging to adapt to the demands of a new job, a counselor may support the client by encouraging them to track their negative self-talk in cognitive reframing logs, allowing them to monitor their thinking and learning while building confidence in adapting to the challenges of cognitive reframing.

Emotional Development

The search for identity and a sense of purpose is a key component of emotional development in early adulthood. Since transitions are both pivotal and inevitable at this time, many individuals at this stage of development are exploring their career paths, relationships, and personal goals, which can lead to both the feelings of excitement and uncertainty. This period of self-discovery may result in heightened emotions as individuals explore their identity and find their place in the world. For example, Kaycee from the introductory case study may express that she is excited for the opportunities in her future while simultaneously expressing fear and uncertainty. This example illustrates her need to search for identity and purpose while navigating career decisions and personal growth.

According to Arnett (2006), emerging adults are becoming more considerate of the feelings and perspectives of others. They begin to shift their relationships with people who were once authority figures in their own world (i.e., parents or caregivers) and start to see them as people, leading them to empathize with them more. Thus, parent-child relationship stress may ease during this stage.

Emotional Intelligence and Self-Esteem

For individuals aged 22 to 25, self-esteem and emotional intelligence are integrally intertwined. Emotional intelligence encompasses the capacity to recognize, evaluate, and manage one's emotions (Cheung et al., 2015). These qualities facilitate the cultivation of happiness and a reduction in stress. Self-esteem, on the other hand, is significantly influenced by the perceived outcomes of success or failure, impacting emotions, relationships, and professional advancements (Cheung et al., 2015). Positive self-esteem is recognized as a harbinger of favorable and prosocial achievements and is closely linked to the overall satisfaction individuals derive from their lives. Emotional intelligence plays a pivotal role in nurturing positive self-perception and significantly molds one's self-esteem.

Anxiety and Depression

Emerging adults face affective obstacles such as feelings of depression, anxiety, and uncertainty, to name a few. These feelings can compound with each other, ultimately intensifying an already complex experience for emerging adults and impeding the development of social connections, perceived academic successes, and confidence in professional roles (Moeller & Seehuus, 2019). Siegel noted the significance of emerging adults feeling "stuck" or "empty," as well as feeling "filled with boredom of just doing the same old things over and over again" (2013, p. 23). For example, a client may express a disillusionment with adulthood by saying, "I go to work and then I just have time to eat dinner and get ready for the next day, and it is time to go to bed and repeat the same thing again. I just want something interesting to happen."

Social and Relationship Development

According to Erikson's theory, positive social/emotional development is indicated by success in social connection (see Chapter 1). The stage of intimacy vs. isolation captures the shift from peer group conformity to developing emotional closeness with others based on what they perceive to be enduring and affectionally intimate relationships (Erikson, 1959, 1968). Detachment or social distancing in interpersonal relationships may occur when social interactions feel dangerous, something Erikson considered to be unhealthy development (Erikson, 1968).

A defining aspect of the social landscape for 22- to 25-year-olds is the lack of previous controls and boundaries. Social norms of behavior are less rigid, individuals do not face as many consequences for their behavior, and ideas about what is acceptable are broader (Arnett, 2006). As a result, 22- to 25-year-olds tend to have freedom to pursue individual preferences, innate desires, and interests that were not available or acceptable during earlier life stages (Panchal & Joshi, 2013; Riggio, 1986). Because of this "freedom," individual differences vary widely during this period of social development.

Individuals during this stage may achieve or work toward social milestones such as attending college, beginning full-time employment, moving out of their caregivers' households, or finding a social network that is not as rigidly constructed as schools are. Milestones and life goals may also be influenced by familial or cultural contexts, where individuals may take on roles as caregivers, immigrate to new countries, or choose to remain in their family homes.

This social freedom may lead 22-to-25-year-olds to develop a greater sense of control over their social skillset (e.g., social expression, adaptability, self-preservation) than they had in childhood and early adolescence (Moeller & Seehuus, 2019; Panchal & Joshi, 2013; Riggio, 1986). Moreover, individuals learn to navigate a wide variety of social settings and cultural differences (Panchal & Joshi, 2013; Riggio, 1986). This can contribute to developing an "autonomous self," which may result in a range of behaviors from pursuing long-term life goals to experimenting with different roles or responsibilities in life that feel fulfilling to the individual (Scharf & Mayseless, 2010). In addition, many emerging adults develop a social identity that is more congruent with their sense of self and refine their social presentation to match this identity (Arnett, 2006).

Intimate Relationships

One of the major life tasks that may occur in this life stage is finding an intimate partner or partners. A committed intimate relationship can result in better mental health; greater social support; and a sense of safety, belonging, and nurturance (Bae & Kogan, 2020). The need for intimacy can be present across genders, and commitment is often an end goal of romantic relationships in 22- to 25-year-olds (Coker et al., 2023).

However, recent social changes have led to a delay in the establishment of long-term committed intimate relationships. Like childbearing, marriage is not necessarily a defining feature of this life stage. Reasons for the delay in childbearing and marriage may be systemic barriers such as the heteronormative model of marriage, states' intolerance towards same-sex marriage, and laws affecting polyamorous relationships (Bartholomay & Pendleton, 2023). The availability of birth control may also impact this trend. Rather than engaging in long-term committed relationships, intimacy is often explored through various romantic and sexual experiences (Broderick & Blewitt, 2020). In fact, a substantial portion of sexual behavior in young adults can be defined as casual, especially in the college population (Hahn et al., 2018). Yet, more recently, there has been a movement toward delaying the sexual debut and taking breaks from partnered sexual behavior. This shift may be due to large-scale sociopolitical events, such as society's response to the 2020 Coronavirus pandemic and the United States' 2022 overturning of *Roe v. Wade* (Match, 2022). While many scholars and policymakers speculate that this shift marks a healthier way to engage in intimate relationships than in previous times, the effects of this movement are still unknown (Match, 2022).

In addition, technology's influence on social communication may also impact intimate relationships. Technologies such as dating applications, online pornography, social networking, and computer-mediated communication are commonly used to obtain, maintain, or find an alternative to intimate relationships (McGee, 2014). Research indicates that using computer-mediated communication, such as texting, can further intimacy by allowing for immediate connection and connection over distance (McGee, 2014). Problems may include the ease of meeting new intimate partners using social networking or the ambiguity of textual communication (the lack of tone and nonverbals that can lead to misinterpretations and misunderstanding) (McGee, 2014).

Loneliness

As many 22- to 25-year-olds leave the security of their social shelter, research shows that loneliness is common. Research specifically in college settings shows that, while students are developing more complex social skills and autonomy, they can also be struck by debilitating feelings of loneliness, which can exacerbate experiences of anxiety and depression (Cacioppo et al., 2015; Moeller & Seehuus, 2019). The construct of loneliness is often tied to the experience of isolation. However, some emerging adults experience loneliness while remaining socially engaged. These individuals may, in fact, be connected to a social environment, such as college or a workplace, but may not be receiving the desired social benefits to mitigate this emotional state (Moeller & Seehuus, 2019). Certain skills refined in emerging adulthood, such as social expressivity, can mitigate this loneliness and lead to connection (Cacioppo et al., 2015; Panchal & Joshi, 2013).

Shifting Parental Relationships

Typically, 22- to 25-year-olds undergo a shift in their relationship with caregivers as they experience milestones like moving out of their childhood homes, entering the labor force full-time, or pursuing higher education. These experiences can foster autonomy and more complex social skills (Arnett, 2006). This shift often leads to healthier, more egalitarian parent-child bonds, moving away from the more strict power dynamics of adolescence (Broderick & Blewitt, 2020). This transition is not exclusive to leaving home but is a developmental shift marked by new expectations including work, marriage, and parenthood (Arnett, 2007).

However, not all parental relationships are positive. Overparenting, characterized by excessive control and assistance, can lead to negative outcomes such as reduced problem-solving abilities, challenges coping with stress, mental health issues, and vocational problems (Broderick & Blewitt, 2020; Inguglia et al., 2015). For instance, a 23-year-old experiencing overparenting may struggle with managing finances or handling medical needs, necessitating support from a counselor to enhance problem-solving skills and emotional resilience. Additionally, in recent years, more 22- to 25-year-olds continue to live with their parents, a trend influenced by the expectations of pursuing higher education before entering the workforce. This trend has been exacerbated by factors like the COVID-19 pandemic's economic impact on employment, college enrollment rates, and the ability to afford independent housing (Creamer et al., 2020; Engemann, 2021).

Culture and Identity Development

Culture and identity development for 22- to 25-year-olds is a complex journey shaped by a multitude of identity factors as individuals strive to comprehend and nurture their sense of self. This may be done through connecting with their heritage, familial values or traditions, or race and ethnicity or by creating their own values, traditions, and beliefs that do not connect with those of their upbringing. Often, 22- to 25-year-olds develop a broader sense of cultural awareness that ultimately can influence and enrich their own sense of identity.

Individuals who belong to minoritized groups often experience discrimination, prejudice, and microaggressions. Meyer's minority stress theory (2003) posits that minority individuals grapple with both external stressors like prejudice and internal stressors such as psychological distress. While experiences of discrimination are directly tied to reduced well-being, strong identification with one's group and a sense of collective self-esteem can help to reduce the impact of discrimination. In fact, research shows that identifying with a minoritized group positively correlates with psychological well-being and a heightened sense of control over one's health and well-being (Hereth et al., 2020; Scroggs & Vennum, 2021).

Racial and Ethnic Identity

Racial and ethnic identity development is a multifaceted process influenced by various theoretical perspectives. Erikson's (1968) framework suggests that forming a coherent identity is crucial during ages 22 to 25. During this period, individuals increasingly use abstract systems to reconcile conflicting aspects of their self-concept, making it an ideal time to explore complex facets of their identity. Marcia's identity status model (1980), adapted for ethnic identity development by Phinney (1989), highlights the importance of exploring alternative possibilities and making commitments in the process. Racial and ethnic identities are multidimensional, encompassing context-specific behaviors and attitudes. Some individuals may hold a stronger racial and/or ethnic identity than others, and 22- to 25-year-olds may not frequently interpret life experiences from an ethnic or racial lens if that identity is not central to their sense of self (Grilo et al., 2023; Syed & Azmitia, 2008).

The definition of racial and ethnic identification emphasizes belonging, shared culture, history, and ancestry (Grilo et al., 2023). Multiracial identity development also acknowledges the importance of understanding the influences on multiracial identity formation and how peer networks can play a role. Childhood experiences, parental influences, and narratives about racial and ethnic ancestry shape individuals' early identity discoveries, which may evolve over time. The intersection of their racial and ethnic makeup and how they are perceived in their environment leads to diverse experiences and internalized messages even by individuals of the same group (Phinney, 1989; Syed & Azmitia, 2008). Importantly, identity formation is depicted as a dynamic, nonlinear process that evolves over time, with individuals shifting their understanding of and the language they use to describe their racial and ethnic identity as they mature and learn more about themselves (Grilo et al., 2023). For example, a 22-year-old client who grew up in an ethnically homogenous environment moves to a different city and begins to live and work with those of other ethnicities for the first time. The client will likely begin to view and describe themselves in different ways as they see themselves through the lens of others.

Gender Identity and Sexual Orientation

The exploration of gender identity and sexual orientation is a nonlinear and intricate aspect of ongoing identity development that occurs across the lifespan and is a common aspect of identity development for 22- to 25-year-olds. Gender and sexual minority (GSM) youth may self-identify earlier in adolescence, but some individuals may not explore or reveal their gender identity or sexual orientation to peers until their early 20s when they are exposed to more diversity among their peers, something that can serve as a protective factor for GSM young people (Scroggs & Vennum, 2021). The development of gender and sexual identity for GSM individuals involves a transition away from heterosexuality toward identity integration within the broader GSM community. This process is influenced by individual and contextual factors and is an ongoing process that extends beyond emerging adulthood (Hereth et al., 2020; Scroggs & Vennum, 2021). As 22- to 25-year-olds often transition away from their family of origin, feelings of social rejection from the majority group can lead to rejection identification, where individuals bond with a minoritized group experiencing a similar challenge. This theme of connecting with peers undergoing parallel experiences is a common thread in GSM identity development. The complex interplay between gender identity and sexual orientation, concepts that are often erroneously conflated in the dominant narrative, can pose challenges for young adults, sometimes compelling individuals to come out multiple times as they develop new conceptualizations of their identity (Hereth et al., 2020). However, GSM individuals who take on this exploration often have a more nuanced and intricate understanding of identity than their peers.

Disability Discrimination

Disability scholars have emphasized that individuals with disabilities face substantial disadvantages due to social barriers, such as discrimination in hiring and inaccessible workplaces and schools (Janus, 2009). For example, college students with disabilities, including those with learning disabilities or hearing impairments, often encounter challenges due to inaccessible environments or instructors who resist making necessary accommodations.

Individuals with disabilities face additional employment barriers, including a reluctance to seek employment due to potential loss of disability benefits and discrimination during the hiring process (Janus, 2009). In the workplace, disabled workers may experience marginalization, stereotyping, and harassment, further hindering their professional integration (Hunter et al., 2022; Janus, 2009). Employment is a vital step toward financial independence and adulthood, with unemployment potentially causing delays in moving out of parents' homes and hindering the development of adult relationships.

Chronic pain, a prevalent issue among 22- to 25-year-olds, can be associated with various health conditions and often leads to pain interference and coping difficulties. Researchers have identified that factors like adverse childhood experiences, sex, and race can predispose people to chronic pain, with conditions like chronic headaches, backaches, and stomach pain being common among college students (Hunter et al., 2022).

Resources and Protective Factors

Individuals aged 22 to 25 benefit from a multitude of resources and protective factors that play a vital role in promoting their overall well-being and a successful transition into adulthood. Higher education, vocational training, and social support systems all positively influence growth and development during this stage of life.

Alongside these external influences, self-focus emerges as a multifaceted protective element within this age group because it empowers individuals to cultivate self-reliance in pursuit of their ambitions and nurtures the invaluable skill of self-advocacy. Over time, as they achieve self-sufficiency, this self-focus gradually transforms 22- to 24-year-old's self-perception to align with the responsibilities of impending adulthood (Arnett, 2006).

Heterogeneity, another protective factor, is defined as the period of life in which the opportunity for varied developmental paths is greatest (Arnett, 2006). Depending on factors such as socioeconomic status and family values, 22- to 25-year-olds have varying levels of choices for different jobs, partners, living arrangements, educational/vocational training, group identification, etc. Navigating these decisions can provide new challenges that result in individual growth for many young people. Emerging adults are able to seek out mental and physical healthcare that aligns with their values, and access to these resources is paramount for supporting 22-to-25-year-olds as they manage stress, anxiety, and other emotional and mental health challenges (Sheffler et al., 2021).

Challenges and Risk Factors

As independence evolves and peak functionality is reached in emerging adulthood, individuals tend to take more risks compared to other life stages (Allred, 2019). This exploratory, yet impulsive, phase often involves engaging in unstable or potentially destructive behaviors, such as unsafe driving, substance and alcohol use, and risky sexual practices (Allred, 2019).

Substance use is a significant concern for 22- to 25-year-olds. Certain predictors of substance and alcohol use include one's living situation and college attendance, two contextual factors that quite commonly occur during the emerging adulthood stage (Blevins et al., 2019). These activities may contribute to other risky behaviors, such as having unprotected sex, participating in illegal and dangerous activities, or engaging in the use of other substances (Broderick & Blewitt, 2020). Some risky sexual practices common during this age include engaging in unprotected sex, having multiple sexual partners, neglecting sexual health and preventative care, and instances of forced or nonconsensual sexual encounters. Risky sexual behaviors may result in outcomes such as contracting sexually transmitted infections such as HIV, unplanned pregnancy, physical trauma, and psychological harm (Blevins et al., 2019).

Yet another risk factor associated with 22- to 25-year-olds is poverty. Since the 1970s, the poverty rate for emerging adults has been steadily rising, perhaps due to the financial strains of independent living and/or lower paying jobs (Hawkins, 2019). Further, emerging adults are often excluded from support services that are afforded to other age groups (Marchand & Smeeding, 2016). As previously mentioned, living in poverty is linked to poor health outcomes, greater levels of stress, and less success with social and vocational pursuits (Hawkins, 2019).

Other challenges specific to 22- to 25-year-olds include navigating new social environments, determining the need for boundaries, and coping with the tendency to procrastinate, all while learning ways to balance their many physical, emotional, and psychological needs. Making autonomous decisions, practicing self-care, and fostering internal motivation are complex tasks that contribute to personal growth within this stage.

Best Practices for Counseling and Therapy

When Counseling Is Indicated

Although many 22- to 25-year-olds are able to eagerly embrace the plentiful possibilities that exist in early adulthood, others may experience feelings of instability, uncertainty, and self-doubt when faced with so many choices. Questioning one's identity, career paths, and/or relationships can contribute to feelings of dread, shame, and even depression or anxiety. When contextual, interpersonal, or intrapersonal factors get in the way of young adults abilities to explore possibilities and successfully navigate in-betweenness, counseling may be indicated. Kaycee provides one example of difficulties navigating typical issues for 22- to 25-year-olds.

Kaycee is struggling with feelings of self-doubt and uncertainty. Her anxiety toward what the future holds has been disrupting her work and personal life as evidenced by her constant restlessness, poor sleep, increased heart rate, and trouble concentrating on anything beyond her worries for the future. Rather than talking about this with her partner Alyx, she avoids conversations that appear to be triggering her anxiety. The more Kaycee has been avoiding this anxiety, the more she notices her symptoms increase at both work and home. When her friends address their job searches, she "shuts down" and goes silent. The way she sees it, "Why should I feel this way when I have a job and a partner? I should feel grateful for what I have." Although she has been avoiding much of what inspires anxiety, Kaycee has clear protective factors worth noting. For instance, Kaycee has supportive parents, loving friends, and a devoted partner who reach out daily to check-in and connect. Additionally, Kaycee finds the most relief from her anxiety when doing activities she loves, such as roller skating, reading, and volunteering at her local art museum

Like Kaycee, individuals in this developmental phase may benefit from therapy to address the vast number of adjustments that occur as a 22- to 25-year-old (e.g., becoming independent, finding a career, engaging in romantic relationships, and improving communication skills). Also, 22- to 25-year-olds may benefit from counseling to reduce the risk of harm to self and learn ways to overcome substance use issues, risky sexual practices, and other barriers to wellness. Some 22- to 25-year-olds may also benefit from therapy centered around navigating the cognitive changes they experience in this developmental period. To do so, counselors may integrate strategies to improve executive functioning, enhance cognitive flexibility, and/or challenge presentations of self-doubt that exist within 22- to 25-year-olds.

Therapeutic Approaches for 22- to 25-Year-Olds

When a 22- to 25-year-old is experiencing impediments toward their well-being in the ways mentioned before, seeking out therapeutic services may be warranted. Some relevant approaches include but are not limited to, person-centered therapy, cognitive behavioral therapy, and solution-focused brief therapy.

Person-Centered Therapy

Clinicians seeking to promote self-esteem and self-direction as well as validate the lived experiences of 22- to 25-year-olds may align with person-centered therapy (PCT), which values autonomy, creativity, uniqueness, and personal development. Using a phenomenological perspective, PCT explores individual experiences through empathy, genuineness, and unconditional positive regard. PCT focuses on the way of being with clients and fostering a growth-producing therapeutic relationship (Rogers, 1995). The PCT approach can assist 22- to 25-year-olds to explore identity development. A therapist working with Kaycee could provide unconditional positive regard, practice accurate empathy, present with congruence in the therapeutic environment, and allow Kaycee to guide the sessions. Doing so would allow Kaycee to explore her self-doubt and uncertainty as well as build self-confidence and decrease her reliance on the opinions of others. PCT provides a safe environment to explore this developmental period and support positive life changes.

Cognitive Behavioral Therapy

Cognitive behavioral therapy (CBT) can also support 22- to 25-year-olds in navigating developmental challenges. CBT addresses the learning of inaccurate perceptions and offers strategies to deconstruct these cognitions, promoting alternative perspectives. Aligned with self-efficacy concepts from social learning theory, CBT aids young adults in building confidence. Techniques like psychoeducation, cognitive restructuring, and relaxation skills can be valuable tools for this age group (Beck, 1976).

During a period of identity exploration and instability, 22- to 25-year-olds can benefit from deepening self-awareness and gaining insight into their thoughts, feelings, and behaviors. Therapists can integrate psychoeducation in collaborative, client-focused sessions, tailoring information to the individual's current developmental stage. Cognitive restructuring helps individuals combat automatic negative thoughts and regain control, fostering an essential space for examining alternative perspectives. Applying this to Kaycee, she may experience thoughts like, "Everything I had in college is over. I will never figure out what to do with my life." In response, a clinician may model the restructuring of this polarized thinking by assisting the client in identifying their associated feelings (e.g., Kaycee's college experience is over, and she must move to a new life phase), and evidence that does not support the original polarized thought. The clinician can offer an alternative thought to complete the cognitive restructuring, or the client can practice doing so. An example of an alternative thought may be, "I feel overwhelmed by this new experience, and I also have time to explore what the future holds." Additionally, the clinician may support managing stress by introducing relaxation strategies, like guided imagery and progressive muscle relaxation.

Solution-Focused Brief Therapy

Solution-focused brief therapy (SFBT) has increased in popularity due to managed care valuing cost efficiency, and the approach aligns well with this development period. The tenets, or rules, governing SFBT include: 1) "If it ain't broke, don't fix it;" 2) "Once you know what works, do more of it;" and 3) "If it doesn't work, don't do it again" (Erford, 2020, p. 1). These rules are of particular use to 22- to 25-year-olds who are self-focused, are feeling in-between, and/or are starting to become open to the possibilities that await them. These three features of this age range deal with decision-making and overcoming past circumstances that may impede future choices. Some of the techniques that would help facilitate the navigation of this developmental phase are scaling questions, exceptions, and flagging the minefield.

Intended to help seemingly impossible tasks feel more manageable, scaling questions can support clients in seeing the potential they have to impact their own circumstances. When used intentionally, scaling questions support 22- to 25-year-olds in gaining confidence and fostering autonomy and a sense of accountability (Erford, 2020). For example, posing a scaling question to Kaycee might sound like, "On a scale of 1 to 10, where 1 represents feeling the most anxious and 10 represents feeling the most at peace, where would you find yourself on this scale when you are addressing the future?"

When using exceptions, therapists aim to find the exclusions within a problem that a client is facing. When utilizing exceptions with Kaycee, the therapist would begin exploring times when the problem does not appear to be bothering her. For example, when Kaycee is actively teaching, watching a show, or listening to music, there might be times when the weight of her anxieties stops feeling so heavy.

Typically implemented near the termination of services, flagging the minefield helps clients identify potential problematic circumstances as a means of steering clear of obstacles. The therapist may utilize this skill by prompting the client with potential challenging situations and encouraging the client consider how to navigate the scenario via the skills learned throughout their therapeutic journey. Flagging the minefield can be especially helpful for 22- to 25-year-olds in the age of instability who feel they have made "wrong" decisions in the past and now struggle with uncertainty about their future choices. The technique can build confidence and a direction forward and can also be utilized as a relapse prevention strategy, which can be useful if working with adults who have engaged in risky and/or impulsive behaviors.

Additional Approaches

Beyond PCT, CBT, and SFBT, a therapist can implement approaches that target developmental experiences specific to 22- to 25-year-olds. For individuals experiencing substance misuse, clinicians may find that integrating motivational interviewing is helpful. Utilizing this modality can support clients in making positive changes by way of investigating their intrinsic motivation and inner strength. To explore vocational wellness and directions, therapists might employ a narrative approach so that the 22- to 25-year-old clients they are working with can tell the story of themselves, their lives, and their career paths. If a client is struggling with a history of trauma and is seeking a way to emotionally regulate, they may benefit from work with counselors who are trained in somatic-based therapies, such as sensorimotor psychotherapy and eye movement desensitization and reprocessing. For the big question of "who am I?" therapists could further find themselves utilizing existential therapy to navigate themes such as meaning, purpose, and freedom. Ultimately, having an integrative approach can tailor the therapeutic experience to the individual development of 22- to 25-year-old clients.

In-Between Sessions Work

To bolster work completed in session, clinicians can consider ways to incorporate work outside of therapy for 22- to 25-year-olds. These individuals benefit from opportunities in-between sessions to explore identity factors, utilize their newfound advancements in critical thinking, familiarize themselves with their wants and needs, and/or examine their decision-making skills. To achieve this, counselors may consider encouraging clients to journal, engage in bibliotherapy, and practice coping strategies.

Conclusion

At a powerful intersection where adolescence meets up with young adulthood, 22- to 25-year-olds live in an age of possibility, individuality, and hope. They get to redefine what they want out of life, who they are, and who will join them in this journey. At the same time, 22- to 25-year-olds face countless developmental obstacles. They are on a path of self-discovery that is marked by instability, adjustment, and ambiguity. This combination of freedom and self-doubt can leave some feeling confused, dysregulated, and anxious. For others, this combination can be a catalyst that thrusts them into the subsequent phase of development. This dichotomy captures the unique challenge 22- to 25-year-olds face – to uncover who you are, what you want, and what you need out of life. In addressing these challenges, clinicians have a wide array of therapeutic approaches at their disposal. By holding awareness of the various experiences individuals ages 22 to 25 may experience, clinicians can better equip themselves to support these emerging adults on their journey of self-discovery and personal growth.

References

Alexander, K. A., Jemmott, L. S., Teitelman, A. M., & D'Antonio, P. (2014). Addressing sexual health behaviour during emerging adulthood: A critical review of the literature. *Journal of Clinical Nursing, 24*(1–2), 4–18. https://doi.org/10.1111/jocn.12640

Allred, C. (2019). High risk behavior in early adulthood. *Ohio Population News, 36*, 1–2. www.bgsu.edu/content/dam/BGSU/college-of-arts-and-sciences/center-for-family-and-demographic-research/documents/OPN/Ohio-Population-News-2019-Risky-Behavior-Early-Childhood-36.pdf

Arnett, J. J. (2006). Emerging adulthood: Understanding the new way of coming of age. In J. J. Arnet & J. L. Tanner (Eds.), *Emerging adults in America: Coming of age in the 21st century* (pp. 3–19). APA Books.

Arnett, J. J. (2007). Emerging adulthood: What is it, and what is it good for? *Child Development Perspectives, 1*(2), 68–73. https://doi.org/10.1111/j.1750-8606.2007.00016.x

Arnett, J. J. (2019). *Human development: A cultural approach* (3rd ed.). Pearson.

Assari, S. (2020). Parental education and youth inhibitory control in the Adolescent Brain Cognitive Development (ABCD) Study: Blacks' diminished returns. *Brain Sciences (2076–3425), 10*(5), 312. https://doi-org.ezproxy.depaul.edu/10.3390/brainsci10050312

Bae, D., & Kogan, S. M. (2020). Romantic relationship trajectories among young, African American men: The influence of adverse life contexts. *Journal of Family Psychology, 34*(6), 687–697. https://doi.org/10.1037/fam0000645

Bartholomay, D. J., & Pendleton, M. (2023). Doing sexuality: How married bisexual, queer, and pansexual people navigate passing and erasure. *The Sociological Quarterly, 64*(3), 520–539. https://doi.org/10.1080/00380253.2023.2179951

Beck, A. T. (1976). *Cognitive therapy and the emotional disorders.* International Universities Press.

Blevins, C. E., Anderson, B. J., Caviness, C. M., Herman, D. S., & Stein, M. D. (2019). Emerging adults' discussion of substance use and sexual behavior with providers. *Journal of Health Communication, 24*(2): 121–128. https://doi.org/10.1080/10810730.2019.1583700.

Broderick, P. C., & Blewitt, P. (2020). *The life span: Human development for helping professionals* (5th ed.). Pearson Education Inc.

Cacioppo, S., Grippo, A. J., London, S., Goossens, L., & Cacioppo, J. (2015). Loneliness: Clinical import and interventions. *Perspectives on Psychological Science, 10*(2), 238–249. https://doi.org/10.1177/174569165570616

Cheung, C. K., Cheung, H. Y., & Hue, M. T. (2015). Emotional intelligence as a basis for self-esteem in young adults. *The Journal of Psychology*, *149*(1), 63–84. https://doi.org/10.1080/00223980.2013.838540.

Coker, J. K., Cannon, K. B., Dixon-Saxon, S. V., & Roller, K. M. (2023). *Lifespan development: Cultural and contextual applications for the helping professions*. Springer Publishing Company, LLC. https://doi.org/10.1891/9780826182791

Creamer, J., Shrider, E., & Edwards, A. (2020, September 15). More young adults lived with their parents in 2019. *U.S. Department of Commerce*. www.census.gov/library/stories/2020/09/more-young-adults-lived-with-their-parents-in-2019.html

Engemann, K. M. (2021). Young adults cope with COVID-19's economic impact. *Federal Reserve Bank of St. Louis*. www.stlouisfed.org/open-vault/2021/march/young-adults-cope-covid19-economic-impact

Erford, B. T. (2020). *45 techniques every counselor should know* (3rd ed). Pearson.

Erikson, E. (1959). Theory of identity development. In E. Eriskon (Ed.), *Identity and the life cycle*. International Universities Press.

Erikson, E. H. (1968). *Identity: Youth and crisis*. Norton.

Eriksson, P. L., Wangqvist, M., Carlsson, J., & Frisen, A. (2020). Identity development in early adulthood. *Developmental Psychology*, *56*(10), 1968–1983. https://doi.org/10.1037/dev0001093

Grilo, S. A., Semler, M. R., & Rameau, S. (2023). The sum of all parts: A multi-level exploration of racial and ethnic identify formation during emerging adulthood. *PLoS One*, *18*(4). https://doi.org/10.1371/journal.pone.0284275

Hahn, H. A., You, D. S., Sferra, M., Hubbard, M., Thamotharan, S., & Fields, S. A. (2018). Is it too soon to meet? Examining differences in geosocial networking app use and sexual risk behavior of emerging adults. *Sexuality & Culture*, *22*(1), 1–21. https://doi.org/10.1007/s12119-017-9449-3

Hawkins, J. (2019). The rise of young adult poverty in the U.S. *Berkley Institute for Young Americans*, 1–7. https://youngamericans.berkeley.edu/wp-content/uploads/2020/01/poverty_FINAL_formatted.pdf

Hereth, J., Pardee, D. J., & Reisner, S. L. (2020). Gender identity and sexual orientation development among young adult transgender men sexually active with cisgender men: 'I had completely ignored my sexuality . . . that's for a different time to figure out'. *Culture, Health & Sexuality*, *22*(1), 37–47. https://doi.org/10.1080/13691058.2019.1636290

Hunter, T., Koch, L., Smith, S. L., & Hampton Hall, A. (2022). Aching to be understood: Vocational rehabilitation implications for emerging adults in chronic pain. *Rehabilitation Research, Policy, and Education*, *36*(1), 34–49. https://doi.org/10.1891/RE-21-14

Inguglia, C., Ingoglia, S., Liga, F., Coco, A. L., & Lo, M. G. (2015). Autonomy and relatedness in adolescence and emerging adulthood: Relationships with parental support and psychological distress. *Journal of Adult Development*, 22, 1–13. https://doi.org/10.1007/s10804-014-9196-8

Janus, A. L. (2009). Disability and the transition to adulthood. *Social Forces*, *88*, 99–120. https://doi.org/10.1353/sof.0.0248

King, P. M., & Kitchener, K. S. (2015). Cognitive development in the emerging adult: The emergence of complex cognitive skills. In J. J. Arnett (Ed.), *The Oxford handbook of emerging adulthood* (pp. 105–125). Oxford University Press.

Kurt, A. A., & Gunduz, B. (2020). The investigation of relationship between irrational relationship beliefs, cognitive flexibility and differentiation of self in young adults. *Çukurova Üniversitesi Eğitim Fakültesi Dergisi*, *49*(1), 28–44. https://dergipark.org.tr/tr/pub/cuefd

Marchand, J., & Smeeding, T. (2016). Poverty and aging. In J. Piggott & A. Woodland (Eds.), *Handbook of the economics of population aging*. Elsevier. https://sites.ualberta.ca/~econwps/2016/wp2016-11.pdf

Marcia, J. (1980). Identity in adolescence. In J. Adelson (Ed.), *Handbook of adolescent psychology* (pp. 159–197). Wiley.

Match (2022). Singles in America: Match releases largest study on US single population for the 12th year. *Cision: PR Newswire*. www.prnewswire.com/news-releases/singles-in-america-match-releases-largest-study-on-us-single-population-for-12th-year-301678813.html

McGee, M. J. (2014). Is texting ruining intimacy? Exploring perceptions among sexuality students in higher education. *American Journal of Sexuality Education*, *9*(4), 404–427. https://doi-org.ezproxy.depaul.edu/10.1080/15546128.2014.976353

Meyer, I. H. (2003). Prejudice, social stress, and mental health in lesbian, gay, and bisexual populations: Conceptual issues and research evidence. *Psychological Bulletin*, *129*(5), 6740697. https://doi.org/10.1037/0033-2909.129.5.674

Moeller, R. W., & Seehuus, M. (2019). Loneliness as a mediator for college students' social skills and experiences of depression and anxiety. *Journal of Adolescence*, *73*, 1–13. https://doi.org/j.adolescence.2019.03.006

Noble, K. G., Hart, E. R., & Sperber, J. F. (2021). Socioeconomic disparities and neuroplasticity: Moving toward adaptation, intersectionality, and inclusion. *American Psychologist*, *76*(9), 1486–1495. https://doi-org.ezproxy.depaul.edu/10.1037/amp0000934

Olmstead, S. B., Conrad, K. A., & Anders, K. M. (2018). First semester college students' definitions of and expectations for engaging in hookups. *Journal of Adolescent Research*, *33*(3), 275–305. https://doi-org.ezproxy.depaul.edu/10.1177/0743558417698571

Panchal, S., & Joshi, H. L. (2013). Happiness in relation to social skills and self-esteem among youths. *Indian Journal of Health and Wellbeing*, *4*(1), 34–37.

Phinney, J. S. (1989). Stages of ethnic identity development in minority group adolescents. *Journal of Early Adolescence*, *9*, 34–49.

Riggio, R. E. (1986). Assessment of basic social skills. *Journal of Personality and Social Psychology*, *51*, 649–660. https://doi.org/10.1037/0022-3514.51/3/649

Rogers, C. R. (1995). *On becoming a person* (2nd ed.). Houghton Mifflin (Trade).

Scharf, M., & Mayseless, O. (2010). Finding the authentic self in a communal culture: Developmental goals in emerging adulthood. In S. Shulman & J. E. Nurmi (Eds.), *The role of goals in navigating individual lives during emerging adulthood* (pp. 83–95). Jossey-Bass.

Scroggs, B., & Vennum, A. (2021). Gender and sexual minority group identification as a process of identity development during emerging adulthood. *Journal of LGBT Youth*, *18*(3), 209–221. https://doi.org/10.1080/19361653.2020.1722780

Sheffler, P., Rodriguez, T. M., Cheung, C. S., & Wu, R. (2021). Cognitive and metacognitive, motivational, and resource considerations for learning new skills across the lifespan. *WIREs Cognitive Science*, *13*, 1–26. https://doi.org/10.1002/wcs.1585

Siegel, D. J. (2013). *Brainstorm: The power and purpose of the teenage brain*. Penguin Group.

Sinnott, J. D. (2014). *Adult development: Cognitive aspects of thriving close relationships*. Oxford University Press.

Syed, M., & Azmitia, M. (2008). A narrative approach to ethnic identity in emerging adulthood: Bringing life to the identity status model. *Developmental Psychology*, *44*(4), 1012–1027. https://doi.org/10.1037/0012-1649.44.4.1012

Taber-Thomas, B., & Perez-Edgar, K. (2015). Emerging adulthood brain development. In J. J. Arnett (Ed.), *The Oxford handbook of emerging adulthood* (pp. 126–141). Oxford University Press.

Whitbourne, S. K., & Whitbourne, S. B. (2016). *Adult development and aging: Biopsychosocial perspectives* (6th ed.). John Wiley & Sons.

Part V

Resources for Practice

Chapter 11

Teen and Young Adult Development

Resources for Practice

Kimberly M. Jayne

The handouts in this chapter may be used to support therapeutic practice with adolescents in multiple ways. Each handout provides a helpful summary and review of key developmental processes and considerations based on an adolescent's developmental age or period including common challenges, when to seek support, and helpful tips for parents/caregivers and adults in an adolescent's life. The handouts follow the age ranges outlined in Chapters 3–10. Counselors and therapists may use the handouts to provide psychoeducation and empower parents, caregivers, family members, and teachers of teens and young adults in supporting and building healthy relationships with the adolescents in their lives. While the primary audience for these handouts is important adults in a teen's or emerging adult's life, counselors may also find them useful for providing developmental knowledge and psychoeducation to adolescent clients. Handouts may be copied and provided directly to clients and families but should not be altered or digitally posted/distributed without permission from the publisher.

DOI: 10.4324/9781003196297-16

THE 13-YEAR-OLD

Physical Development

- Physical changes related to start or continuation of puberty (voice changes, breast changes, changes in size and shape of penis, changes in size and shape of vulva, menstruation, ejaculation)
- Changes in skin including acne and stretch marks
- Changes in hair texture and growth of facial hair, pubic hair, underarm hair, and body hair
- More sweating and body odor
- Growth spurts, growing pains, and changes in overall body height, size, and shape
- Need 8–10 hours of sleep a night
- Go to sleep later and need to sleep in later in the morning due to changes in circadian rhythm

Brain and Cognitive Development

- Seek novelty and new experiences
- May feel bored more easily
- More likely to take risks or be impulsive
- More influenced by peers
- Less fearful or aware of risks and consequences
- More capacity for perspective-taking and empathy
- More likely to perceive interactions or experiences negatively
- Continuing to develop more self-control and self-regulation

Emotional Development

- Frequent changes and fluctuations in mood
- More irritability
- More intense emotions
- Heightened emotional reactivity
- More aware and attuned to the emotions of others
- May experience more feelings of worry and anxiety
- More emotionally impacted by peers and friends

Social and Relationship Development

- Seek more independence and autonomy from parents/caregivers and adults
- More conflict with parents/caregivers
- Increased desire for privacy
- Intense focus on peer relationships
- Value and prioritize approval from peers and friends
- Seek belonging and acceptance from peers and friends

- Seek information and advice from peers more than adults
- May have romantic interests and experience sexual attraction
- Increased interest in sexual pleasure and behavior with self and others
- May challenge parent/caregiver rules or expectations
- Seek an active role in their social groups with peers, families, communities

Culture and Identity Development

- Wide and varied exploration and experimentation with identity and interests
- Explore different social groups and different activities
- More awareness of their own cultural identity and others' cultural experiences
- More focus on fitting in with peers and social status
- Express individuality and explore personal values and beliefs
- May question or reject parent/family values and traditions

Common Challenges

- Inadequate or inconsistent sleep and sleep-deprivation due to technology and social media use, early school start times, and irregular sleep schedules
- Navigating menstruation cycles as well as the physical symptoms and social implications of menstruating
- Navigating spontaneous erections and ejaculation and social implications
- Navigating social dynamics and relationships with peers and friends
- Use and impact of social media and technology on daily life and friendships
- Navigating romantic attraction and relationships and sexual behavior including exposure to and use of pornography
- Navigating transition from middle school to high school

When to Seek Support

- Teen experiences intense sadness, low mood, or anxiety that is persistent and negatively impacts their life
- Teen has big or sudden changes in mood, energy, personality, or behavior beyond what is developmentally expected
- Teen expresses feelings or thoughts of self-harm or suicide
- Teen experiences ongoing social isolation or bullying or is bullying others
- Teen engages in repeated risk-taking behavior that is unsafe
- Teen is experimenting with or using alcohol or other substances
- Teen experiences a significant change or traumatic experience, including loss, disruption in the home or school environment, violence, or a medical emergency
- You need parenting support to address communication, conflict, or other concerns in your relationship with your teen
- You or your teen need support related to their identity development
- Teen tells you or another trusted person they want or need more support

Tips for Supporting 13-Year-Olds

- Help teens create healthy sleep routines, practice sleep hygiene, and create agreements related to technology and social media use at night
- Understand teen sleep needs and rhythms often don't align with school and social expectations
- Help teens prepare for menstruation through education, discussions, and providing supplies to care for their bodies
- Help teens prepare for erections and ejaculations through education, discussions, and making a plan for navigating spontaneous erections and nocturnal emissions
- Have consistent, open conversations about alcohol and substance use, healthy relationships and sex, risk-taking, and decision-making
- Discuss internet and social media safety and establish agreements and limits for technology and social media use at home and school
- Listen and validate teen's emotions and perspectives and give them undivided attention when they initiate conversation
- Normalize and support teens through the typical ups-and-downs of social and romantic relationships
- Respect teens' need to express individuality and independence from adults, parents, and family and try not to take it personally
- Spend time learning about teen's interests and doing activities together that they enjoy and value

THE 14-YEAR-OLD

Physical Development

- Continue to experience physical changes related to puberty
- Have changes in skin and body hair
- Experience growth spurts, growing pains, and changes in overall body height, size, and shape
- Need nutrient-rich foods to support growth and may often want to eat foods that are fast and low in nutrients
- May be less physically active and gravitate to more sedentary activities
- Need 8–10 hours of sleep each night
- Go to sleep later and wake up later in the morning due to changes in circadian rhythm
- May masturbate and explore sexual pleasure and behavior

Brain and Cognitive Development

- Seek novelty and new experiences
- Seek immediate gratification
- Have fluctuations and inconsistency in reasoning and logic
- May estimate outcomes of situations or consequences of actions inaccurately
- More interested in advanced ideas and concepts
- Desire to understand things at a deeper level
- Are present-focused and concerned about immediate gratification and immediate consequences of behavior
- Gain more awareness of others' perspectives and experiences
- Build skills to plan for the future and consider long-term goals

Emotional Development

- Many fluctuations in feelings and mood
- May seem more annoyed or irritable
- More emotionally reactive
- Higher emotional highs and lower emotional lows
- Tend to misread or perceive interactions and others' emotions negatively
- Sensitive to criticism
- Tend to react emotionally rather than logically under stress or pressure
- Express emotions verbally and physically

Social and Relationship Development

- Focused on peer relationships and friendships
- Strive for belonging and acceptance from peers
- Sensitive to peer pressure and influence
- More likely to confide in and seek advice from friends

- Navigating new and complex social dynamics
- Frequent changes, inconsistency, and conflict in peer relationships
- Highly influenced by social media
- More interest in romantic relationships
- May explore and engage in more intimate and sexual behavior with peers
- May feel embarrassed or avoid interacting with parents/caregivers in public

Culture and Identity Development

- May express values and beliefs that are different from their family
- May dress and/or behave differently or in ways that seem "out of character"
- Explore different activities, interests, peer groups, and means of self-expression
- May explore gender identity and expression
- Aware of racial and gender stereotypes and discrimination
- More interested and passionate about social issues
- May opt-out of family traditions and/or organized religion

Common Challenges

- Feel insecure or express low self-esteem
- Navigating more complex social dynamics and frequent transitions in peer relationships and friendships
- Navigating transition from middle school to high school
- Experiencing more stress related to academic, social, and family expectations
- Not getting adequate sleep or being chronically sleep-deprived
- Use and are impacted by social media and technology in daily life and friendships
- Risk-taking behavior and impulsive decision-making, especially under social pressure
- Experiment with alcohol and other substances
- Moodiness and conflict with parents/caregivers

When to Seek Support

- Teen is not showing typical signs of beginning progressing through puberty
- Teen experiences intense sadness, low mood, or anxiety that is persistent and negatively impacts their life
- Teen has big or sudden changes in mood, energy, personality, or behavior beyond what is developmentally expected
- Teen demonstrates concerning changes in behavior related to food, is under-eating, or is over-eating
- Teen expresses feelings or thoughts of self-harm or suicide
- Teen experiences ongoing social isolation or bullying
- Teen engages in repeated risk-taking behavior that is unsafe
- Teen is repeatedly experimenting with or using alcohol or other substances
- Teen experiences a significant change or traumatic experience, including loss, disruption in the home or school environment, violence, or a medical emergency

- You need parenting support to address communication, conflict, or other concerns in your relationship with your teen
- You or your teen need support related to their identity development
- Teen tells you or another trusted person they want or need more support

Tips for Supporting 14-Year-Olds

- Listen first without offering advice or trying to solve their problems
- Be curious about and validate their emotions, experiences, and perspectives
- Schedule time to talk together about important topics rather than surprising them with a big conversation
- Discuss characteristics of healthy relationships with friends and romantic partners
- Have consistent, open conversations about risk-taking, decision-making, peer pressure, substance use, sexuality, and safe sex
- Discuss and establish agreements related to social media and technology use and safety
- Give teens opportunities to contribute to their families and communities by sharing age-appropriate responsibilities and decisions
- Establish clear expectations and limits for teen's behavior with empathy and care for when they test boundaries and make mistakes
- Understand mistakes are a part of learning and help your teen learn from their experiences
- Respect teen's need to express individuality and independence from adults, parents, and family and try not to take it personally
- Spend time learning about teen's interests and doing activities together that they enjoy and value

THE 15-YEAR-OLD

Physical Development

- Have started most body changes related to puberty by age 15
- Experience and are adjusting to changes in body size, shape, hair, voice, menstruation
- Need 8–10 hours of sleep each night
- Stay up later at night and wake up later in the morning
- Need nutrient-rich food to support growth
- May make more independent and socially-driven decisions about food
- May skip meals or eat at irregular times due to engagement in social activities or social media
- More concerns about appearance and body image

Brain and Cognitive Development

- Brain is still growing and is more sensitive to new and exciting and rewarding experiences
- May feel bored more often and more easily
- Structures of the brain that help with decision-making, planning, and impulse control are still developing
- Activities and experiences in which teen spends the most time and energy create stronger neural connections in the brain
- Developing more critical thinking skills
- Able to see and imagine others' perspectives
- Can hypothesize about the unknown and make inferences
- More self-focused and spend more time thinking about themselves
- More concern about grades and academic performance

Emotional Development

- Intense emotions and fluctuations in mood
- Have higher expectations for self and feel more stress
- May respond to stress by withdrawing, acting like they care less than they do, or "being lazy"
- More self-critical and sensitive to criticism from others
- Worried that others are paying attention to their flaws and shortcomings
- More anxious and insecure

Social and Relationship Development

- Friendships and relationships with peers are really important and often feel challenging
- Eager for social connection and friendships with peers
- Friendships and relationships begin and end more frequently
- Social dynamics may be confusing, unstable, and unpredictable
- Continue to develop social skills and learn how to navigate social situations independently

- Highly influenced by social media
- Use slang frequently in communication
- May feel pressure to behave in certain ways to fit in with friends or peers
- May be exploring romantic relationships, dating, physical intimacy, and/or sexual activity
- Spend less time with parents and family

Cultural and Identity Development

- Explore and try on different identities
- Experience contradictions and rapid changes in their sense of self
- Sense of identity highly influenced by peers
- May rebel against family culture or values if not given freedom to express individuality
- More awareness and interest in social and ethical issues
- Sense of identity is more connected to personal values and beliefs

Common Challenges

- Low self-esteem and body image issues
- Being highly self-critical and sensitive to feedback
- Learning how to drive and getting driver's license
- Managing more independence and responsibility
- Navigating transition from middle school to high school including change in social dynamics and status
- Experiencing more stress related to academic, social, and family expectations
- Not getting adequate sleep or being chronically sleep-deprived
- Use and are impacted by social media and technology in daily life and friendships
- Risk-taking behavior and impulsive decision-making especially under social pressure
- Experimentation with alcohol and other substances
- Moodiness and conflict with parents/caregivers

When to Seek Support

- Teen experiences intense sadness, low mood, or anxiety that is persistent and negatively impacts their life
- Teen has big or sudden changes in mood, energy, personality, or behavior beyond what is developmentally expected
- Teen demonstrates concerning changes in behavior related to food, is under-eating, or is over-eating
- Teen expresses feelings or thoughts of self-harm or suicide
- Teen experiences ongoing social isolation or bullying
- Teen engages in repeated risk-taking behavior that is unsafe
- Teen experiments with or uses alcohol or other substances repeatedly

- Teen experiences a significant change or traumatic experience, including loss, disruption in the home or family environment, violence, or a medical emergency
- You need parenting support to address communication, conflict, or other concerns in your relationship with your teen
- You or your teen need support related to their gender or sexual identity
- Teen tells you or another trusted person they want or need more support

Tips for Supporting 15-year-olds

- Be curious about and validate their emotions, experiences, and perspectives
- Schedule time to talk together about important topics rather than surprising them with a big conversation
- Be available and present and willing to shift plans when possible when your teen wants to open up to your or spend time together
- Discuss characteristics of healthy relationships with friends and romantic partners
- Have consistent, open conversations about risk-taking, peer pressure, substance use, sexuality, and safe sex
- Support teens in creating healthy sleep and meal routines
- Understand teen's sleep needs and rhythms often don't align with school and social expectations
- Avoid challenging or dismissing their self-critical statements; rather listen, share context that broadens their perspective, and model positive self-talk
- Discuss and establish agreements related to social media and technology use and safety
- Discuss and establish agreements related to driving and safe driving practices
- Establish clear boundaries and limits for behavior and respond with empathy and care when teens break rules or test limits
- Show interest in your teen's interests and activities and prioritize spending time together doing things your teen enjoys

THE 16-YEAR-OLD

Physical Development

- Continue to experience hormonal changes related to puberty
- Teens with ovaries reach their adult weight, height, muscle, and bone mass
- Teens with testes continue to grow in height, size, and overall body size
- May receive unwanted attention due to being perceived as older and more physically mature
- Need 8–10 hours of sleep a night
- Need nutrient-rich foods to support growth
- May eat meals at irregular times or have inconsistent food routines

Brain and Cognitive Development

- Activities and experiences in which teen spends the most time and energy create stronger neural connections in the brain
- Neural connections are strengthened during sleep
- Emotional and memory centers of the brain develop more quickly than reasoning and control centers
- Continue to develop capacity for stronger reasoning and self-regulation
- Brain is sensitive to new, exciting, and rewarding experiences
- Increased capacity for understanding and solving complex problems
- Able to engage in more abstract and hypothetical thinking
- Able to reflect on their own thinking and understand the perspectives of others
- Learn through trial and error
- Often inconsistent in their decision-making, alternating between considering and ignoring consequences

Emotional Development

- Experience intense emotions and frequent fluctuations in emotions
- More emotional reactivity and irritability
- Decisions and behavior are often emotionally driven and/or impulsive
- Recognize and identify emotions in themselves and others
- Difficulty expressing and regulating their emotions
- Navigate more complex emotional dynamics and experiences with peers and social groups

Social and Relationship Development

- Very focused and motivated by peer relationships
- Socially active and spend a lot of time with friends and peers
- Relationships with peers are stronger and more intimate

- Tend to form relationships with peers who share similar interests, beliefs, values, and behavior
- Sensitive to social expectations and pressure to conform from peers
- Seek advice and support with problems from peers
- Interested and/or engaged in romantic and/or sexual relationships
- Use slang frequently in communication
- Spend less time with parents/caregivers

Culture and Identity Development

- Gravitate toward media and content that aligns with their own direct experiences and/or personal and family beliefs
- May feel ambivalent about their own identities and culture
- Actively explore identity and express individuality
- More aware of race, gender, sexuality, and other aspects of identity
- May experiment with gender expression through clothes, hairstyles, activities, and social interactions
- Exploring sexuality and more likely to articulate sexual or attractional identity to others

Common Challenges

- Preoccupied with appearance and social status
- Learning how to drive and getting a driver's license
- Managing greater independence and responsibility
- Engaging in risky behavior and/or impulsive decision-making
- Navigating changing social dynamics, communication, and conflict with peers, friends, and/or romantic partners
- Navigating communication and conflict with parents/caregivers
- Balancing school, social life, job, and/or family expectations
- Experiencing stress related to current pressures, responsibilities, and future-planning

When to Seek Support

- Teen experiences intense sadness, low mood, or anxiety that is persistent and negatively impacts their daily life
- Teen has big or sudden changes in mood, energy, personality, or behavior beyond what is developmentally expected
- Teen demonstrates concerning changes in behavior related to food, is under-eating, or is over-eating
- Teen expresses feelings or thoughts of self-harm or suicide
- Teen experiences bullying, discrimination, harassment, violence, or social isolation
- Teen engages in repeated risk-taking behavior that is unsafe (e.g., unprotected sex, reckless driving, stealing)
- Teen experiments with or uses alcohol or other substances repeatedly

- Teen experiences a significant change or traumatic experience, including loss, disruption in the home or family environment, violence, or a medical emergency
- You need parenting support to address communication, conflict, or other concerns in your relationship with your teen
- You or your teen need support related to their gender or sexual identity
- Teen tells you or another trusted person they want or need more support

Tips for Supporting 16-Year-Olds

- Encourage teen to participate in groups and communities that support their unique identities
- Share experiences and stories from your adolescence to relate to them and model vulnerability
- Be available, present, and flexible when teen wants to talk or spend time together
- Support teen in creating healthy sleep and meal routines
- Understand teen's sleep needs and rhythms often don't align with school and social expectations
- Discuss characteristics of healthy relationships with friends and romantic partners
- Have consistent, open conversations about risk-taking, substance use, sexuality, and safe sex
- Discuss and establish agreements related to social media and technology use and safety
- Discuss and establish agreements related to driving and safe driving practices
- Help teen manage stress related to school, job, extracurricular, and social pressures
- Support teen in exploring goals and career and educational opportunities they may want to pursue after high school
- Show interest and learn more about their hobbies, activities, interests, and friends

THE 17-YEAR-OLD

Physical Development

- Puberty is nearing completion
- Changes in voice and body hair may continue
- May engage in less physical activity and recreation
- May eat less nutrition-rich foods and meals
- Inconsistent and irregular meals and routines
- May consume more sugar and caffeine for quick energy
- Need 8–10 hours of sleep a night

Brain and Cognitive Development

- Activities and experiences in which teen spends the most time and energy create stronger neural connections in the brain
- Neural connections are strengthened during sleep
- Neural networks that are no longer used or needed are pruned
- Tend to think more irrationally and idealistically
- Capacity for complex and critical thinking increases
- Able to think more abstractly and hypothetically
- Continue to develop better problem-solving skills
- Tend to have stronger organizational skills
- Low tolerance for others' different or opposing beliefs and opinions
- More self-awareness and ability to reflect on self and own thought processes
- May have more understanding of consequences and still make impulsive decisions
- Need more time to process and make informed and reasonable decisions

Emotional Development

- Experience intense emotions
- Moods and feelings are unpredictable and shift rapidly
- May engage in risky and impulsive behaviors
- Make decisions based on their emotions and immediate rewards or consequences
- More prone to sadness
- Stronger ability to regulate emotions
- Deeper capacity for empathy and understanding of others
- Emotions are highly impacted by social interactions with peers

Social and Relationship Development

- Socially active and focused on relationships with peers and friends
- Increased interest in romantic and sexual relationships
- Seek more independence and autonomy from parents and adults

- Influenced by peers and friends in their social groups and through social media
- Able to communicate more like adults
- Use slang regularly in communication

Culture and Identity Development

- Explore identity and roles and may try out new personalities and behaviors
- Explore personal beliefs and values
- Express individuality through interests, dress, hobbies, and extracurricular activities
- More awareness of social, political, and cultural experiences and issues
- Consider their identity in relationship to their beliefs and values
- Aware of and able to articulate their sexual and/or affectional orientation
- Explore values, beliefs, and identity in relationship to opportunities and goals beyond high school

Common Challenges

- Preoccupied with appearance and social status
- Low self-esteem
- Body image issues
- Uncertainty about identity and future-planning
- Balancing school, extracurricular activities, social life, job, and/or family expectations
- Planning and preparing for educational and/or career options after high school
- Navigating changing social dynamics, communication, and conflict with peers, friends, and/or romantic partners
- Experiencing stress related to current pressures, responsibilities, and future-planning

When to Seek Support

- Teen experiences intense sadness, low mood, or anxiety that is persistent and negatively impacts their daily life
- Teen experiences intense stress or pressure related to academic, social, or family responsibilities and has difficulty coping
- Teen demonstrates concerning changes in behavior related to food, is under-eating, or is over-eating
- Teen expresses feelings or thoughts of self-harm or suicide
- Teen experiences bullying, discrimination, harassment, violence, or social isolation
- Teen engages in repeated risk-taking behavior that is unsafe (e.g., unprotected sex, reckless driving, stealing)
- Teen experiments with or uses alcohol or other substances repeatedly
- Teen experiences a significant change or traumatic experience, including loss, disruption in the home or family environment, violence, or a medical emergency
- You need parenting support to address communication, conflict, or other concerns in your relationship with your teen

- You or your teen need support related to their gender or sexual identity
- Teen tells you or another trusted person they want or need more support

Tips for Supporting 17-Year-Olds

- Encourage teen to participate in groups and communities that support their unique identities
- Share experiences and stories from your adolescence to relate to them and model vulnerability
- Listen and validate their experiences while helping them explore and make decisions that reflect their goals and values
- Be available, present, and flexible when teen wants to talk or spend time together
- Support teen in creating healthy sleep and meal routines
- Discuss characteristics of healthy relationships with friends and romantic partners
- Have consistent, open conversations about risk-taking, substance use, sexuality, and safe sex
- Discuss and establish agreements related to driving and safe driving practices
- Help teen manage stress related to school, job, extracurricular, and social pressures
- Support teen in exploring goals and career and educational opportunities they may want to pursue after high school
- Show interest and learn more about their hobbies, activities, interests, and friends

THE 18- TO 19-YEAR-OLD

Physical Development

- Physical development and changes related to puberty are coming to completion
- Preoccupation with physical appearance and meeting social expectations related to body image
- Need 7–9 hours of sleep a night
- Changes to routines related to exercise, sleep, and nutrition due to education and career transitions
- May discontinue or be inconsistent in preventative health behaviors and medical care

Brain and Cognitive Development

- Continue to develop and strengthen decision-making and problem-solving skills
- May make impulsive decisions with consideration of immediate rather than long-term consequences
- May draw false conclusions or have difficulty predicting realistic outcomes
- Focused on planning for the future and achieving goals
- Increased awareness of self and others
- Use abstract thinking skills and perspective-taking to solve problems
- Guided more by personal ethics, ideals, and values in decision-making

Emotional Development

- More emotionally mature at times
- Emotionally sensitive and reactive
- Moods and feelings are intense
- More capacity to regulate emotions
- More awareness and empathy for the feelings and experiences of others
- Tend to interpret others' emotions more negatively or intensely
- Increased awareness of own emotions and ability to articulate emotions
- May blame others for or externalize their problems

Social and Relationship Development

- Focused on peer and social relationships
- Increasing independence and autonomy from parents/caregivers and family
- Socially active and regularly engaged with peers, friends, and/or romantic partners
- Compares self to peers and concerned with social status
- May engage in sexual and romantic relationships
- May struggle to balance independence from parents/caregivers with ongoing need for support

Culture and Identity Development

- Continue to explore identity and develop a cohesive sense of self
- More awareness and concern for social, ethical, and political issues
- More awareness of cultural and racial identity through increased exposure to diversity
- May explore gender and sexual identity more freely and openly
- Express and explore identity more outside of their home or family context
- Increased exploration of personal values and beliefs apart from parents/family
- Often question beliefs, values, traditions from childhood
- Explore long-term goals and plans for the future

Common Challenges

- Navigating social relationships including friendships and/or romantic and sexual relationships
- Balancing social activities, relationships, daily responsibilities, and educational or career expectations
- Increased access and exposure to alcohol and other substances
- Navigating transition from high school to career or college
- Leaving structure and support of home and/or educational environments
- Navigating legal status including new responsibilities and consequences as a legal adult (in the US)
- Conflict and communication with parents as gaining more independence and changing roles and routines

When to Seek Support

- Young adult experiences intense sadness, low mood, or anxiety that is persistent and negatively impacts their daily life
- Young adult experiences intense stress or pressure related to academic, social, or family responsibilities and has difficulty coping
- Young adult expresses feelings or thoughts of self-harm or suicide
- Young adult experiences bullying, discrimination, harassment, violence, or social isolation
- Young adult engages in repeated risk-taking behavior that is unsafe (e.g., unprotected sex, reckless driving, stealing)
- Young adult engages in binge drinking or repeated substance use/misuse
- Young adult experiences a traumatic experience, including loss or death of a family member or friend, car accident, sexual assault, or violence
- You need parenting support to navigate your changing relationship, roles, and communication with your young adult
- Young adult needs support making decisions and navigating choices related to jobs, career, education, and relationships
- Young adult tells you or another trusted person they want or need more support

Tips for Supporting 18- to 19-Year-Olds

- Encourage young adult to participate in groups and communities that support their identities and goals
- Listen and validate their experiences while helping them explore and make decisions that reflect their personal goals and values
- Balance providing support and promoting independence
- Use their preferred methods of communication (e.g., text, email, phone, videochat) to connect
- Have open conversations about healthy relationships, risk-taking, substance use, and safe sex
- Discuss and establish agreements related to driving and safe driving practices
- Discuss and collaborate on communication and sharing responsibilities in the home environment and establishing new routines and boundaries
- Show interest and learn more about their goals, hobbies, activities, interests, friends, and/or romantic partners
- Ask open-ended questions about their life and interests
- Provide emotional support as young adult's make mistakes and only offer advice when it is requested

THE 20- TO 21-YEAR-OLD

Physical Development

- May continue to gain weight
- Tend to be physically healthy
- Tend to be less physically active and engage in more sedentary activities
- May engage in risky behaviors like binge drinking and/or smoking
- Less likely to engage in preventative healthcare
- Need 7–9 hours of sleep each night
- May not prioritize exercise, sleep, or nutrition due to social, academic, and career pressures

Brain and Cognitive Development

- Neural connections related to memory and social cognition continue to strengthen
- Able to understand and interpret others' emotions more accurately
- Risk-taking behavior starting to decrease
- Sensation-seeking behavior starting to decrease
- Less reactive and impulsive when making decisions
- Stronger decision-making and problem-solving skills
- Focused on goals and future-planning

Emotional Development

- Increased ability to regulate emotions
- Increased awareness and understanding of own and others' emotions
- Emotional instability due to many frequent transitions and changes
- More feelings of stress and overwhelm related to big and frequent life changes and instability
- Tension and angst related to being in-between adolescence and adulthood

Social and Relationship Development

- More changes and shifts in friendships and social relationships due to moving, going to college, and/or job changes
- Less sensitive to social pressure from peers
- May engage in romantic and sexual relationships
- May seek more intimate, committed, or long-term romantic and sexual relationships
- Friends are major source of social support and intimacy
- Tend to be friends with people with shared interests, identities, and behaviors
- More autonomy and independence from parents/caregivers and family
- May rely on parents/family for practical, financial, and emotional support

Culture and Identity Development

- Exploring and defining personal identity and values
- Exploring new possibilities and choices related to life goals and opportunities
- Increased exposure to diverse ideas and experiences
- Continue to explore and integrate understanding of race, gender, and sexual identity
- Able to more freely pursue interests and social groups that reflect identities and values

Common Challenges

- Navigating legal access to purchase and consume alcohol (in the US)
- More likely to engage in social and/or binge drinking
- Navigating many new relationships and social groups independently
- Navigating endings of friendships, romantic, and/or sexual relationships
- Navigating risks related to sexual activity (e.g., STIs, pregnancy)
- Navigating transition from college if completing or discontinuing formal education
- Navigating more decisions and responsibilities related to housing, jobs, relationships, time-management, and finances
- Confusion and conflict related to changes in familial and social roles and relationships
- Experiencing pressure related to achieving adult milestones in education, career, relationships, and finances
- Increased risk of mental health issues and substance issues
- May not seek support or counseling due to drive for autonomy and independence

When to Seek Support

- Young adult experiences intense sadness, low mood, or anxiety that is persistent and negatively impacts their daily life
- Young adult experiences intense stress or pressure related to academic, social, or family responsibilities and has difficulty coping
- Young adult experiences feelings of loneliness or social isolation
- Young adult expresses feelings or thoughts of self-harm or suicide
- Young adult experiences bullying, discrimination, harassment, or violence
- Young adult engages in repeated risk-taking behavior that is unsafe (e.g., unprotected sex, reckless driving, criminal activity)
- Young adult engages in binge drinking or repeated substance use/misuse
- Young adult experiences a traumatic experience, including loss or death of a family member or friend, car accident, sexual assault, or violence
- You need parenting support to navigate your changing relationship, roles, and communication with your young adult
- Young adult needs support making decisions and navigating choices related to jobs, career, education, relationships
- Young adult wants to work on communication or relationship with intimate partner
- Young adult tells you or another trusted person they want or need more support

Tips for Supporting 20- to 21-Year-Olds

- Encourage young adult to participate in groups, activities, and communities that support their identities and goals
- Listen and validate their experiences while helping them explore and make decisions that reflect their personal goals and values
- Ask open-ended questions about their life and interests
- Provide nonjudgmental support and only offer advice when it is requested
- Balance promoting independence and providing support
- Use their preferred methods of communication (e.g., text, email, phone, videochat) to connect
- Have open conversations about healthy relationships, risk-taking, substance use, and safe sex
- Discuss and establish agreements related to driving and safe driving practices
- Discuss and collaborate on communication and sharing responsibilities in the home environment and establishing new routines and boundaries
- Show interest and learn more about their goals, hobbies, activities, interests, friends, and/or romantic partners
- Take care of yourself and focus on fulfillment in your friendships, intimate relationships, career, hobbies, and personal goals

THE 22- TO 25-YEAR-OLD

Physical Development

- Physical development is considered complete with growth of wisdom teeth
- Reach physical maturity
- Tend to be physically healthy
- Peak fertility
- Less likely to engage in preventative healthcare
- Need 7–9 hours of sleep
- May not prioritize exercise, sleep, or nutrition due to social, educational, relationship, and career pressures

Brain and Cognitive Development

- Prefrontal cortex nears full maturity
- Able to consider multiple perspectives
- Able to think more abstractly, creatively, and critically
- Increased ability to consider and solve complex problems
- Learn from trial and error and navigating new experiences and opportunities independently
- Less either/or thinking
- Able to adapt thinking and behavior in response to new or changing environments and circumstances
- More rational and less emotionally driven or impulsive decision-making and behavior

Emotional Development

- Heightened and complex feelings related to frequent changes, instability, and new opportunities
- May feel overwhelmed by responsibilities and decision-making
- Increased capacity for emotional awareness and empathy
- Able to regulate emotions
- Increased emotional intelligence
- Able to articulate emotions and advocate for own needs

Social and Relationship Development

- More self-sufficient and independent
- Focused on personal values and goals that align with values
- Seek intimacy in friendships and/or romantic relationships
- May seek long-term or committed romantic and/or sexual relationships
- Increased social freedom and opportunities to develop new relationships
- Experience more frequent shifts or transitions in relationships

- More understanding of parents/caregivers perspectives and identities beyond their parental/caregiving role
- Decrease in stress and conflict in relationships with parents/caregivers
- More mutual and reciprocal relationships with parents/caregivers

Culture and Identity Development

- Continue to explore and define their own identity, beliefs, and values
- Express values and beliefs more freely and confidently
- Explore identity and express individuality
- More exposure to diverse ideas and experiences through travel, career, education, and relationships
- Tend to have a broader understanding of own and others' cultures and identities
- May seek deeper connection with cultural traditions and heritage
- Seek community and relationships with others who share similar identities and values
- More congruence between internal sense of self and expression of self to others
- More stable and cohesive sense of self

Common Challenges

- Navigating job/career decisions, instability, and transitions
- Navigating transition from college/formal education
- Navigating decisions and responsibilities related to intimate relationships, reproductive health, housing, finances, and parenting
- Ambiguity related to identity and life choices
- Feeling stuck or lost or disillusioned by realities and responsibilities of adulthood
- Loneliness and/or less social support

When to Seek Support

- Young adult experiences intense sadness, low mood, or anxiety that is persistent and negatively impacts their daily life
- Young adult experiences feelings of loneliness or social isolation
- Young adult expresses feelings or thoughts of self-harm or suicide
- Young adult experiences discrimination, harassment, or violence
- Young adult engages in binge drinking or repeated substance use/misuse
- Young adult experiences a traumatic experience, including loss or death of a family member or friend, car accident, sexual assault, or violence
- Young adult needs support making decisions and navigating choices related to jobs, career, education, relationships, and/or parenting
- Young adult is questioning identity or sense of self
- Young adult is having difficulty achieving personal goals or meeting responsibilities
- Young adult wants to work on communication or relationship with intimate partner

- Young adult is have difficulty in communication, relationship, expectations, or roles with parents
- Young adult tells you or another trusted person they want or need more support
- You need parenting support to navigate your changing relationship, roles, and communication with your young adult

Tips for Supporting 22- to 25-Year-Olds

- Encourage young adults in building strong relationships and social support systems
- Listen and validate their experiences while helping them explore options and make decisions that reflect their personal goals and values
- Ask open-ended questions about their life and interests
- Provide nonjudgmental support and only offer advice when it is requested
- Use their preferred methods of communication (e.g., text, email, phone, video) to connect
- Balance promoting independence and providing support
- Discuss and collaborate on communication, sharing responsibilities, and establishing new routines and boundaries if/when living together
- Show interest and learn more about their goals, work, hobbies, interests, friends, and/or romantic partners
- Understand they are experiencing different generational and social pressures and realities than you did as a young adult
- Treat them like an adult and practice open communication and reciprocity in your relationship
- Be a model and a mentor by engaging in activities that support your health and wellness and focusing on fulfillment in your friendships and/or intimate relationships, career, hobbies, and personal goals

Index

Note: Page numbers in **bold** indicate a table on the corresponding page.

For Product Safety Concerns and Information please contact our EU
representative GPSR@taylorandfrancis.com
Taylor & Francis Verlag GmbH, Kaufingerstraße 24, 80331 München, Germany

www.ingramcontent.com/pod-product-compliance
Lightning Source LLC
Chambersburg PA
CBHW081738270326
41932CB00020B/3315

* 9 7 8 1 0 3 2 0 5 0 4 2 3 *